Stories of Our Lives

Stories of Our Lives

Memory, History, Narrative

Frank de Caro

Utah State University Press
Logan

© 2013 by Frank de Caro

Published by Utah State University Press
An imprint of University Press of Colorado
5589 Arapahoe Avenue, Suite 206C
Boulder, Colorado 80303

All rights reserved

 The University Press of Colorado is a proud member of
the Association of American University Presses.

The University Press of Colorado is a cooperative publishing enterprise supported, in part, by Adams State University, Colorado State University, Fort Lewis College, Metropolitan State University of Denver, Regis University, University of Colorado, University of Northern Colorado, Utah State University, and Western State Colorado University.

ISBN: 978-0-87421-893-0 (paperback)
ISBN: 978-0-87421-894-7 (e-book)

Library of Congress Cataloging-in-Publication Data
De Caro, F. A., 1943–
  Stories of our lives : memory, history, narrative / Frank de Caro.
    pages cm
  ISBN 978-0-87421-893-0 (pbk.) — ISBN 978-0-87421-894-7 (e-book)
 1. De Caro, F. A., 1943– 2. Folklorists—United States—Biography. 3. Folklore—United States. 4. United States—Social life and customs. I. Title.
  GR55.D4A3 2013
  398.092—dc23
  [B]
                                        2013019962

Contents

	Acknowledgments	vii
	Be Sure to Read This First: A Preface	ix
1	The Golden-Haired Maiden	1
2	7002 Ridge	16
3	Foreigners Arrive	26
4	The Lake	42
5	Beyond 7002	67
6	Becoming the East Village	90
7	Tinkly Temple Bells	113
8	Life in a Cornfield	142
9	Mexico	152
10	Long Ago and Far Away: Another Passage to India	176
11	Katrina: We Leave, We Return, Stories Abound	198
	Contexts and Meanings: A Brief Afterword	210
	About the Author	215

Acknowledgments

Part of chapter 11 appeared previously, in somewhat different form, in the *Louisiana Folklore Miscellany* (volumes 16–17, 2008). And as of this writing material from chapters 1 and 10 is due to appear in *Western Folklore*. My thanks to these publications for their interest.

A number of people have read this book in an earlier draft and kindly offered additions and suggestions and I thank them all: Beatrice Palmer, Barbara Gray, Jack Mulvehill, Rosan Jordan, Kevin Mulvehill, Carl Patrick, Mary Jane Mulvehill, Margo Culley, Urban S. Mulvehill Jr., John McAlevey, and Kathleen Gray. Laura Clapp kindly sent me some of her stories.

At Utah State University Press John Alley encouraged this book at an early stage and Michael Spooner and Karli Fish gave close attention to the project. At the University Press of Colorado, my thanks go to managing editor Laura Furney and marketing manager Beth Svinarich for their fine handling of the book, and to copy editor Diane Bush for providing such excellent editing.

Be Sure to Read This First
A Preface

With individual stories, the statistics become people.

—Neil Gaiman, *American Gods*

I am . . . ambivalent about memoirs because of what I have learned about memory. Yet I also realize that we are constantly constructing our memoirs, polishing and tweaking our life stories, making order out of randomness every time we recount the events of the day.

—Laura Lippman, "Shut Up, Memory"

This book is partly a memoir, but a memoir with a difference and a premise: that our life memory is informed by and greatly influenced by the oral stories that we tell or have told about our lives and the stories others have told us about their lives or the past or the nature of culture and the world. Such stories may coexist with more generalized memories and documentary sources, like letters and diaries, that help us to remember or reformulate our pasts. But certainly the stories we tell and listen to play an integral role in constructing our temporal selves. This premise may be self-evident—especially to folklorists, who are aware of the social importance of personal narratives, family saga, and communal legends—but seldom has it been demonstrated for individual lives.

This book, then, in part attempts to demonstrate and use some of my own life memories and stories as specimens to suggest the applicability of the premise. If all memoir is to some degree a self-indulgence, I further indulge myself as a folklorist by calling attention to the centrality of oral narration in my own life. Thus, in addition to providing the types of recollections found in all memoirs, this book includes my thoughts on the meanings of certain stories to my life and my sense of self. This admittedly makes for an odd sort of book.

This memoir relies heavily on bits and pieces of oral history and oral narratives, accounts of past events that were passed on to me, accounts that

I have passed along to others, and most particularly, stories—accounts of the past that have crystallized into "finished" narratives. In the case of this memoir, however, I seek to specifically call attention to such narratives and emphasize their significance in creating personal records of our lives.

The oral stories that come to us—in conversations and special recountings by relatives or friends, whether in passing or specially recalled—have considerable power to convey knowledge and meaning. I doubt that most of us are consciously aware of this power when we first begin to hear such stories, usually quite early in life. I know that I wasn't. Yet that power is there. Because stories make events cohere into some sort of plot, because stories are often repeated so that their message is emphasized again and again, and because stories often speak of happenings somehow regarded as special, they take what might be the mundane facts of life and turn them into something transcendent. A story tells us: here is something significant, something worth remembering, something to internalize. A story calls attention to some aspect of memory that we and others think important to never forget. In this book I talk about the stories that are part of my personal memory and the memories of other people I have known and consider what they are telling me about my personal worldview and the worldview of those around me, about what I have been told about and have noticed about existence and the world and my passage through it. I mostly have no recordings of the stories I've heard or told and simply re-create them on the page, though in a few cases I format transcriptions of recordings as block quotations (without quotation marks).

When I say that I re-create stories, I mean more than one thing. I occasionally reproduce a story—delinated by quotation marks—in what I imagine to be something like the language in which I or someone else might tell it. In most cases, however, I simply work the story into my larger text, hoping that I have retained something of the dramatic quality of oral narration (though not all told stories are necessarily "dramatic"). When I write here of something being a "story" or of some incident having become a "story" for me, I mean that this narrative is a tale I have told or that someone else has told—that it is a part of my or someone's oral repertoire. Of course, other elements of this memoir are based on bits and pieces of oral history, which are perhaps stories in utero. Certainly the family history that I recount consists not merely of well-formed stories but is also drawn from other pieces of family oral history.

What I do here, then, is also explain why particular stories might be important to me (what they "seem to say"), although readers of this book may come up with their own explanations and though my explanations may very much be partial ones. In the case of stories which are not mine alone—legends and family saga, certainly—my perspectives may be quite different from those of other people who share the stories; and my versions will doubtlessly be different from theirs in greater or smaller ways.

In approaching both life memory and oral narration in this manner, I was influenced, at least indirectly, by my graduate study at Indiana University with Professor Jerome Mintz. Probably partly for managing pedagogy, he centered our required fieldwork course around studying and doing life histories—a technique favored by anthropologists that gave us (or me, at any rate) a great appreciation for the importance of the individual tradition bearer and the relationship of folklore to his or her particular life. And I see my work related to that of my colleagues in folklore—William A. "Bert" Wilson and Barbara Kirshenblatt-Gimblett—in that the three of us have been working with material quite personal to us. Wilson's work, involving interviews with his mother, certainly has been more rigorous and systematic and more in line with what folklorists have done historically. And Kirshenblatt-Gimblett's book about her father's memory paintings, written in collaboration with him, has dealt with a quite different genre of material, a visual arts one.[1] But I think we share the general trend in folklore and the social sciences toward producing work that is more self-reflexive. The extent to which our work has produced "fictions" is a theoretical issue that I shall leave unaddressed.

When I became consciously aware of the importance of oral stories in my life I cannot say precisely. My graduate study of life histories certainly influenced me, but well before that I remember being interested in stories. Of course, I enjoyed hearing and reading them as a child—what child doesn't?—but I began writing stories, sometimes dictating them to my mother, by age six or seven. I wrote fiction in high school and college and then received a grad degree in creative writing, primarily short stories. And though a variety of forces took me into the study of folklore, I cannot help but think that somehow stories led me into that field where the study and appreciation of narrative is central. Some particular stories seem to have lurked in my mind forever—perhaps more so than for many of us.

If you endeavor, when entering the web of memory that is your life, to take into account the oral stories which are part of that memory, you will realize that not only is your remembering wound up in stories of your own, but it is implicated, too, in the stories of others, whether individuals or groups, especially family stories. Some of this memoir of mine is really a recounting of family history, including what Mody C. Boatright called family saga; our memories and certainly our identities are much embedded in family past and memory, and parts of our lives are inextricably bound to family narrative.[2] Family narrative, of course, tells us where we came from.

In the course of life we also hear many stories from other people, most of which we probably forget, some that we remember and may even retell, a few of which seem incorporated into our own lives. These may be the stories of close friends or stories in which we have a peripheral role or that speak of a context we personally know. As a folklorist I have sought out the stories of some people to gain insight into their lives and cultural identities. Sometimes we hear rumors and legends that have played an important role in influencing how we think or feel. At any rate, often the stories of others become very much a part of us and are important to us. Certainly stories told by others pop up in this memoir. I mean to say that my life memory is made up of constituent memories that are sometimes wound up in the stories I and others tell, and that such stories deserve consideration when thinking about how lives are remembered. Indeed, formal biographies are often full of the anecdotal, but do we always recognize the importance of the humble anecdote in rendering lives?

But what role, exactly, do oral stories play in memory—what do they mean?

In part, they are a sort of mnemonic device. We remember some things *because* we have formulated and told stories about them; this helps us to remember the events and people and conditions the stories are about. But our stories are also a construct that provides a particular vision—or series of visions—of ourselves and the world. Stories "provide inspiration . . . and new frames of reference to both tellers and listeners," as folklorist Amy Shuman notes.[3] That is, they shape for us a particular perspective. Memory itself does that, and in remembering we edit and reformulate the past, partly because memory is fallible, partly because we prefer certain memories to others or prefer to remember them in certain ways, partly just to order and make sense of what we remember. The stories we tell, because they are only a part of memory, simplify this process, transforming memory into a limited number of themes that we seek to project to others and ourselves. The stories may embody an accurate recounting of the past, and what they embody may be particularly important to us, being what we choose to share. But they are a somewhat scaled-down version of things. That means that they leave out a lot but also that they distill something crucial; by looking at their themes we can tell a little about the fundamental visions of our lives and surroundings and personal pasts.

I see my family oral history, for example, as expressing definite themes related to how the family became part of the greater American experience.

First merging with the fabled pioneer saga: great-grandparents crossing the Plains in a covered wagon, a grandmother who undergoes the virtually mythic experience of being kidnapped by Indians. Then economically rising in the world: a grandfather who lands at the Battery in New York City, practically penniless, sleeping on park benches, who goes on to own his own business. Some think of these themes as the American Dream itself. I see these themes emerge in the stories of both my mother's and father's families—probably they are common to many Americans. Stories from my grad school days at Indiana University speak particularly of student poverty—something that can be savored as having been temporary and as something shared that provided solidarity—and of the tumultuous times of student protest and strongly held ideologies, cherished perhaps because of having gone on to a more settled, more ordinary life. Stories from my long sojourn at Louisiana State University in Baton Rouge tend to stress the eccentricities of colleagues and friends and the cultural uniqueness of the state in the face of the rather bland suburban lifestyle of Sunbelt Baton Rouge. Stories stemming from my and my wife's frequent trips to Mexico often suggest—again, perhaps because so many of these trips occurred against the backdrop of our somewhat humdrum existence in Baton Rouge—whiffs of adventures in strange cultural realities, encounters with the out of the ordinary. In the stories we were a bit like the Vicks VapoRub salesman whose self-published memoir of being inadvertently caught up in the Mexican Revolution, and thus swept into something exciting, my wife, Rosan Jordan, turned up in her researches into Americans in Mexico in the 1920s and 1930s.[4]

As a folklorist I've been concerned quite consciously and directly with the stories other people tell, and my interest in their stories in a way makes them a part of my own life. Thus, I remember and write about not only my fieldwork in Britain and Ireland with British people who had lived in India under the colonial Raj but their specific stories and how I see those stories render meaning. And in writing about the displacement wrought by the disastrous levee failures in New Orleans in the wake of Hurricane Katrina in 2005, I concentrate on filtering the experience through the urban legends we heard upon our return to the Crescent City—surely a folklorist's way of dealing with recollection.

In using particular stories I have, of course, chosen to manipulate the thread of discussion. However, I think that I have included virtually every significant story I can remember from my repertoire and prefer to believe that, though every narrator preselects his or her themes by remembering certain stories, I have not tried to overstate what themes the stories contain.

In his book *Fragile Things* Neil Gaiman, an author virtually obsessed by stories and storytelling, tells us that he once planned a collection of short stories he would have called *These People Ought to Know Who We Are and Tell That We Were Here*; each would be narrated "by one of a variety of dodgy and unreliable narrators" telling about their lives and that "they too were here."[5] Perhaps we are all dodgy and unreliable narrators, but I believe that all of us do have the right to narrate our lives, to emphatically state that we were here and did this or that. That someone should set down his or her memoirs has in the past seemed to imply that the author was someone of consequence whose actions were of some importance to the rest of the world. We are moving beyond such assumptions, and I certainly make no such presumption about myself. I do think that the more any and all of us write about our lives, however extraordinary or everyday, however outstanding or typical, the more we will understand about each other, and the more people in the future can understand about the realities of our own present-day existence. Somebody, somewhere, some time, for some reason will want to know what we can tell them. In calling this book *Stories of Our Lives* (and including in "*my* memoir" stories not my own) I mean to suggest that all of our lives are of interest and that the stories all of us tell—however particular to our own circumstances, however trivial they may seem to others—are revealing about our selves, our societies and cultures, and our larger human existence. As Gaiman puts it in his poem "Locks," "We owe it to each other to tell stories."[6]

Indeed, it is our growing realization of the power inherent in storytelling that has led to the popularity of projects that have facilitated the recording of personal oral stories—like the Family Folklore Project at the Smithsonian Institution, the Veterans History Project organized out of the American Folklife Center at the Library of Congress, and StoryCorps, the independent nonprofit that has received funding from the Corporation for Public Broadcasting, which cooperates with National Public Radio and the American Folklife Center. These projects have sought to reach a wide array of potential narrators; the Family Folklore Project, for example, records people in a special tent at the Festival of American Folklife, and StoryCorps provides personnel and equipment to schools, churches, and other institutions where recording can take place. These attempts to record people's personal stories certainly reflect the growing popularity of looking to our own narratives, and they reflect, I think, a growing awareness of the value of stories in enlightening us about our lives and our worlds.[7]

NOTES

1. William A. Wilson, "Personal Narrative: The Family Novel," in *The Marrow of Human Experience: Essays on Folklore*, ed. Jill Terry Rudy (Logan: Utah State University Press, 2006), 261–81; Mayer Kirshenblatt and Barbara Kirshenblatt-Gimblett, *They Called Me Mayer July: Painted Memories of a Jewish Childhood in Poland before the Holocaust* (Berkeley: University of California Press, 2007). Wilson (264) notes, "I do not believe we can understand the emotional force narratives might exert in the lives of others until we have dealt with that force as honestly as possible in our own lives." I feel a particular connection with these authors in terms of our use of material very personal to us, but I do not mean to ignore recent work by other folklorists who have moved in new and less conventional directions by using less academic kinds of writing, such as memoir and autobiography, like that by Sw. Anand Prahlad in the *Journal of American Folklore*, volume 118; or that by Elaine J. Lawless, Joanne B. Mulcahy, Kirin Narayan, Jens Lund, and others, in a volume I edited, *The Folklore Muse: Poetry, Fiction, and Other Reflections by Folklorists* (Logan: Utah State University Press, 2008); or Kirin Narayan's memoir, *My Family and Other Saints* (Chicago: University of Chicago Press, 2007). Previously, Jeannie B. Thomas, in *Featherless Chickens, Laughing Women, and Serious Stories* (Charlottesville: University Press of Virginia, 1997), used many stories from her own family and discussed her family's background in her consideration of oral narrative and humor. Even earlier, Kathryn L. Morgan made great use of her own family's narrative traditions in *Children of Strangers: The Stories of a Black Family* (Philadelphia: Temple University Press, 1980).

2. Mody C. Boatright, *The Family Saga and Other Phases of American Folklore* (Urbana: University of Illinois Press, 1958).

3. Amy Shuman, *Other People's Stories: Entitlement Claims and the Critique of Empathy* (Urbana: University of Illinois Press, 2005), 1.

4. Hugh Dixon McKay, *Stranded in Mexican Revolution, 1923–1924* (Wilton, CT: n. p., 1969).

5. Neil Gaiman, *Fragile Things: Short Fictions and Wonders* (New York: William Morrow, 2006), xi.

6. Gaiman, 179. In suggesting that everyone should write a memoir, I am obviously at odds with someone like Jonathan Yardley, who in reviewing a memoirist, writes in *The Washington Post*, April 29, 2009, that his subject has "done enough interesting things to have earned the right to write his memoirs." Or perhaps I just think that we are all interesting enough in one way or another by virtue of having lived.

7. The Family Folklore Project at the Smithsonian Festival of American Folklife produced such publications as *"I'd Like to Think They Were Pirates": Stories and Photographs Collected by the Family Folklore Program of the Festival of American Folklife* (Washington, DC: Smithsonian Institution and National Park Service, 1975) and *Family Folklore Collected by the Family Folklore Program of the Festival of American Folklife* (Washington, DC: Smithsonian Institution and National Park Service, 1976). For information on StoryCorps, see http://storycorps.org. For information on the Veterans History Project, see www.loc.gov/vets.

Stories of Our Lives

One

The Golden-Haired Maiden

IT IS 1979 AND I AM SITTING IN a pub in Youghal, County Cork, Ireland, with six other people, five of whom have personal connections to an imperial past. Our informal conversation quickly turns to the subject about which I have come to interview one of them, though I will wind up taping four out of the five later and will hear their stories.[1]

At the bus station in Waterford yesterday evening the stage was set for oral performance. We tell the station agent where we're going, and he looks completely puzzled, as though we have asked for a bus that goes to Moscow or San Francisco. Then he realizes that we have merely been mispronouncing the name of our destination. We are not going to *U-gall*, as we have been saying, but rather to someplace more like *Yawl*. This linguistic confusion and its resolution sets him off on a lengthy paean to the joys of being a bus conductor, of announcing destinations, of pointing out to his riders—especially any tourists aboard—the sights being passed. "Oh, 'tis grand," he says repeatedly, "'tis grand." His lilting tones stoke our stereotypes of the Irish love of elaborate, musical speech and remind us of the Irish fame for verbal art, though the conductor on our journey the next day turns out to be more taciturn.

The stage should be set, too, for the post-colonial. Ireland has, after all, been called Britain's original colony. And it gained independence early—in 1921, well before the spate of post–World War II British colonial departures that began with the independence of India and Pakistan in 1947.

But we have not come to Ireland to encounter grand oral performances, but rather the prosaic, everyday speech of interviews. And though we are very much interested in the colonial, there is nothing "post" about the colonial we seek. Nor, for that matter, is the Irish context directly involved. We stopped in Ireland on the route of a larger project that will also take us through England and Scotland that requires talking to British men and women who lived and worked in imperial India before independence—as colonial administrators, soldiers, businesspeople, and in other capacities. My interest is in part personal and comes out of my Fulbright grant in India in the 1960s, an experience that made me curious about earlier generations of Western sojourners on the subcontinent, who certainly left their mark upon the cultural landscape in various ways.

But my fellow interviewer and I are both folklorists, and our current project is also part of an interest in the expanding conception of the parameters of folklore, of seeing folklore as something possessed and communicated by virtually all human groups—not just "peasants" or "the common people" or "country folk," not just wizened mountaineers and star-crossed Delta bluesmen. Although our purpose here has a connection to oral history, we see our endeavor as folkloristic and ethnographic, as an exercise in what Margaret Mead and Rhoda Métraux once called "the study of culture at a distance."[2] The distance is temporal as well as spatial, for the subculture of our focus no longer exists either in situ or the present time because the colonialists of India mostly came "Home" to the British Isles when their world in Asia ceased to exist.[3] We want to know what sort of folklore existed in that world and, in passing, see something about the lore of a politically and socially elite group. To mention the various purposes of this project, however, merely provides a sort of prologue and—though the stories of the sahibs will play an important role here—this project on Anglo-India is but one focus of this book. Rather, the book is intended as a meditation on the importance and value of narratives, oral narratives especially and personal narratives in particular—by which I mean the structured and repeated stories that virtually all of us tell about our lives and the events and forces (personal, historical, and cultural) that have shaped our lives. In doing so, I mean to draw upon both research and stories of significance to me personally or other people I've known. Such stories form us and communicate who we are and constitute parts of larger narratives such as life histories and social epics. In the past I think folklorists have performed a singular service to the study of history and culture by repeatedly calling attention to such "humbler" narratives, though I also hope to suggest more about the meanings these stories possess in our repertoires of narratives while placing some into contexts as part of my personal and family repertoire, necessarily against the backdrop of memory and memoir.

We sit in the pub—a rather upscale one—and eat tasty fish sandwiches made on excellent rolls with Ian, the informant we have come to see; his wife, Davida; her brother-in-law, Howard; and Howard's brother, Arthur; as well as Davida's sister (and Howard's wife), Marian (Arthur has never married).[4] All three men belonged to the small, elite Indian Civil Service, or ICS, the corps which provided imperial India with its key administrators. I am particularly struck by a story Arthur tells, about what happened to him after he left India following Partition (we have learned that our informants seldom speak of the independence of India and Pakistan, but rather reference the partition of one entity into two nations as the culminating event of the British Raj). Arthur's story went something like this (we had no tape recorder at our pub lunch, so I am re-creating it here[5]):

"Well, I had gone on to Egypt when I left India [Arthur said]. I was making my way south. I thought that perhaps I would reach Kenya, you see, and might try coffee farming there. But when I reached the cataracts of the Nile, I ran into an English chap and he said to me, 'I say, aren't you wearing a Marlborough tie?' And I said I was. Marlborough was my old public school.

"And he asked, 'Were you at Marlborough?'

"'Yes, of course,' I said, or something of the sort.

"'Why, so was I,' he said, and we chatted a bit about Marlborough and the people we might have known in common, though we had been there at rather different times.

"'Well, what are you doing now?' he finally asked.

"I told him I had left India and was heading for Kenya and might try coffee farming, but he had another idea, you see.

"'I'm in the Uganda Judicial Service,' he said. 'Why don't you come to Uganda and join the Judicial Service?'

"And so that's just what I did."

It is the quintessential old school tie story. In the middle of Africa—still very much a colonial place, though India has become something else—he is literally wearing a tie. This itself is a rather extraordinary fact, and by it his identity is recognized as an alumnus of an elite "public school," and hence, not only as someone with an important link to the man he has run into but as someone suitably qualified—even without further inquiry—to assume an important position as a judge in African colonial courts.

It is a story about an encounter full of assumptions about the character and abilities of someone who attended a certain kind of school and who thus is a member of a certain class, and about the rightness of his taking a position in which he will judge the affairs of inferior, colonized people. It is also a story that reveals what a small world we deal with in our interviews—this world of the British upper classes whose members assumed a certain right to govern others. Its inhabitants have all gone to the same schools, wear the same ties, encounter each other in far-flung if unlikely places, trust each other, make assumptions about each other, and take care of each other's interests.

In reality, Arthur's significant ICS experience might also have entered into any consideration of him as a suitable candidate for this new career.[6] But the story does not take that into account, but rather focuses on the smallness of the (imperial) world, class solidarity, and the one-of-us-ness that unified certain phases of the British colonial endeavor. Arthur seldom expressed these ideas directly in the course of our interviews, yet they were certainly revealed in his story of the beginnings of his second colonial career. Indeed, the narratives embedded in our larger interviews often revealed much, and much that was never stated directly, suggesting the revelatory power of oral narratives as people encode into their stories, even the most "simple" ones, what they might not otherwise say.[7]

The great importance of stories in human communication has been recognized increasingly by contemporary scholarship. Those who engage in narratology—from whatever academic disciplines they may come—have written repeatedly of the great significance of story in human cultures. Cognitive scientist Mark Turner, for example, goes so far as to say that "story . . . is the fundamental instrument of thought," while linguist Charlotte Linde calls narrative "perhaps the most basic of all discourse units."[8] Turner and Linde are referring, of course, to stories of all sorts, and narratology has given particular attention to the grand narratives of literature, film, and historical writing. Yet folklorists deserve special credit for having looked at the most humble stories, at the folktales and legends of people often socially marginalized. But in recent years they have also given close attention to the most everyday stories, the personal narratives that people tell about themselves in and sometimes about ordinary situations. Folklorists are not the only ones to study such narratives (one thinks, for example, of the pioneering work of William Labov), but they have taken to these stories with a particular appreciation for them and a particular intensity of interest. Certainly in the larger scheme of things such narratives are easily ignored. Yet frequently they provide telling insights into worldview and cultural attitudes and assumptions so that our attention to them can be very rewarding from the standpoint of cultural understanding. As I have said, my Anglo-Indian informants' personal narratives often pointed to underlying ideas that they seldom—if ever—addressed directly.[9] They did provide what Clifford Geertz calls "hindsight accounts of the connectedness of things"—accounts that were often less self-conscious and less deliberately constructed than other, direct statements, but which made important connections as the narrators looked at their colonial lives in retrospect, telling stories that obviously had personal meanings for them that also seemed to comment on larger themes and issues.[10]

For example, during our interview with Howard and his wife, Marian, she recounted the following story (which *was* recorded and is quoted here as a precise transcription), which centers on her father, also an ICS man; the setting is a family holiday in Kashmir:

> We just spent our time on the water. Beautiful lakes. We learned how to swim there . . .
>
> But there was, curiously enough, over there a myth [that] there . . . was something that dwelt in the lake, a female who used to attract people, and, you know, Daddy was practically drowned under our very eyes . . . He was turning most peculiar, and it was this thing, this goddess if you like . . . was asking for him. And it was only that we were out in the boat and the *mangi*—that's the head sort of boatman over there—he threw out his . . . paddle, and Daddy was able to grasp, get hold of it, and we rescued him. And, you know, he'd never go out again like that because he said he used to feel drawn towards the water, and it was quite the usual thing, apparently, that this . . . It had to claim a victim or two. And you'd never think on these beautiful, calm lakes surrounded by hills and mountains that anything like that could happen.

Although our informants discussed quite openly some of the dangers of life in India—sometimes making light of them—this story suggests *hidden* dangers and fears they did *not* discuss. The danger here is not something specific and concrete, like disease or a marauding tiger, but rather something virtually unrecognized by the educated Western belief system, and which suggests a dread of unknown forces that might suddenly destroy the European. The setting is a hill station, one supposedly among the safest for Europeans because it was away from the heat and dust and teeming Indian masses on the plains at lower altitudes and because the cool climate during the hot-weather season would seem more familiar and congenial to natives of England and Scotland. Yet the protagonist is practically sucked to his death nonetheless. The "goddess" perpetrator may be "demon" India herself, which both attracts and frightens the British, and the story can certainly be seen as reflecting a generalized fear of the consequences of the British presence here—a fear that logically would have been quite real, if perhaps suppressed, and indeed one that was never brought up to us in the responses to our many questions.[11] The story also suggests a certain assimilation of Indian folk beliefs, something virtually never touched on in other aspects of the interviews, though our questions tried to probe the connections between British and Indian on the cultural level.

I have included these two sahib stories here partly because I just like them. I grew up, an American in New York City, with the idea of the British Empire as not only unimaginably vast and sprawling—such that an Englishman might shift from one part to another with seemingly little effort—but also as being run by an elite; and Arthur's shift to Africa and his encounter there reinforced my conceptions. Like many of us, I admit to a certain fondness for the macabre and the supposed nearness of supernatural forces, and the story of the Kashmir lake appeals to just that. But I also recognize thematic concerns in both stories that demonstrate how stories can communicate. That possibility for communication is not only found in stories from the other side of the world but from far more homey ones, such as those that many families maintain to pass on the familial past and familial values. Rather, as my retired Anglo-Indian sahibs partly spoke of their past experience through stories, so did the members of my family partly remember the collective familial past through passed-down oral narratives; and certainly those stories I heard for much of my life had a far more pronounced effect upon me than did stories I recorded years later, even if both kinds could be understood as conveying meaning. Unlike the generically personal narratives just given, my family's stories are more communal—like the traditional tales folklorists have historically most comfortably studied, a similitude that Mody Boatright recognized as "family saga."[12] Nonetheless, I see a relationship between them and personal narratives in that both kinds of stories sort of fly under the radar in that they are transmitted so informally and are ubiquitous but seldom collected or published as such. Because they are common within particular personal and familial contexts, non-folklorists tend to pay them little attention, though in fact they can tell us a great deal.

My family (I will discuss only stories of my mother's "side" in this chapter) has a number of stories, but a particular group of them—all involving my great-grandparents Charley and Annie Brown "out West"—have enjoyed particular popularity among my relatives who, I think, see them as particularly significant.

Charley's father, William C., was a Brooklyn police captain who later engaged in land investments, mostly on Long Island, and who at one point, acquired from the Kansas Pacific Railway a parcel of land in Kansas; in the late 1870s, Charley and Annie went west to work it, and two of their children, including my grandmother, Myrtle Belle Brown, later Mulvehill, were born there. We assumed they had gone west in a covered wagon, pulled like iron filings by the great westward magnet. Stories of their time in the West (they stayed only a few years before going back to New York) had become central family legends by the time of my childhood in the 1940s. They were the stories we all knew and that held us spellbound—though there may have been a few dissenter in-laws who discounted their truth and refused to feel their potency—and they form a sort of fragmented, sketchy saga. Their telling had no particular order, nor were they necessarily told as a group, though I think of them now as a continuous narrative. My grandmother herself almost always told these stories, and after she passed away in the 1960s, they were well fixed in our minds. The stories went like this (and they have become so much a part of me that I do not even remember particular retellings, so I am not so much trying to re-create them as to limn their essential "facts"):

One night my great-grandparents went to bed. The mattress—really the focus of the story—was simple, a sort of sack filled with corn shucks to provide what must have been a crinkly, rustling comfort. Charles Brown, no doubt tired out from a hard day in the West, fell asleep, but his wife kept feeling something—not Charley—moving around in the bed. In fact, the movement seemed to be coming from inside the mattress itself, like little, spasmy earthquakes rumbling up from this soft substance beneath her. She awakened her husband, complained. He, however, dismissed her complaint and rolled over into sleep once more. But she continued to feel these motions and woke him again and finally got him up and looking. They poured the shucks out of the mattress and investigated. There must have been a light—a candle? a kerosene lamp?—and in the pile of limp shucks, a great black snake could be seen wriggling, an uninvited guest at the slumber party, probably swept up with the shucks when the mattress was stuffed into being.[13]

In another story, Charley told Annie about people living in the area who dwelt sort of underground in a house partly dug out of the earth, partly with aboveground walls made of earthen blocks fashioned from the excavated dirt. She disbelieved him, arguing that no one could be so poor as to live such half-buried lives, enclosed by such impermanence and filth. He took her to visit a sod house, and then she believed.

On another occasion (this was a separate story, though one naturally invoked by the previous story), Annie heard of some sod house–dwelling neighbors who had been struck down by the dreaded smallpox. Their food was running low and no one would go near them for fear of the disease. She, however, hitched up the wagon to bring food and clothes and medicine to the sick family. What she brought she hung in sacks in a tree near the house of contagion, with a note instructing the family to burn the clothing and sacks when they recovered. They survived and were grateful.

Figure 1.1. Myrtle Belle Brown Mulvehill as a young woman.

 And once, Annie left Myrtle Belle's brother, Harry, playing by himself while she attacked laundry in a washtub, laundry she then hung billowing to dry in the sparkling Kansas sun. Suddenly she heard Harry scream—a scream that rendered the air electric with dread. She raced to him. He had found his way to a big anthill and plunged into it with toddler joy, and the insects had now counterassaulted, stinging and stinging his tiny body that to their ant world must have seemed a hovering, threatening giant. His pain was great, but his mother brushed him off and he survived.

But these are virtually prologue stories that only lead to the supreme stories, wherein the temporarily westering Browns encounter—go toe to toe with, involuntarily present tribute to—the mythic Plains Indians, who come riding out of the shimmering dust.

Sometimes, my grandmother would say, beginning with a little background, bands of Indians would ride down on a farmstead. They wouldn't hurt any whites but would steal anything that wasn't nailed down, rampaging around the yard and outbuildings. But the Browns—and no doubt other wily folk—would keep them out of the house by wrapping their faces in cloth like mummies and come outside yelling "Poxy! Poxy!," feigning the specter of smallpox that the Indians feared.

This story served as a scene setter, taking the listener into the Wild West, with marauding Indians pouring out of the distance, menacing white settlers—though the settlers, including the Browns, remain sort of semi-spectators themselves; these Indians didn't actually hurt any whites. This encounter indeed introduced Indians, though it seems a puny enough encounter compared to Myrtle Belle's own, through which she not only enters the family saga but steps briefly onto a larger stage of American legend in what seemed to us the supreme story:

She had gorgeous golden hair. So naturally, the darker Indians were attracted to her. And they acted, snatching her up and riding off with her, not once but twice—once on horseback, once in a wagon. Once Charley Brown chased her abductors and got her back. Once a neighbor somehow grabbed her before she disappeared into the borderland of captivity. And so she got to go back East and grow up and become our progenitress, riding Brooklyn streetcars instead of a war pony, living in the still shadow of emerging skyscrapers rather than with the prairie wind wild in her golden hair.[14]

The extent to which people think about and analyze their family stories—such as these—and wonder about what they "mean" no doubt varies but in general is probably limited. Doubtless all family stories tell their listeners something about the family's place in the world, providing some knowledge of origins and evolution that people want to have about their own realities. The stories supply something satisfying and in some way important but not intellectualized. As Elizabeth Stone notes in her book *Black Sheep and Kissing Cousins: How Our Family Stories Shape Us*, family stories:

provide the family with esteem because they often show family members in an attractive light or define the family in a flattering way. They also give messages and instructions; they offer blueprints and ideals; they issue warnings and prohibitions . . . Family stories underscore . . . the essentials, like the unspoken or admitted family policy on marriage or illness. Or suicide. Or who the family saints and sinners are, or how much anger can be expressed and by whom . . . Family stories convey the bad news, but they also offer coping strategies as well as stories that make everyone feel better . . . They say what issues—from the most public and predictable to the most private and idiosyncratic—*really* concern a given family.

But it's the folklorists who come along and start worrying about these meanings and significance and mine stories for larger social and cultural understandings.[15] I'm personally grateful that they do, and it's probably because I am a folklorist that I have mulled over the meaning of my own family stories, as well as those stories of my British informants. I'm grateful that my predilections for studying folklore have impelled me to do so, giving me a more structured sense than I might otherwise have of why the stories endured and what they tell me.

Although in fact, these stories are not chronologically the earliest from my mother's side of the family, they are in a real sense the ur-stories of origin and do seem to me stories of genesis—not literally genesis into life but into the "myth" and realities of the American experience. They fling the family—or the Brown redaction of it, with its obscure national origins (Germany, England, Scotland, and Ireland all having been proposed)—not merely into America but into the heart of a "mythic" center of the American past: contact with Native Americans, the fabled aboriginal inhabitants who have exercised such a potent influence on America's past and our American identity. There is Myrtle Belle's brief incorporation into a key American legend—that of the golden-haired maiden who attracts and is captured by swarthy savages—a narrative with a multitude of psychosocial ramifications. And there are the predators who swoop down on farmsteads—though their raiding is relatively benign and easily dealt with—drawing family members into (fairly safe) hostile encounters such as set before us so many times by Hollywood Westerns and dime novels.

But the larger group of stories connects the family to one of the key encounters of the American imagination in the country's history: pioneering the great West. In fact, the family spent comparatively little time as pioneers before going back East. They may even have failed as pioneers; no oral or documentary information explains why precisely they retreated back to New York, where they merely resided on rural Long Island, which was still primarily farm land, or were humble dwellers in the growing city of Brooklyn, which would soon be gobbled up by the more voracious metropolis that reached out from Manhattan. But the importance of the stories is that they testify that the family was there, however transitorily, sharing in something so essential and undergoing the sanctifying hardships of pioneer life: stinging insects, sod houses, smallpox. The stories clearly situate the family into a meaningful cultural and historical milieu and give us a recognizable place in the national saga. In a larger sense, they provide some understanding of how stories function to provide individuals and groups with meanings and they speak about relationships between people and greater historical events and social meanings.

My attitude toward the personal narratives of my sahib informants is more distant than that toward my family stories, to which I have a strong emotional attachment. But for both, I seek meanings and am grateful that folklorists have persisted in seeking meanings for oral narratives of many kinds, including the humbler sort that are especially ephemeral. Folklorists do many things that, if often unsung, have great value in life. In particular, they document those who might otherwise be lost to history; they document local contexts; they document the artistry of the vernacular, whether verbal or visual or artifactual. And they give us—one hopes that the "us" includes many who are not folklorists—some sense of how both everyday and nonelite creations, whether stories or songs or something else, provide insights into the human condition, proving that such important insights come not only from observing our more grand genres and celebrated productions but from all human communication and expression and creativity.

In recent times, folklorists have insisted that in interpreting oral culture we observe the contexts of communication. No folklore exists—certainly narratives do not—in a vacuum, but rather in some social and cultural milieu that influences what is communicated and how. Stories have certain purposes: to entertain, to teach, to express, to sanction behavior, to speculate on the divine or supernatural. That is, stories function within larger social or personal narratives: what an individual wants the story of his self to be, what group members want as the big story about their values, their worldview, their destiny. What follows in this book, then, I frame in part as memoir, as recollections of my life that include the embedded stories as part of those recollections—stories that I tell or have told or that other people do or did, stories that are not the whole of memory but which constitute parts of it that have, for whatever reasons, crystallized as central, oral communicators of memory and that have been shaped to communicate particular ideas or impressions or viewpoints. What follows is hardly an autobiography, but rather some vignettes of my life that are stories themselves that include or relate to personal narratives. Although obviously I have felt the desire to tell something about my life, or rather a few parts of it, as a folklorist, I am intrigued by how personal narratives and other kinds of oral stories play a role in life-projection and in expressing a variety of ideas.

I begin at a sort of personal chronological beginning.

NOTES

1. My collaborator on the "sahib project" (the sixth person at the table in the pub besides myself) is my wife and fellow folklorist, Rosan Augusta Jordan. Our joint publications stemming from this research are "The Wrong *Topi*: Personal Narratives, Ritual, and the Sun Helmet as a Symbol," *Western Folklore* 43 (October 1984): 233–48; "Comentarios acerca del Folklore de una elite colonial," *Cuadernos del Instituto National de Antropología* 13 (1988–1991): 47–57; *British Voices from South Asia* (Baton Rouge: Louisiana State University Libraries, Special Collections, 1996); and the online exhibition "British Voices from South Asia," www.lib.lsu.edu/special/exhibits/e-exhibits/India.htm. Additionally, using material from the project, I published "Differential Uses of Narrative," *Fabula* 29, no. 1 (1988): 143–49, and she published "Foodways in British India: A Letter from R.C.A. Edge to Rosan Jordan," *The Digest: An Interdisciplinary Study of Food and Foodways* 7 (Fall 1987): 4, 21.

2. Margaret Mead and Rhoda Métraux, eds., *The Study of Culture at a Distance* (Chicago: University of Chicago Press, 1953).

3. That *home* was spelled with a capital *H* was a standard joke. A variation had *England* spelled with a capital *H*.

4. Although I have used only first names to identify these people, because of Howard's—and possibly Davida's—sensitivity about material we recorded, I nonetheless have used pseudonyms (although a number of other persons recorded in connection with this project and who are quoted either in this or other chapters, are identified by their real, full names). Arthur's actual public school was not Marlborough. In discussing stories told by members of this group at this point in the book, I do not mean to suggest that their stories were more significant than those told by others I interviewed. They do, however, constitute a neat grouping for this chapter; I include many other stories told to us in the course of our Anglo-Indian research in chapter 10.

5. In this book, I mostly discuss stories not tape-recorded. Some stories from my Anglo-Indian informants in Ireland happened to come up in informal contexts when taping was not taking place. In the case of my family stories, taping has never seemed appropriate (though that perspective may seem wrongheaded to other folklorists). In the later chapter concerning the sahib project, a number of stories are quoted in full from recordings (which are indicated by block passages with no quotation marks), but one or two are summarized. Passages in quotation marks are my renderings of stories, intended to suggest an approximation of an oral story, a sort of imaginative re-creation.

6. An ICS district officer had local judicial responsibilities, and he would have had considerable experience as a judge in certain legal areas.

7. Another story, recorded from Sir George Abell, relating to his time as private secretary to the next-to-last Viceroy of India, Lord Wavell, also evokes the small-world character of the exclusive British public schools (in this case, Rugby) and ultimately, the imperial world. Here even the most exotic-seeming, grand-scale elements of the empire get folded into shared experience, as though the empire itself is a mere extension of school days:

When I was secretary to Wavell, the Tibetan government sent a legation—I think it was a conventional thing to do. They sent one to each viceroy once to pay their respects and ask that their good relations with India should remain the same. They came from the north over the Himalayas, you see. Always under pressure from the Chinese. They came to Delhi and their conventional clothes are a round, sort of velour hat—a homburg—a round felt hat. Then they have white trousers underneath a long black coat and their hair is kept long and they plait it, wind it round their heads and put the hat on top, and they wear the hat indoors. And six of them, or eight of them, turned up. A deputation of leading Tibetans to see the viceroy, and he received them according to tradition in the Durbar Hall, which was a place like a great lake of marble with huge pillars round the sides. And there were members of the bodyguard standing up against each pillar with lances in their hands and huge turbans on their heads. White britches and black boots. This was a very formal occasion. Indeed, everybody frozen and these eight little men in the middle to make their presentation to the viceroy, which consisted of a silver teapot. On these occasions they also have a white shawl, which they put across their arms, and they bring it out and it's sort of a ritual gift. And they all have these white shawls over their hands, and one of them had the silver teapot in his hands, and they walked across this lake of marble, as I said, people looking all around, bodyguard there, viceroy on the throne. And they got halfway across, and the man who'd got the silver teapot dropped it on the marble with a clang. Total silence. We thought, "Oh, no. The whole party's broken up, what's going to happen now?" None of them smiled, none of them cried out. They just halted and stopped. The man who dropped the teapot put it back on his arm. They walked up and made their presentation to the viceroy, and so the formal part of the thing ended. And it was rescued by the extraordinary calm of these characters who looked right out of this world. Nobody'd ever seen anybody looking like this before.

This was to be followed by a luncheon party given by the viceroy. Now I was at the party and I knew no language that I thought these strange characters from the other end of the world would know. And I wondered what would happen if I sat next to one. Sure enough, I sat next to one of these senior members of the Tibetan government, and I thought, "Now, shall we try French, or shall we try Hindustani, English, or what?" And I thought, "Probably we shall have to mumble in our food and say nothing." And then this man next to me—he'd taken his hat off, he'd still got the plait round here—he turned to me and said, "I was at Rugby. Where were you?"

Although some of the stories I recorded for the sahib project probably fall into the category called "small-world stories" by Amy Shuman (*Other People's Stories: Entitlement Claims and the Critique of Empathy* [Urbana: University of Illinois Press, 2005], 89ff), I do not mean to discuss any in those terms. Neither Arthur's story nor Sir George Abell's story seem to me stories of "coincidence and fate," though those may be elements in the narrative. I mean to suggest that the imperial world, because of connections in the metropolitan country and of class solidarity, really tended to be rather circumscribed as a society, and that Anglo-Indian stories of various kinds indicate this. The narrators certainly did not use the coda "Small world, isn't it?" and probably did not intend their stories in that spirit.

8. Mark Turner, *The Literary Mind* (New York: Oxford University Press, 1996), 4; Charlotte Linde, *Life Stories: The Creation of Coherence* (New York: Oxford University Press, 1993), 67.

9. The term *Anglo-Indian* has for some years most commonly referred to persons of mixed European (especially British) and Indian ancestry (people who would at one time have been called "Eurasians") and their culture. I am mostly using it, however, in its older sense of referring to British people residing in India or British society in India; I use *Anglo-India* to refer to their "world" and its society and culture. One informant quoted in this chapter, however, does use *Anglo-Indian* in its "Eurasian" sense.

10. Clifford Geertz, *After the Fact: Two Countries, Four Decades, One Anthropologist* (Cambridge: Harvard University Press, 1995), 67.

11. After our interview with Howard and his wife, back at the rather grand house of Ian and Davida, Ian and Davida told us the story of something that had happened to Howard in India, an account that, unusually, also emphasized the dangers faced by the British in India. A brief summary of the story is as follows: Howard was serving as a district officer in Bengal, a province that experienced much political unrest, and one night a mob attacked his bungalow. He went out to face down the mob, ordering them to halt and disperse. When they did not and instead advanced further, he fired his pistol over their heads. They kept coming, however, and attacked and beat him terribly and left him for dead, and he still suffered trauma from the event. According to Ian, Howard had made a terrible mistake. He should have shot one or a few of the people in the front of the mob, an action that dispersed a threatening crowd and that was, Ian noted, "standard procedure." For years Howard's action was widely known as "Howard's error."

Howard had not told us the story himself, perhaps because he did not wish to speak of a painful incident. But this story told about him by others nonetheless had a nearly anomalous place in the corpus of our interviews—not only because it speaks rather frankly of imperial dangers. Although our informants lived during a period of intense political agitation by Indian nationalists pushing for the British to quit India, our informants said very little about it. In their memories, Indians looked kindly upon them, hoped they would never leave, and maintained only cordial relations with them. Little was said about hostility or tense relations or the political waves that swirled around the era. The story of the attack on Howard constituted a counter-message of discord slipping through that silence, and it could only cause us to think about what we were not hearing from our informants and what they chose to repress.

I do not mean to imply that personal narratives are useful only because they sometimes reveal things that are somehow unconscious and not readily expressed in other ways. But often stories are striking encapsulations of ideas and experiences and thematic points, and personal narratives are a particularly immediate and accessible source for assessing the ideas and attitudes behind the actual narration.

A more typical story of relations with Indians comes from C. A. K. Innes Wilson, head of the Survey of Pakistan following Partition, who told us:

> When I left Pakistan in 1954, which of course was long after Independence, my own department, they were quite reluctant to see me go because I was the end of an era. I went up to Rawalpindi, and at my hotel I was met by a deputation of several hundred women dressed in burkas. I was quite charmed to see this concourse. I asked the driver to go and find out. He said it was a deputation. I said, "Let two of them come forward," and two came forward and took back the tops of their burkas, and they were gray-haired Pakistani women. They said, "Our husbands told us to tell you to stay. You're our last British officer."

12. Mody C. Boatright, *The Family Saga and Other Phases of American Folklore* (Urbana: University of Illinois Press, 1958). For folklorists, the definitive work on the personal narrative

has been Sandra Dolby Stahl, *Literary Folkloristics and the Personal Narrative* (Bloomington: Indiana University Press, 1989). Other work by folklorists in which personal narratives play a significant role include Shuman, *Other People's Stories*; Timothy R. Tangherlini, *Talking Trauma: Paramedics and Their Stories* (Jackson: University Press of Mississippi, 1998); and Eleanor F. Wachs, *Crime-Victim Stories: New York City's Urban Folklore* (Bloomington: Indiana University Press, 1988). Tangherlini and Wachs deal with the narratives of particular groups or situations.

13. An unpublished family genealogy compiled by my cousin John H. (Jack) Mulvehill presents a version of this story that takes place while camping on the journey west. That probably makes more sense, but I remember it being told (or at least conceived it that way) as taking place while they were actually living in Kansas; the availability of corn shucks does suggest a settled farming environment, not trail conditions.

14. In 2007 my cousin Urban S. Mulvehill (during dinner at an excellent Chinese restaurant near Lincoln Center) told me that he had once asked our grandmother about the incident. She had said then that, in fact, the incident had happened to *another* young girl in the same wagon train they had taken west. That certainly suggests that the family was picking up on the more widely known rumors/legends of Indian captivity and that the story is part of a folkloric process; it may also suggest the setting for the story as being on the trail west.

15. I do not mean to say that only folklorists do so. See, for example, Elizabeth Stone, *Black Sheep and Kissing Cousins: How Our Family Stories Shape Us* (New York: Times Books, 1988); for quotations here, see 5, 7, 17.

Two

7002 Ridge

Of course, I was born in a place and grew up in a place and I have always felt strongly influenced by place. My early place was New York City. Like virtually everyone, I must have started hearing stories while still young, must have awakened to the power of narrative as I learned about how people communicate. Yet when I think of the quintessential New York story—the story that most evokes my early place—I think of one that I heard only many years later, after I had left the city. Stories have this power to reach back and suddenly illuminate both past and present, to seemingly pull together our sense of ourselves and our history, our grasp of place. This chapter does contain other stories from this specific time period, but what I refer to as "Paul's story" seems to capture something larger.

I heard this story from my wife's cousin Paul Pettigrew, who at the time was the superintendent of a rural school district in Oklahoma. A former speech and drama teacher in his native Texas, he loved the theater and made intermittent pilgrimages to Broadway and Off Broadway. I do not actually remember him telling this story in the first person, but I have retold it, rendering him a character in his own tale. After first explaining Paul's identity to those who might not know him, I would tell it something like this:

"On one of his New York trips, Paul is walking down the street. Somehow I remember it as Sixth Avenue, but I may have made that up.

"And he passes this bizarre figure, like a street guy, wearing a sandwich board and dressed up like a Norseman, complete with a horned helmet.

"Maybe it was Moondog, the street poet—who did use to hang out on Sixth Avenue, near the jazz venues on Fifty-Second Street—or maybe not, I really don't know.[1]

"Anyway, as Paul passed him, so do these two really blasé New Yorkers, and they give the street figure a quick glance, and one of them says to the other:

"'Hunh. Another Viking.'"

Another Viking indeed! What more could be said? What more, that is, by a New Yorker, blasé to the point of some cosmic indifference, wrapped in a world full of everything, including an oversupply of Vikings, wrapped in a worldview which has viewed it all—every vice, every treasure looted from somewhere else, every shade of human color, especially every fantasy.

But I myself viewed the New York of my childhood and youth (the late 1940s through the early 1960s) not with the jaded sense that I had already seen it all, but rather with the awed and wondrous sense that my city held, in powerfully concentrated form, all that anyone ever needed to see—a confabulation of sights and experience that out-of-towners needed a lifetime of traveling to accumulate: dinosaur skeletons, mysterious gothic mansions behind great iron fences, kosher shops with strange letters posted in their windows, rows of piers that extracted from ships' holds the world's wares, enough restaurants to eat a different meal every day of the year, fleets of chauffeured limousines to serve the needs of the rich and smart, and endless miles of subterranean track to serve the needs of the rest, who would take them to neighborhoods with residents who might be beyond their imaginings. Riding the Sea Beach Express—later prosaically renamed the N Train—to Coney Island, one even saw small farms, refutations of the urban that nonetheless confirmed the vastness of this urbs, certified its evident power to encompass existence itself.

While I seem to stress its wonders, the New York world of my childhood and youth was, of course, a mixture of the exotic and the mundane. And the mundane predominated because the exotic can only glow against the deep shadow of the everyday. I lived in one of the six-story brick apartment buildings that architecturally defined the Brooklyn of a certain era; ours had certain pretensions to grandeur—an awning; doormen; a "super" named Mr. Carlson, who always wore a three-piece suit; a resident congressman; and a handyman called Jim, who periodically washed our sixth-floor windows while dangling from a safety belt like a floating, stationary parachutist. The awnings were repeatedly torn off in storms and eventually not replaced.

Mr. Carlson turned into several successors who did not wear suits of any sort; and eventually—after I had left but while my mother still lived there—had become a Puerto Rican named Julio, who shocked the old-timer tenants by holding pig roasts in the basement and playing Hispanic music that floated up through the courtyards and whose son was sent to prison, I think, for murder, or so my mother's stories would have it. The lobby furniture—with slipcovers that changed with the seasons, along with the rugs—simply disappeared at one point, and no one knew whether it had been sold or stolen or simply disintegrated in storage. One year the indifferently decorated Christmas tree just failed to appear and thus ceased to be an institution.

The doormen, too, were let go until only one remained, on the night shift, who was called Charley by most, but Charles by my mother, grandmother, and me because it sounded more dignified or perhaps just more servant-like. His full name was Charles Fleetwood. He wore a black tie and black jacket while on duty and lived in a basement apartment that guarded the rear entrance to the building—its grimy, blank windows overlooked a sort of cemented courtyard where the children of the building played. His nearly skeletal frame paced energetically and he rode a bicycle all over the neighborhood—far beyond it, for all we knew—a fact that marked him as odd at best; we seldom saw an adult on a bike. He claimed to be a Yale man and that he had grown up at the Mayflower Hotel in Washington, where his father had lived while managing the business affairs of the Queen of Hawaii. Once he gave us a dusty, faded typescript to read, a sort of novella he'd written against the background of Gillette Castle, the medieval fantasy erected by the razor tycoon on the Connecticut River. Gillette, Charles said, had been a family friend who had encouraged him to write the piece and said he would help with publication, but nothing ever came of it. Even as a kid, reading the novella, I understood that our doorman did not have the literary gift, though he certainly had this fund of stories.

His bony frame, combined with a funereal disposition and a half-smile that suggested inner secrets, made him a chilly note in our lives, a Charles Addams character without the light Addams touch. To the building's kids especially, he was an unsettling, quasi-authority figure poised to pounce upon our infractions—the skates in the lobby, too much noise out front. Yet he protected us—literally guarded the door—and controlled access at least during the hours of darkness and was a human presence that saw us off and, in his way, welcomed us home. He coached a local boys' basketball team, apparently to some effect, and the team's members would come by enthusiastically looking for "Mr. Fleetwood." He delighted in riding his bicycle backward. The building's owners attempted to get rid of him, provoking tenant meetings to save our last doorkeeper. We saved his job once or twice, but eventually he too was sent packing, and the building seemed to sink slowly to some more ordinary level of existence.

I remember one event in which he entered my life, have it as both a vivid personal memory and a story I've told:

"It was late at night and I was home in the apartment, undressed for bed, with my mother and grandmother, and the doorbell rang, and it was

Charles standing there in an overcoat. He insisted that I had to come with him, so I put on a coat over my pajamas and I guess shoes of some kind, and I followed him out to the alley that went behind the apartment building.

"He told me to look up, and I saw a night sky that sparkled with an unusually fine array of stars. The darkness seemed especially vivid, and the stars sort of stood out.

"He knew the stars, and he pointed out constellations to me. I've never actually had the imagination to connect those little dots of light into the Pleiades or Pisces, so I'm afraid I probably just stared blankly. But I was also impressed by the awesomeness of it all, of the universe, and I gazed at it in that spirit too."

Even then I found it amazing that this man had gotten me—practically snatched me out of bed—to see the immensity of existence above and beyond the six-story buildings and the streets of my city.

Charley Fleetwood did, I suppose, straddle the mundane and the exotic. He spent his life, as we knew it, standing around the lobby of an ordinary New York apartment building—an increasingly ordinary one, as its pretensions slowly dropped away—eyeing all comers, polishing what little brass there was, coolly greeting those he chose to greet. Yet he stood out as a local character whose odd reality was a bit resplendent against the backdrop of humdrum Bay Ridge, and there were those hints of a different past. I have no idea whether the narrative bits of his putative past that he shared with us were true, but they seemed to loom out of a grander, certainly WASPier world where noble gestures—his father, Charles was proud to tell us, had died of a chill he caught when he removed his hat for the national anthem at the start of one bitterly cold Army-Navy game—bespoke the steely resolve of a more splendid age.

The roof of the building, too, seemed to hover on the edge of the exotic, much as we would sometimes hover on its literal edge, looking over it and seeking the slight dizziness of fearful heights while clutching the security of the parapet itself, wondering sometimes what it would be like to start down the outside stairway that descended to a series of fire escapes. The building was taller than most around—a row of graceful brownstones ran down Ovington Avenue, which ended at the front of our building, and blocks of single-family houses set along quiet, one-block-long streets flanked its rear (one of which even had a white frame house with shutters that looked plucked out of some old New England seaport)—so that the roof offered an impressive vantage point. It was an ordinary, flat Brooklyn roof with tar on the top that would soften in the summer heat; we shivved Popsicle sticks into its thick spots and wriggled them in the soft blackness. The two ends contained wooden platforms with clotheslines, and in warm weather the tenants flew the flags of their washing to dry in the still sun or gusty breeze. Ordinary life went on there, but what a transcendent view. Just below were the Brooklyn rooftops, and a little further away, the rotund, gray-girdered shape of a great gas storage tank. The roof provided a different perspective at least, showing angles and relationships not perceived from one's usual, grounded vantage. But beyond stretched a whole swath of world, the empire beyond 7002 Ridge Boulevard: the Statue of Liberty, the curve of the Staten Island shoreline, the Lower Manhattan skyline, and all the way to the Empire State Building in Midtown. The view was not, however, a matter of landmarks, obscure or celebrated, but of expanse and possibilities: the harbor promising the sea lanes of the globe; the New Jersey horizon barely hiding the curves of a land that rolled on practically forever; and the jagged outer wall of the City (as we called Manhattan, as in "I'm going into the City tomorrow") whispering of endless pleasures to be had within the gates.

People gathered on this roof, as people did in the Brooklyn of those times. One Fourth of July evening, when my mother's brother, Uncle Urban Mulvehill; his wife, Aunt Margo; and cousins Mag and Urbie lived in the building, we all lit sparklers and shot off firecrackers placed on the parapets and thus lit the darkness with trim, powerful flashes and slow, fountain-like sparks while the Statue of Liberty glowed appropriately as a backdrop and pyrotechnicians more adept than we set off radiant bombs over the harbor and lit up distant skies. But mostly people went to hang clothes and talk and enjoy the view. It seemed that we knew all eighty-odd families who lived in the building and that we were a tiny, vertical village, though surely there were virtual strangers among us, and I remember only a handful of actual people.

Among them were Harold and Madeline Blunt—Captain and Mrs. Blunt, as we always thought of them then. He was a sea captain of sorts, captain of an Esso tanker that cruised the coast down to the Carolinas, a beefy man with the mustache of a British Army officer. Once, when I expressed my interest in boats and sailing, he took me up to the roof to show me how to shoot the sun with a sextant. Like Charley's attempt with the constellations, I'm afraid that I only stared rather blankly through the magnificent instrument he put into my hands and came to doubt my possible future as a navigator. Mrs. Blunt—née Carter—was likable despite her imperious self. She insisted that she was a *Mayflower* descendant and she did really belong to the Daughters of the American Revolution. Once she told us her story of sending a Catholic proselytizer packing by declaring, "I am a direct descendant of Martin Luther!"; and she certainly seemed to believe that she was.

She was especially friendly with my mother, in part because we had some claim to being an "old" Bay Ridge family, at least old enough for Mrs. Blunt. My mother, Bee, remembered when Fourth Avenue had mostly been fields and the family had lived in a fine brownstone on Seventy-Fourth Street with servants and a few Protestant connections and once was listed in something called the *Brooklyn Blue Book*, a little intermittent volume that passed for the borough's social register. Mrs. Blunt was certain my mother could get into the DAR if she would only check out her Long Island ancestors; she did get her involved in Colony House, a settlement house that enjoyed the patronage of Brooklyn's female elite. My mother even became corresponding secretary, an office with duties mostly involving periodically sitting at a card table and addressing hundreds of postcard meeting notices. What interested me about this, however, was that Colony House itself was located in mysterious and vaguely ominous Downtown Brooklyn. Someone would point out its street while we rode past on the Third Avenue bus to shop at the renowned Abraham and Strauss, and it seemed dark and narrow. More interesting was the Colony House thrift shop on Atlantic Avenue, where Bee put in a volunteer day every month or so, and which thus took her into another world. The shop became especially interesting after the staggeringly notorious bank robber Willy Sutton was captured in this very neighborhood and someone at the shop recalled that he used to buy his ties there. When, not long after Sutton's capture, the young man who had spotted him and turned him in—Arnold Shuster, whose local fame was instant—was shot down in the streets, the genteel shop became a notorious place in my mind, and my mother, and her gripping accounts of Colony House stories, certainly became a more interesting person to me.

Other residents at 7002 included the Iveses: he an ebullient man who bustled about, often doing favors for others; she someone I seldom saw and who later became a genuine recluse, never leaving her apartment. In the years after Mr. Ives's death and before she moved to Baton Rouge, Bee spent a lot of time with her, providing a contact with the outside world and securing from her a florid bronze statue of an angry Latin drawing his knife that I indelicately named "The Dago Card Player."[2] There was Mr. Brooks, a tall, dignified dealer in foreign exchange who once brought me a bag full of exotic coins—odds and ends—which I kept as a treasure for many years, certain that one day one of the coins would prove tremendously valuable. There was Congressman O'Toole, who, when a small fire broke out in one of the apartments and firemen poured into the building with their gleaming axes and hoses the size of big pipes, hustled about as if he were directing the whole operation. There were my contemporaries such as Paul Kaye, who acquired from some mail-order catalog a very real-looking toy tommy gun made of metal such as no one had ever seen before, and who would tell none of us from whence it came; and Paul Wright, who had a notable penchant for being hit by cars—never, seemingly, to any great injury—because he had great stores of nervous energy and dashed across streets without looking any way, let alone both ways. There were the Ivingses, with their daughter, Marilyn (a little older than I), and son, Billy (a little younger), who also acquired the first known television set at 7002. When I would later tell the story of my first encounter with television, I would also tell about these neighbors I remembered.

I don't remember any warning about the advent of television. For some reason, we were not a radio household, and my earliest contact with the mass media consisted mostly of bringing in the three (three!) evening (!) newspapers that stacked up at our door—the *World Telegram and Sun*, the Hearst *Journal-American* (my own special favorite because of its *pages* of comics and because the front-page headlines were set in *red* type, an ironic color given the paper's obsessive anti-communism), and the Brooklyn *Eagle*, by then a pale ghost of its glory days when Walt Whitman edited it or when globe-trotting Brooklynites fondly stopped by its offices in Rome for news of home, as my aunt Frances recorded in one of her diaries from the 1920s. Television—that is, television as a mass phenomenon—must have been lurking somewhere but came as a surprise to me. I was simply informed that the Ivingses had invited me over to watch it and to just go ring their bell; I was expected. I did so and was ushered into their living room, which had become a place of darkness, full of the indistinct shapes of other building residents silently facing a small moving picture that I remember gave off a greenish glow.

Surely I had no inkling that this was more than the latest gadget, that by entering the Ivingses' door and encountering my first moving image of Howdy Doody or whoever, I had stepped definitively beyond their apartment and into the new age—but I was suitably impressed. Unlike some of the other 7002 kids who wore out their welcome at the Ivingses' small screen, I don't recall ever going back there to watch it again. Unlike my friend James Dorfman, who insisted on being taken to the DuMont studios to be in Howdy Doody's Peanut Gallery and often spoke of having seen the Video Ranger in person, I did not become particularly enamored of the medium. But I must have had increasing opportunities to watch it, for I was vaguely discontented until we acquired our own TV set with a seventeen-inch screen—for a while at least, the king size of screens, the ruler of the airwaves. And I finally became addicted to Jackie Gleason and "Your

Show of Shows" and the TV cowboys with their various grizzled sidekicks and their animals with names that evoked speed and valor. Television, of course, did not replace oral storytelling, but rather gave me stories of my early encounters with it.

TV, of course, was a nighttime phenomenon. Our days did not transpire before the flickering screen. Our days were on the streets and in courtyards and alleyways and parks. Behind 7002, metal picket and high chain link fences defined a concreted, rectangular space in which to play games. "I Declare War" involved chalking off spaces and writing the name of a country in each one. Each square contained one player. A player would proclaim, "I declare war on . . . England" and throw a rubber ball hard into England's space, and England's "player" would have to chase it. We also flipped or pitched "baseball" cards (I best remember gum card sets featuring World War II scenes, state license plates, and Indians). "Flipping" cards was a contest in which you spiraled a card to the ground to rest beside another player's, winning his if you matched it heads or tails; "pitching" involved skimming cards toward a wall, the card closest to the wall won the batch. I considered hopscotch (sketched out in cabalistic chalk designs) and jacks to be girl games, and I looked upon them with some fascination because they were incomprehensibly beyond my male sphere, as was jump rope (made further esoteric by the formulae chanted as the rope or ropes spun around the hopping players like eggbeaters). Beyond 7002, I tried marbles once or twice in Bliss Park, losing all of mine as others shot them out of a gently sloping hole we'd scratched out. I did this mostly because Bee—thinking of her own childhood—imagined marbles as a grand boy's game. But the glory days of Brooklyn marbles culture seemed to be over by my childhood, and neither I nor anyone I knew was much interested—fortunately, for I was even then a born collector and loathe to gamble any little glass spheres on my meager skills with a shooter.

We played Kings wherever a fair piece of wall abutted a sidewalk. A sort of miniaturized street version of handball, players used their palms to tap a rubber ball—preferably a Spalding, properly referred to as a Spaldeen—against the wall to bounce into the opposing player's court, defined by one square of sidewalk, and he had to return it. When a player missed, his opponent was assigned the letter *k* or *i* or so on, until whoever first reached the word *kings* won the game. If we had a friend with a stoop, we could play stoop ball; but I most yearned to play stickball, the street version of baseball that used only a broom handle bat and a Spaldeen, and perhaps—but probably not—baseball mitts. We almost always played it in the middle of the street, so that the diamond had a most irregular and narrow shape, with bases sketched in chalk or just designated as this fire hydrant or that tree. Because moving cars interrupted the game and parked cars posed omnipresent obstacles on the field of play, we thought it a dangerous game suited only for the tougher element. I indulged in stickball only rarely but always to my delight, feeling, I suppose, gritty and challenged by the odd conditions and it being, well, very urban.

But my urban world did imperceptibly change. The Ivingses moved to Florida, which we scorned as a place of sand and year-round mosquitoes. One summer, while we were staying at Beech Lake in Pennsylvania, a letter arrived with the news that Uncle Urban and Aunt Margo were moving to Connecticut, taking, of course, my cousins—my almost constant companions—with them. These were isolated happenings to me, but they also signaled the winds of suburbanization that were sweeping the nation in the Fifties, carrying people to tidy houses set on soft lawns punctuated by flagstones and crabgrass. We stayed on, perhaps becoming out of place, as time rolled around us and we pushed on into new eras. I did not definitively leave 7002 until 1965, when I moved to East Third Street, in the reluctantly hip East Village.

The stories that relate to this period call attention, I think, to the possibilities beyond the everyday world I inhabited. I lived a normal life of children's games and TV shows—even if TV was just beginning and had the excitement of novelty, it was settling into the predictable—and newspaper comic strips and the usual playmates with toy guns. Some stories and what I'll call fragments of stories were there to transcend the everyday and the mundane, suggesting to me grand realities beyond, like the very view from the roof of 7002. There was Charles Fleetwood's hint of a more gracious world where he had once lived: he of Yale and the Mayflower Hotel, his father the Queen's manager, his connection to Gillette Castle, and his father's death from a noble action while at a great American event. There were Captain and Mrs. Blunt and her stories—admittedly designed probably to stress her social superiority—about her *Mayflower* and Martin Luther connections, stories that suggested a local attachment to a wider world.

Even the seamier stories and accounts offered me glimpses of more interesting realities. My mother's telling me about Willie Sutton's virtual closeness to us through the thrift shop where she volunteered presented such a "reality," of gangsters and stickups and hideouts. Her account was much amplified by the newspaper stories that followed his capture—which, of course, occasioned her account in the first place—and that reported on the tragic murder of Arnold Shuster. Likewise her account (noted just below) of living in the same building with some of the Dodger baseball players and their domestic affairs told of a more glamorous world and our closeness to it—a world far from my own games of stickball or Kings.

These were all stories and fragments of stories that I heard and remembered and have repeated. My own story of being taken outside by Charles Fleetwood to look at the heavens is, I think, also a story about being opened to amazing realities and marvels that we can encounter just by looking up. Paul Pettigrew's story encapsulates and reinforces the idea that I lived in the midst of wonderful things in New York, things I was being exposed to and was increasingly aware of, even if I did live in the provinces of Brooklyn.

Doubtless, as a very young person, I looked to understand avenues for growth, and these stories seem to me to be about possibilities for growth. As our literal, commonplace world in fact declined—the loss of the doormen and the pig roasts in the basement, which could have been seen as the exciting arrival of a new culture but were viewed as threats to an existing world order—other realities beyond could replace what was being lost. The stories hinted of these possibilities. I'm sure that I heard other stories during this time period, and those I've mentioned may have other meanings as well. But I remember and have retold these because they seem important, for I needed to know about the possibilities for expanding my world. Those possibilities seemed to me to be tied particularly to my marvelous place—New York—though certainly the stories of the time were not necessarily about New York as such.

I'm not sure when we moved to 7002, though it is my earliest memory of home. When I was born my parents lived on East Nineteenth Street in Flatbush, in a building that also housed Peewee Reese and another Brooklyn Dodger (maybe Phil Rizzuto), in the days when ball players had more human stature and less fabulous money. One Dodger couple lived right above my parents and Bee always remembered they made ungodly noise fighting. When my father joined the army during World War II, my mother moved in with her mother, Myrtle Brown Mulvehill, at 7002 Ridge, and after he was killed in France, that arrangement just continued, though we eventually moved from a one-bedroom on the sixth floor to a two-bedroom on the first. Where we came from before 7002 is, of course, other stories.

NOTES

1. The often-noticed blind street poet and musician Moondog was Louis Thomas Hardin, who died in 1999; after 1978 he had lived in Germany but was long a fixture on Manhattan streets. He wore a "Viking"-style helmet as part of his persona.

2. Our connection to the Ives family extended beyond 7002. They had operated the "casino" in Beech Lake, Pennsylvania, where the Mulvehills, at one time, took to going in the summer, as noted in a later chapter.

Three

Foreigners Arrive

THOSE OTHER STORIES, WHICH I HEARD "ALL MY LIFE" at 7002 Ridge, start in the second half of the nineteenth century, on the Kansas frontier—stories already recounted in the previous chapter—and in Battery Park in the City of New York. These seem to be the stories of my personal beginning, linking me and my "people" to the national story, situating me and us in time and the great flow of America, giving me my personal connection to larger forces, extending my own life and identity back beyond the 1943 of my birth. Such stories stretch us into other times and other places and even other personalities. Although they may be the stories of my personal beginnings, they are family stories, and family stories enjoy both collective and individual meanings. Family stories put us as individuals into bigger pictures.

These are my stories of maternal and paternal genesis; genesis of a nonliteral sort—not into life but into the myth and reality of the American experience that shaped me and us. If the Browns and Myrtle Belle had not emerged on the Plains, encountering Native Americans as they went, and if Frank De Caro, my grandfather, had not arrived under the classically humble circumstances noted below, I would not exist in my current form and cultural identity, as the stories explain.

FRANK DE CARO ARRIVES IN NEW YORK

Shift back from the Kansas prairies to New York, but not to Brooklyn or the Browns. The Browns, whose western saga appears in the previous chapter, are said to have returned from the West when Myrtle Belle was two years old, so around 1882. Perhaps they had failed as pioneers, or perhaps they grew bored by the relentless monotony of the prairie or were unsettled by the reassuring normalcy of the developing midwestern accent. Although the stories of what happened during Myrtle Belle's time Out West had a powerful

Figure 3.1. Frank De Caro, 1886.

impact on our collective, familial imagination, we hear little more of her in stories until she is old enough to be courted. We *do* hear a little of the life the Browns returned to, and I remember particularly those stories told by my Great Uncle Harry Brown, my grandmother's brother. What I don't remember is just how he actually told his stories, so they, like the Kansas stories, have become more narrations of the "facts." Living in Bay Ridge, on a portion of New York harbor, Myrtle Belle's brother, Harry, became a good sailor, taking sailboats out into the Narrows, the strait that separates Bay Ridge and Staten Island and joins Upper and Lower New York Bays. He was so good that a wealthy young man with a boat, but insufficient sailing skills, hired him to sail him and his bride through New York harbor and up the Hudson. When Harry told the story, he included details that I have since forgotten—for what seemed important was the mere fact that he had done this. And, though sadly, I remember few details here too, I do recall my same great uncle telling stories of when he stayed out on the farm of Brown relatives on Long Island, said to have been located somewhere on the tract that became Camp Upton for the World War I military and later, Brookhaven National Laboratory. The stories of the Hudson sail and the Browns' Long Island farm seemed to broaden the East Coast world, which was inevitably smaller than the wide prairies that Myrtle Belle and her family had returned to.

But, to shift perspectives: let's go back to New York City, approximately two years after the Browns came back East. In 1884 my paternal grandfather (and namesake) arrives from southern Italy, from a town called Giffoni Valle Piana, in the province of Salerno, where he was born in 1866.

I think that he must very much have been one of those neo-Americans who remake and redefine themselves from the outset. I say that because his life before he stepped off the boat as a very young man is a virtual blank to me. There were no stories. Except for the most fragmentary pieces—the name of his town, the vague suggestion that his great-grandfather had been a wealthy merchant who lost money in a shipping mishap, the fact that he had trained as a tailor—there was no information, or none that ever entered my ears then or since. Of close relations, only a sister also came to the New World—contrary to the Italian obsession with *famiglia*, they must not have been close; we had largely lost track of her family by the time of my youth—so that my grandfather seems in retrospect a rather isolated figure, with no strands of Italian family tradition to fill in the stories of the old country he did not seem to have. Hence, it was as if the sea had suddenly cast him upon the shores of America like the foam-born Venus naked upon the half shell, ready to clothe himself in whatever new garments came to hand. Two early photographs show him in the quasi-military uniform of

Figure 3.2. Francesco De Caro (*arrow*) in uniform with Italian-American group.

some Italian-American fraternal or social organization, and he is identified as Francesco Antonio; before long, he became Frank Anthony forever—his name change, like so many other American name changes, marking his cultural and personal transformations.

Here is the story of his (re)birth and, along with the saga from Kansas, the second story of my essential beginnings. As a child I heard the story many times; but even more than with other family stories, I have conceived a sort of visual representation of the events, so that I do not hear the story being told so much as see these things happening in my imagination.

Frank got off the boat. I do not so much see this as see him suddenly on shore. I imagine him processed through the great, red brick, industrial-strength immigrant receiving station of Ellis Island, though in fact, Ellis Island did not begin to function as an immigrant terminus until 1892; so he must have come through Castle Garden on the Battery itself, but Ellis Island is easier to reimagine. He was supposed to be met by some distant relative or *compare* at the Battery, but the man never showed up. I see my grandfather as strangely calm, little perturbed by this unfortunate turn of events. He wandered around a bit, some absurdly small amount of money in his pocket (seventeen cents is the amount that comes to mind), and spent the night—his first night in America—sleeping on a bench in Battery Park: no *Avalon*-like pyrotechnics, no fireboat salutes. The next day he somehow managed to meet up with the distant relative and find his first place in the New World.

This happened in 1884, and as a story, it might be seen as a "typical" immigrant tale: the newcomer lands with nothing, has an inauspicious arrival, and finally manages to be taken in by his community. It sets up the larger narrative for better things to come—and they do—for Frank, like many others, is being reborn into a New World.

COURTSHIP AND RISING IN THE WORLD

As with Myrtle Belle, there are practically no stories about Frank for some years, until he courts my grandmother, Anna Menkhoff, in the 1890s. It is as if Myrtle Belle and the first Frank Anthony—who were never to meet until the next century, through their children, probably around 1920—incubated for a while, growing into their roles as ancestors; hence they are not of much significance in family memory or story until they met their future spouses and embodied the potential for creating the rest of us who came after. Perhaps that is the same logic of narrative that in the New Testament mostly hides the child Jesus until He is ready to assume his sacred role.

I imagine them as they inhabit fin de siècle New York. Where precisely each of them lived remains mostly unknown to me, though Frank Anthony evidently lived in East Harlem—then an Italian enclave—some of the time.

Figure 3.3. Anna Menkhoff, probably in costume for a ball.

It was an extraordinary time for New York: a period of expansion, both outward and upward, a time of building and immigrant masses and local energies that both matched and stimulated the energy of America itself—industrializing, electrifying, moving people on rails and in boats, corrupting and reforming—a world of both naked money-grabbing and decorously promulgated, lofty ideals. Interestingly enough, they inhabit the same New York as Jack Finney's illustrated time-travel mystery novel, *Time and Again*, where events transpire in 1882.[1] Perhaps they ride the same horse-drawn streetcars, eat at—or stare into—the same gas-lit restaurants, watch the same Dakota apartments rise on the far edge of the city at West Seventy-Second Street, overshadowing the small-holdings and squatter settlements that still dotted Manhattan at the time.

But around 1891 Frank DeCaro meets Anna Menkhoff.[2] Probably a few years later Myrtle Belle Brown meets John Henry Mulvehill.

By 1891 Frank DeCaro had his own tailoring business on West Thirty-Fourth Street in Manhattan. A photograph shows him standing in front of it—where a sign announces CUSTOM FRANK DE CARO TAILOR and a street number, 511—with another man, who according to family tradition is Antonio Meucci, the Italian inventor of the telephone who was cut out of the credit that went to Alexander Graham Bell; although a little research indicates that this seems not to be Meucci at all, whose image is widely available and who would have been older. Standing a little way off is a black man, about whom family tradition says nothing. Perhaps he was an employee or perhaps just one of those hangers-around who were drawn to posing in group photos in those earlier times when the medium encouraged ritual public posing. Whatever the case, Frank DeCaro must by then have discovered something of the multicultural reality—black and white included—of the American continent. As had Anna Menkhoff, whom Frank would soon marry. At least according to a family story—I do not recall having heard it, but my cousin John McAlevey e-mailed me a summary of it in 2010; he remembered it well and had often told it—the first word she spoke in the New World was *schwarz*, black, when she saw for the first time in her young life African American people in New York.

Indeed, this new multicultural reality would shape the rest of his life, one that initially brought with it certain difficulties. An important family story concerns how Italian Frank and German Anna joined together despite cultural pressures to stay apart. This story was certainly well known to all in the family, though my aunts, Frank and Anna's daughters, probably told it to me. The story, however, was closely tied into a letter that Frank eventually wrote to the Menkhoffs, and which was framed and available for viewing. The story went like this:

On Thirty-Fourth Street, where Frank's business was located, in fact, said to have been in the very block where Macy's, the "World's Largest Store," sits today, was the *konditorei* run by August Menkhoff and his wife. August was a baker by trade and training, and they had emigrated from Germany only a few years before. I imagine lots of people coming into the shop from the busy New York streets; perhaps there is even a shop doorbell that chimes each time the front door is opened.

Foreigners Arrive

Figure 3.4. Frank De Caro, custom tailor, on West Thirty-Fourth Street, late nineteenth century.

In the shop worked the Menkhoff daughter, Anna. She had even noticed Frank DeCaro passing by and has been struck by his good looks. There are a number of theaters in the area, and she thought that he might even be an actor. Then *he* actually came into the shop and noticed *her*, for she, too, is quite attractive and of course, a Nordic blond.

They were attracted to each other and struck up an acquaintance that turned into a romance, initially in the shop, then in the surrounding neighborhood. The Menkhoffs, however, did not approve Anna's evident attraction to an Italian and a Catholic, or perhaps just a non-German. Hence, Frank ran smack into the multicultural reality of ethnic identity and ethnic exclusion and cultural politics of a very personal kind.

He asked her parents for permission to marry her. But he was refused. He had already been coming into the *konditorei*, of course, and the pastries and cakes that he buys from Anna have sent signals about meetings and other messages, though what particular thing a torte or a napoleon meant has not come down to us. Finally, in September of 1891, Frank and Anna slipped away together and secretly got married, against Menkhoff personal and cultural wishes. To inform his in-laws and indeed, to state his case for these rash actions, Frank sent the Menkhoffs the letter, which was later prominently framed as a kind of document that backs up the oral history:

> Dear Sir and Lady
>
> Today your daughter has become my lawfully wedded wife and it has made me the happiest of men. Still it was also sorrow for me as well as Annie that we were married in this style but as you were so much opposed to our marriage we had not the courage to inform you of it. Your opposition was formed by the firm believe that your daughter would be unhappy with me, because I belong to another nation and because I am brought up in the catholic church, but let me assure you that I will never neglect Annie for my countrymen nor anybody else. I love her so deeply and truly and always will love her the same. . .
>
> I am now . . . better situated than the time I asked for your daughters hand and also know that I will better my situation more and Annie will never need to go working as I will earn enough to live comfortable. Dear parents (allow me to call you this) we are happy; all is missing is your forgiveness for taking this step against your knowledge and wishes. We could not part and two weeks almost broke our heart. How would it be for a lifetime? I give you a most solemn promise that I will always be a loving and true husband and a dutiful son to you. Though I have taken Annie from you any time you wish her help in business she will be willing to help you and I will gladly give up a little comfort to help you. I respect and honor you as I do my own parents and again I beg forgive.

Later the Menkhoff parents moved in with the young couple and, according to family accounts, found Frank to be a fine son-in-law.

The story is such an indicator of growing American realities: the old cultural boundaries, despite strong feelings about them, slowly collapse; the northern and the southern merge; the New World breaks apart the parameters of the Old and fuses the pieces into its own design of overlapping ethnic scraps that somehow merge and hold together.

The letter is indicative too of something personal, but in the American vein. Frank speaks of being "better situated" than he once was, expresses his belief that he will better his situation even more, and promises a comfortable life for Anna. Indeed, he has pretensions. Somewhere along the line he becomes the more aristocratic-looking de Caro. He fills a scrapbook with letters from Italian consuls and engraved invitations to consular functions. He receives jeweled stickpins from the King and Queen of Italy. The tiny nation of Montenegro, across the Adriatic from his native country, knights him for his participation in relief efforts.

His business—conducted with a partner for many years as De Caro and D'Angelo—manufactures flags, banners, and uniforms; fashions elaborate tapestries for religious organizations; makes tiny buttons for fascist societies; and provides other goods and services for the Italian-American community. One of the firm's undated catalogs depicts their Grand Street building as very grand indeed, like a small department store or even a railroad depot.

In the summers he sends his growing family to the country. There are a few photographs of them in rural places, but only one story that I can recall. The story probably had several meanings and several purposes in being told. It establishes the family as upwardly mobile, able now to vacation in the country. It suggests the great determination Anna had. And it tells us about how the family ventured out beyond New York City. I probably heard the story from my aunts, who would have mentioned details I have forgotten, like just where the family was and how often the family went away and how long they stayed. So I can only re-create its bare bones:

"So we were away in the country [one of my aunts might have started] and in fact, we were due to go home to Brooklyn the next day. But Frances had been playing a few days before with one of the local country girls, and it turned out that this girl had scarlet fever or diphtheria. Now those were both dreaded diseases then, though you don't hear much about them anymore. And then it was the practice to quarantine people who had come into contact with anybody who had one of those diseases, and Mother [Anna Menkhoff de Caro] was afraid that we'd be stuck there, quarantined because of Frances [my aunt]. So she got us up really early the next morning and had to just sneak the family out of there and back to the city. I think she found someone who would drive us the whole way."

They begin renting a lovely nineteenth-century house on Lake Waramaug in Litchfield County, Connecticut, where other stories will take place. It's the place that brings together the progeny of the Golden Maiden and the darker-haired son of Italy.

But back to New York in the late 1890s. Or, rather, to Brooklyn, which becomes part of New York City only in 1898, in a tight election that may have been rigged. Myrtle Belle is a grown woman, working as a linen buyer at Abraham and Strauss, the behemoth department store, the downtown Brooklyn equivalent of Macy's. She has met John Henry Mulvehill, probably from residing in the same Brooklyn neighborhood—the area just beyond Park Slope, which has developed as Brooklyn has crept out along Fourth

Figure 3.5. John Henry Mulvehill (*right*) with his son Urban and a friend, Luna Park, Coney Island, ca. 1912.

and Fifth and Sixth Avenues toward what are still the open fields of Bay Ridge. He is of Irish extraction, his father and grandfather having arrived in New York together from, according to family tradition, near where the River Shannon flows into the sea. They have come around 1840, probably disembarking from a ship of the Black Ball Line, swift transatlantic packets that figure centrally in at least one Anglo-American sea shanty. According to a story—told, so far as I can remember, only by my mother's cousin Jed Mulvehill—one of them was a bootmaker and came to America because of political troubles with the British authorities; as a wanted man, he had to embark on his emigration ship disguised as a woman, wearing a dress. That story offers both a very particular reason for emigrating—one which adds a touch of the romance associated with Irish rebellious politics and lifts at least one member of the family above the usual assumptions of economic hardship as compelling the shift to America; and it offers a suggestion of the great difficulties that emigration might entail.

But, decades later, in 1890s New York, the story goes:

Myrtle Belle knew the Mulvehill family and knew John's sister, Nellie Mulvehill (the name, according to the story, then being pronounced, in the Irish way, as *Mulveal*). Myrtle ran into Nellie, and for some reason they have not seen each other for some time. She asked, how are all the Mulvehills (Mulveals)? Nellie replied, they're all fine, but now they're pronouncing their name *Mul-ve-hill*.

It's a subtle story but a suggestive one. It is a story of the Americanization (or is it Anglicization?) of a name. But it suggests more than that familiar process. It suggests not so much acculturation—this is the second generation after all—as upward mobility, the leaving behind of not only a foreign name but a déclassé one, one that sounds like dead meat, the adoption of a more harmonious and classy-sounding alternative. It is taking place around the same time Francesco is becoming Frank, and I see it as a story equivalent to Frank's telling his reluctant in-laws that he is prospering and will be well able to care for Anna. His assurances to the Menkhoffs, and the Mulvehill pronunciation change, speak of moving up in the world and ambition and doing what is needed to fulfill ambitions in the America of the time. The fact that the pronunciation change story is virtually the only one to survive from this period hints that this is an important story, not merely indicating a quirk in family history, but something a bit more monumental: getting ahead, moving to something better, reaching critical mass.

Myrtle Belle and John Henry marry in 1900—not once, but twice—initially in a Protestant church because he is Catholic, she is Baptist; subsequently in a Catholic church.

Many years later, my mother, Bee, told me a fragmentary story about learning of where one of those weddings took place.

"Grandma [Myrtle Belle] and I were at Wanamaker's. That was, I think, a Philadelphia department store, but they had a big store in New York too, on Eighth Street in Greenwich Village. And we were in the dressing rooms area, but there were big windows looking out on Grace Episcopal Church, just up Broadway. And Mother told me that was where she had gotten married the first time."

This is one of the more puzzling family stories, partly because documentary research identifies the actual site of the wedding as All Souls Episcopal on East Twenty-Second Street. Perhaps Myrtle Belle was confused or, given subsequent events noted in the following chapter, preferred to forget as much as possible about her marriage, including the wedding. Perhaps she preferred to reimagine a grander setting, for Grace Episcopal is one of the most stylish houses of worship in New York. Why the story has come down at all is a mystery, for it adds little to the family saga. Perhaps my mother was just intrigued to know something concrete—if incorrect—about her parents' past, and such fragments of oral history do serve to fix events in definite places and thus give them an added reality.

Nothing is said of Myrtle Belle and John Henry's courtship by any stories, but we can imagine that his prospects for success may have played a role in his attractiveness; pictures do show him as a handsome man, and evidently he had charm. He does indeed get ahead by going into the insurance business, just as Frank's tailoring and flag-making firm also steams ahead, becoming a force in the Italian-American community even well beyond New York.[3]

INTO AMERICA

The ambitions and successes of both men, Frank and John Henry, drive both of them to Lake Waramaug, propelled into the prosperous upper middle class, whose members seek summer refuge in the coolness of the country, allowing their families to spend the entire season out of the city. The de Caros (by this second American generation, they are mostly inclining toward the small *d*) never bought such a house, just rented the same gracious farmhouse near the landmark Hopkins Inn year after year, eventually summering at a hotel—the Interlaken Inn—farther north in Lakeville. The Mulvehills' summer home remained in the family for many years, though at first they, too, rented.

But another story says something about just how they got there:

Some time in the 1920s, Myrtle Belle and John Henry's second son, Vincent, broke his arm. It was a complicated break and had to be set carefully. The doctor, who undertook to set the thing, properly explained that the procedure, which involved the use of sandbags to provide tension, would be quite painful and that two men would be needed to hold Vincent down on the table while the procedure was undertaken. John Henry agreed to be one and got a friend or neighbor to be the other.

The arm was successfully set, and the doctor recommended that, for Vincent's therapy, the family go away in the summer to a lake where Vincent could row a boat to exercise the arm.

That story always seemed dramatic to me, probably because of the detail of the sandbags, which evoked complicated procedures, though I could never quite imagine what those might be. As a family story, perhaps it meant to say something about Vincent's suffering or John Henry's resolve, but mostly it just forwarded the family narrative to new and important places.

This attempt at physical therapy took the family to several places in the summertime, including an old boarding house in Beech Lake, Pennsylvania, which was attached to a farm run by a family named Olver. The Mulvehills went here for several years and once even took young Horace Olver, one of the sons of the family, back to New York with them. The story about that time was one that my grandmother and mother both enjoyed telling, rather like so:

"One year we were about to leave Beech Lake and come back to the City, and as we were getting ready to leave we discovered that Horace was ready to come home with us. Somebody in the family had made a chance remark to Horace that he should come see us in the City some time. He had taken that as a definite invitation, and he was all set to come, his suitcase waiting by his side. That was a surprise to us, but it was okay, and he came.

"He came for a few days or a week. I'll never forget that he had all of his money tied up in a handkerchief. He had a marvelous time."

Clearly they liked the story because it was about a hick in the big city and appealed to their urban sensibilities, but I think that it also gave them an added feeling of connection to Beech Lake and the Olvers in the heartland of the countryside. Nonetheless, the family eventually switched their allegiance to a place called the Loomarwick Inn on Lake Waramaug, where the de Caros lived in the summer by the 1920s. The Mulvehills liked this lake "in the foothills of the Berkshires," and in a later season found a house to rent. They subsequently bought the house, fronting on the lake, along with a barn that became a garage, in 1926, and it became a central place in the family consciousness and a focus for stories.

So by the mid-1920s, both families are summering at "the Lake." The stories that "get" them there, the stories that recount the families' developments and other related events in the period before the 1920s, are relatively few. For the Mulvehills: the Kansas prairie stories, Harry Brown's sailing activities and his visits to Long Island, the Irish ancestor emigrating disguised as a woman, the name pronunciation shift, John and Myrtle Belle's marriage, Vincent's broken arm, and Horace's visit to the city. For the de Caros: the night spent on a Battery bench, the discouraged romance between Frank and Anna, the elopement leading to a statement of increasing prosperity and a happy family, escaping a quarantine in the country after the family starts going into the American interior in the summer.

The stories are few (and history must be filled in with documentary sources or other, more generalized pieces of memory and oral history), but nonetheless, I see them as a loosely unified narrative chain that constitutes a sort of saga that has its own progression and internal logic, as having definite, limited thematic thrust, communicating not just bits and pieces of a past but particular, related messages.

They are stories, first of all, of connecting with America, a concern perhaps for all Americans who realize that their families came from "someplace else," whether recently or in a more distant past. The prairie stories connect to the great American wilderness, the central historical processes of pioneering and westward movement, and the mythic original inhabitants, the mysterious, wild Indians who have figured so prominently in the American imagination. They tell the family: we were here, participating in this essential American undertaking. But the immigration stories also make an important connection to the essential experience of getting here, of coming from the Old World. Many immigrants to the United States did not find the transition easy. One ancestor, hunted by an oppressive British authority, barely makes it. He has to go aboard ship disguising his very identity (not a bad metaphor for the acculturation to come), humiliating himself by wearing a dress, denying his manhood (not a bad metaphor for colonialist oppression). The other ancestor, Frank, comes virtually penniless, forced by circumstances to spend his first night in America sleeping in the open on a hard bench. These are veritable statements of the hardships of immigration by which so many Americans and American families came to be, but of hardships that were ultimately overcome. He and the woman who later becomes his wife, like the westering Browns, encounter American Others—not Native Americans but black people.

And indeed, the stories, as a group, are also stories of overcoming. The immigration stories assert the family's participation in the process, but other stories go on to speak of the successes encountered beyond, the upward mobility that some would see at the heart of the American Dream. Frank may have come with only seventeen cents in his pocket and had to sleep in the open, but a few years later he can promise growing prosperity to his bride's parents. The Mulvehills pronounce their name in a way more befitting their status. As the families move on in the big, bustling, economic engine of the city, however, they also continue to merge with the fundamental American heartland. There are memories of not only the prairies but also the Brown farmstead on Long Island and a voyage up the fabled, sylvan Hudson; and, as they literally move into the countryside in the summer months, stories tell of encounters out there: of escaping an epidemic or actually bringing home a country boy to see the bright lights of New York.

Finally, the stories speak of encountering the American cultural mix—not only the Native Americans who still occupy the Plains but also other ethnic groups. Frank runs right across ethnic borders, falling in love with an Other, meeting opposition from her group at first, then successfully bridging the gap with her, pulling cultures into alignment, as the nation as a whole learns to do.

So I do see these early family stories as commenting on family involvement in the American endeavor. The actors become my ancestors while they also embed the family in a larger context. Of course, I realize that in one sense these stories are only mine—that I am the only result of these two families eventually merging in my parents—thus bringing together the golden-haired girl of the West and the darker foreigner; other family members may have different stories of other ancestors and may have a different perspective on these stories. But this is, after all, *my* memoir and *my* attempt to come to terms with the stories. I see their accounts of my ancestral beginnings—at least as recounted in stories—as connecting me to the American past and American cultural experience. I think they do the same for others. Once the family is firmly rooted in America, its members can do other things and other stories can emerge.

NOTES

1. Jack Finney, *Time and Again* (New York: Simon and Schuster, 1970).

2. He would spell his last name DeCaro, De Caro, and de Caro, with the family as a whole tending toward de Caro as time went on, probably because it seemed fancier; de Caro appears on my own birth certificate.

3. I've enjoyed telling the story of how in the 1970s or 1980s, when Rosan and I were walking near Jackson Square in New Orleans, we ran into Leo Marcello—an LSU grad student who later taught at McNeese State and was known as a poet—as he enjoyed coffee and beignets at Café du Monde. We chatted, and he said he'd been meaning to ask me if I was related to the de Caro of De Caro and D'Angelo. It seemed that the Italian society in the small western Louisiana town where his family had lived had a banner with the De Caro and D'Angelo label.

Four

The Lake

Lake Waramaug became a key focus for family memories.

The lake, my mother or grandmother would say to people who couldn't place it, is "about twenty-five miles north of Danbury." People might know Danbury, Connecticut, because of its noted hat factories or its fair, which had begun modestly enough in 1821 and developed into a sort of lavish, intermittent amusement park and racetrack that drew people from miles around. The route north from Danbury went to New Milford, a picture-perfect New England town with a green that once graced a *Saturday Evening Post* cover, and then on to New Preston, once on a *New Yorker* cover, the village that sits virtually at the foot of the lake itself. The lake—at about seven-hundred acres, the second-largest natural lake in the state—zigzags through several coves and sits mostly ensconced by verdant hills that create a sort of bowl effect. The borders of three townships—Kent, Washington, and Warren—meet in the middle.

Waramaug is said to mean "place of the good fishing" in the local Indian languages, though this refers not to the lake itself but to a spot below New Milford where the Great Falls impeded shad going up the Housatonic River at a certain time of year; hence, the fishing was good then and there. This was the place where Chief Waramaug, who died in 1735, had his "capital." He took his name from the place, and the lake was within his territory; he placed lookouts atop The Pinnacle, a mountain that overlooks the lake, to watch for incursions by the powerful Mohawks farther west. By the beginning of the eighteenth century, however, white colonists began moving into the area to farm, evidently welcomed by Waramaug and his people as providing a useful barrier against the Mohawks. After his death, the lands around the lake were reserved for his people, but by 1738 these lands were being auctioned off to whites; villages and farmlands appeared and water-powered mills popped up along the Aspetuck River after 1745. George

Washington passed through in 1781 on his way to the Hudson Valley, but what is really important for the Mulvehills and de Caros is that, after 1840, when the Housatonic Railroad opened a station at New Milford, the lake began progressing toward becoming a summer destination.[1]

In 1864 a family from—interestingly enough—Brooklyn found lodging at the Hopkins farm on the lake, and soon several boardinghouses were taking in guests. People began building summer houses. In the 1870s the Bonynge family from New Jersey visited the lake and made it their summer destination, staying at a place called Lakeview Farm. In 1898 they bought the farm and later built the house they called The Maples and that the Mulvehills would later buy from them. The house the de Caros rented was originally a farmhouse built around 1840.

Probably sometime in the nineteenth century, a legend of Chief Waramaug's daughter, Lillinonah, of whom there is no historical record, began to circulate:

Lillinonah found a young white man lost in the woods, brought him home, and they fell in love and married. Later he went to visit his own people and did not return for so long that she despaired of his ever coming back and decided to pilot her canoe suicidally over the Great Falls. He returned just as she was doing so, leapt into the canoe with her, and they both plunged over the falls to their deaths. Great Falls became known as Lovers Leap (along with countless others in the United States with similar stories attached to them).

I never actually heard this story told and did not sense any strong Native American connections to the lake. A family from Bridgeport built a mansion along the Housatonic on the site of Chief Waramaug's grave in the 1890s, supposedly demolishing his grave marker and placing the house's fireplace right on top of the grave itself. In the 1950s the Connecticut Light & Power Company created an artificial lake and named it Lillinonah.[2] So much for the Indians, though in the twenty-first century, a Native American group laid claim to a large swath of Kent Township, to the surprise and consternation of local whites.

Back in the twentieth century: The lake house (as a name, The Maples lived on somewhat desultorily with the Mulvehills, eventually passing out of use) was—and is—a graceful Edwardian structure that rambles a bit without losing a certain convenient compactness. It was always painted white, but its shutters changed from light green to black sometime in the 1940s. The ground floor rooms have more openness than many houses of the period. The double fireplace has a mantel of rustic fieldstones in the living room and a mantel of more manicured-looking brick in the central hallway facing the dining room. The second floor has five bedrooms, and there are more rooms on the third floor—called the attic by some at one time. Gracious porches run along the front of the house and extend partway down each side. With the house came some classic Stickley arts and crafts furnishings and a collection of antique weapons that long decorated the living room walls, many of which were lost in a 1980s burglary. Like other country houses of the period, the house has a certain grandness, but with an attitude of being comfortable and welcoming, not opulent or overbearing.

The barn, once white like the house but painted red after World War II, housed cars as well as old farm tools left over from the Bonynge era, with living quarters for the chauffeur on the second floor. And in 1929 John Henry and Myrtle Belle built a large boathouse right on the lake, with docking facilities, changing rooms, a large recreation room, and a porch overlooking the water.

ROARING TWENTIES

I write of the lake and the house at some length because it is, as I've said, an important focus of family consciousness and conversation and a backdrop for stories as well as an era. In the 1980s, many years after John Henry and Myrtle Belle were gone, a young cousin and his wife filmed a documentary tour of the house, like televised visits to famous stately homes. They did so to try out a new camera and record their grandmother, Lillian Mulvehill. The video highlights the importance of the house to the family vision over time.[3]

For myself, the lake has particular importance as a place of my own origins. Those origins involve a canoe, rather neatly reversing the legend of Lillinonah, wherein the canoe facilitates a demise, not a beginning. Frank and Anna de Caro had a son, born in 1908, and named him Frank Emanuel—his middle name was a tribute to Italy's King Victor Emmanuel. John Henry and Myrtle Belle Mulvehill had a daughter, born in 1907, and named her Beatrice, or Bee—never Bea—who particularly liked to recount the story of how she and Frank E met:

As young teenagers they both happened to be canoeing on the lake, and both canoes found their way into Sucker Brook, a small tributary that feeds into the lake. In the confined space of the brook they could not help but meet. In close quarters, he somehow managed to get her paddle away from her, teasing her by refusing to return it. She eventually got it back and they both paddled off, but my mother and father had thus irrevocably met.

Although both were from Brooklyn, they lived virtually at opposite ends of the borough—she in Bay Ridge, out along the Narrows, he in

The Lake 45

Figure 4.1. The Mulvehill house at Lake Waramaug, Connecticut, 1920s.

Windsor Terrace, hugging the southwestern edge of Prospect Park. But for Lake Waramaug and its development as a summer haven for New Yorkers who could afford to spend the season there, they likely would not have come together. Indeed, as time went on, the two families of Bee and Frank E's generation merged in friendship, palling around with each other both in Connecticut and New York. For example, oral history has it that my uncle John Mulvehill, in the earlier days of the families' getting together, happened to call on the de Caros in Brooklyn and met my aunt Frances de Caro for the first time. He came away staggered by her good looks and indeed raved about them, though no relationship between them ever followed.

The stories I heard about the lake—certainly primarily from my mother—centered around the good times that were had, and I think that Bee meant to, consciously or not, construct a picture of a sort of Roaring Twenties, F. Scott Fitzgerald lifestyle. Once, for example:

Mrs. Sefton, a fellow Brooklynite who rented a house on the lake at one point and whose daughter would marry Uncle Urban Mulvehill, complained

Figure 4.2. Bee on the steps of the lake house, 1920s.

to Myrtle Belle that while driving up from the city, her car had been overtaken by a madly speeding roadster that had practically forced her car off the road. It turned out to have been Uncle John Mulvehill and his friend John Clark—who would marry another Sefton daughter—rushing ahead with a load of bootleg whiskey, that key ingredient of the Twenties.

The stories were supplemented by other, more general accounts: how guests filled the house to the brim every weekend, the dances at the country club, the circle of carefree young people who also summered at the lake. One early morning, a story went, one of the maids, who was obviously agitated, woke my grandmother Myrtle Belle. The maid had come downstairs that day and found three tramps sleeping in the living room! Myrtle Belle hurried downstairs to investigate and learned that the sleepers were cousin Jack Mulvehill and two friends he had brought up for the weekend. They had arrived late the previous night and, finding no one awake, just bedded down. The lake house was a place of hospitality where family and friends just dropped in for the good times and congeniality of like-minded folks.

They would make their way to a little gas station and grocery on the road between New Preston and New Milford because the owner made illegal booze in a house up the hill behind the store. Sometimes they had to hightail it out the back way due to a real or imagined raid. Uncle Urban seems to have been a particular harum-scarum, and the family loved the oral lore about how he drove the family's speedboat, a lovely Hacker Craft named the Myrtle Belle, aground on at least two occasions and drove his car into the lake on at least one, and perhaps as many as three, occasions. His brother John managed to get the car out of the lake, though one winter season, both of them, on a lark, decided to drive out on to the lake's frozen ice, to see if it would hold. Once, as one of Bee's brothers drove into nearby Washington Depot, local farmers in another car cut them off and collided with the car. The farmers thought they'd get some money out of the rich New York summer residents but never did.

It was a carefree time of fun and play, the stories say, and a time of bonding and prosperity, riding high the wave of national wealth and insouciance of the 1920s. Years later, I sat in the Boulders Inn overlooking the lake with my aunt Lil de Caro Santo, who had been the social director at the Hopkins Inn for a summer in the Twenties. "We ruled this place," she said a trifle imperiously, gazing across the waters and cutting through time, a look of absolute nostalgia spreading across her face. And in his wartime letters to Bee, Frank E writes longingly of Lake Waramaug several times as a place of great happiness, probably more so after the Great Depression and into the darkening days of war. In his very last letter from France, where he would soon be killed, he recalled "that day in Sucker Creek" and "the paddles across the lake on moonlight nights." "They were golden days," he said in this letter of September 11, 1944, a few days before his death.

THE FORMIDABLE MYRTLE BELLE

Another theme in stories crystallized around Myrtle Belle, and it added to our perception of her. Now she was no longer the golden-haired child of the prairies, nor the young woman asking after the Mulvehills. She had taken shape as an intimidating and dominant personality, perhaps in contrast to John Henry, who, as we shall see, becomes a more shadowy figure. I did not need stories to see her as formidable, for Bee and I lived with her at 7002 Ridge from just after my father's death until her death in 1963—I had firsthand experience. Then she seemed always to be bustling about—running our little household, cooking our meals, dealing with the building's personnel, changing the curtains or putting slipcovers on the furniture according to the seasons, varying her clothing from her array of housedresses for domestic chores to the frocks and gloves and veiled hats of an obviously grande dame in the outside world. Of course, in former times, she ran both the brownstone in Bay Ridge and the lake house like establishments, shifting family, servants, and life from one to the other and back as the seasons dictated.

But several stories solidified my sense of her formidableness both within and beyond the family realm.

During one epidemic, her son Urban came down with scarlet fever—not an inconsiderable illness then. He was quarantined and recovered perfectly well. Then the health inspectors showed up at their doorstep on Seventy-Fourth Street. It would be necessary to take and burn all the furnishings of the room where he had been confined in his illness to prevent further contagion; even the wallpaper would have to be stripped from the walls. Myrtle Belle was not going to have any such disruptions of her house, so she showed them to a small spare room and told them it had been the sickroom, and they duly tore it apart.

At one point, in the village of New Preston, a man named Paul Kraselt opened a grocery store. Because he was not a local or perhaps because of his Jewish ethnicity, business was slow, and he was having a hard time making a go of it. But Myrtle Belle took a liking to him and evidently respected his efforts, and she began to shop at his store and steer other business his way. That his business soon picked up might be due partly to the numerous guests at the large lake house and partly because of Myrtle Belle's status in the locality. He prospered and was forever grateful.[4] One day years later, when my uncle Edward Mulvehill owned the lake house, Myrtle Belle happened to be sitting in a car in nearby New Preston. When told she was outside, Paul dashed out to see her and talked to her for a long while through the car window. I thought he was going to kiss her hand.

I take you back to Brooklyn, for a final story about Myrtle Belle. The Mulvehills knew a family that had emigrated from Belgium. The husband of the household was a diamond cutter, a highly skilled trade customarily passed on from father to son. Evidently the son wanted to go his own way and was horrified at being forced into diamond cutting. He ran away due to the unbearable pressure from his family. Remorseful, they despaired of ever finding him. Myrtle Belle took a sympathetic interest, set out to visit shelters and other places a runaway youth might find refuge, enlisted the help of newspaper acquaintances who had wide knowledge of the city, and managed to find the young man. Perhaps because she was not his parent, she was able to persuade him to return home. The Belgian family was greatly thankful and presented Myrtle Belle with a pair of metal vases made from artillery shells fired at the great World War I battle of Ypres. Those vases blended in with the antique weapons that hung on the dark paneling and were arranged around the living room of the lake house. Although the events of the story took place in New York, I always associated the story with the vases and the lake.

These stories of Myrtle Belle perhaps say a number of things, but I always thought their intention was to evoke a picture of an ancestor as formidable, righteous, and able to get things done, to provide family members with an example of correct behavior.

BEE GOES TO EUROPE

Indeed, the lake house serves as a handy metaphor for an era when other events took place and other stories took form. In 1926, for example, my mother commenced her grand tour of Europe, a pilgrimage that shaped her understandings for the rest of her life. She attended school then at the Berkeley Institute, a private high school in Brooklyn's Park Slope neighborhood that also offered a subsequent year of college, and she had reached the summer before her final year.[5] The school's principal always offered an escorted European tour for students in the summer prior to their last year of classes; it substituted for an art appreciation course. Bee set out on the tour along with seven or eight other students, the principal, the principal's mother (who served as an extra chaperone), and the mother of one of the girls. They left in late June aboard the S.S. *Orduna* of the Royal Mail Steam Packet Company and stayed in Europe until August 26, coming home on the S.S. *Republic* of the United States Lines. Along the way she fired off a barrage of postcards, developing a formulaic style that served her impulsive card-sending proclivities for the rest of her life. She sent many to Lake Waramaug, where the rest of the family had settled in for the summer. Although she took along a diary, there are no entries in it after the first three days on the *Orduna* ("All my relatives saw me off. Lovely ship. . . . Sea a little rough. . . . Played bridge. Had drink in bar. Interesting bar steward. Talked with him till eleven. . . . Walked on deck; sighted a ship in distance. . . . It is beginning to rain. They rigged a bathing pool on deck." The "rain will spoil our swim" is the final entry). The postcards (quoted verbatim here) remain the sole written record of her journey and include these messages:

> We visited here [Stratford-on Avon] this morning. It is the quaintest town you ever saw.

> We were here this after-noon [Anne Hathaway's cottage]. It is very pretty and quaint. I just adore England.

> I went swimming in the North Sea yester-day [in Holland]. It was very cold but refreshing. They have bath houses on wheels & horses draw you right down to the water. You should have seen the suits. Quite hot.

> I'm still having a gorgeous time seeing the world. I'm sending you a picture we had taken on a glacier in Switzerland.
>
> We took a steamer to the Isle of Capri to-day. It is a darling little place. We went into this grotto, which is one of the most gorgeous sights I have seen. Only 2 in a small rowboat can enter the grotto, & we had to lay on our stomachs & shoot through the opening. It was very thrilling.
>
> Venice is divine. The gondolas are adorable. Yester-day we took a trip to the Lido & went for a swim in the Adriatic.
>
> Venice is wonderful except for the mosquitoes.
>
> Greetings from Florence. . . . I'm about worn out trotting around seeing old art galleries & churches here. They say it will be worse in Rome.
>
> We visited the Colloseum this morning. It certainly reminds me of the Yankee Stadium. We also went down into the catacombs, with an old monk as our guide. A little candle was our only light. Certainly was spooky.

Her memories of the trip remained strong, and she told a few particular stories that seemed to encapsulate her experience. I think she meant to project herself as mischievous and free-spirited, fey and a bit feckless, which fit perhaps with her vision of herself as a child of the Roaring Twenties and its heedless good times.[6] She told this as her sole story about her Atlantic crossing:

"On the boat we were all supposed to be in bed in our staterooms by a certain time, and the principal and her mother would come to check on us. But I had met this nice boy who was taking a similar trip to Europe with a group organized by a famous rabbi, Rabbi Wise. And one night we were just sitting, talking, somewhere high up on the ship, maybe even up near the smokestack, and it got late, and the principal noticed I was missing from my room. She alerted everybody, and there was a big search all over the ship, and I guess finally they found us. The principal threatened to make me sleep in her stateroom for the rest of the trip over."

This was a story that emphasized "improper" behavior that went against the rules, even for a minor infraction that was perhaps even inadvertent. In London she was rude to one of her father's associates, though I think that she always saw her behavior as more rebellious than discourteous. Perhaps she did feel guilty about her actions, for she told me this story many times; it was virtually her only story about England:

In London she had been invited out to dinner and the theater by a man named L'Estrange Malone and his wife. L'Estrange Malone was the author

Figure 4.3. Bee (*second from right*) with members of her group, St. Mark's, Venice, 1926.

of children's books whose day job was as some sort of agent for her father's New York insurance company.[7] But when the Malones called for her at her hotel, she was nowhere to be found. She had blithely decided to go off somewhere with some of her fellow students. The Malones were not happy, but she apologized. They took her out another night, and Malone promised to dedicate a character in one of his books to her.

She told me this story at least once while we looked at Malone's books on a shelf at the lake house.

Then in Italy another young man she met somehow figured in a story, or perhaps it was more of an allusion to a story. This young man had been overheard saying something critical about Benito Mussolini and had been taken in by the police for investigation! That was not, of course, something that happened to Bee or another in her party but was meant to imply, I think, that she had at least met someone who was reckless. And this put her a little closer to the edge of danger, like in the "foreign intrigue" movies she later came to love.

Other stories, though, were the little details of the tour that might strike someone who only turned nineteen while on the trip. Bee "climbed" the Matterhorn—though it is said that the local guides, used to hauling tourists up the mountain, could manage to drag a cow up the slopes—and ate chocolate bars and stuffed newspapers inside her coat for added warmth. To get into the grotto on Capri, she had to lie on her stomach as the boat slid beneath the low opening. This event, which she related on one of her postcards, obviously made a strong impression on her as something "thrilling"—she passed into something "gorgeous" rather like an initiate moving on a narrow path into the mysteries beyond.

Two other stories impressed a listener as to the importance of her family—and her father in particular. In Rome, John Henry had arranged (indirectly) for an audience with the pope for her group as well as a private audience for her. A business acquaintance of his—a New York stockbroker—had contacted the vice rector of American College, who had written to someone he knew at the Vatican; Bee saved the letter of introduction she carried. The pope, in fact, received them after he had met with her alone in private. He told her that he was sure she would become a good woman and gave her a head covering made of lace. Surely this had been a pro forma meeting such as he often engaged in, but as a devout Catholic in later life, Bee cherished the experience and often told the story.

But earlier in the trip, in England, she had already chanced to demonstrate her father's significance in the world, and this was another of her favorite stories:

Another business associate of her father, a Mr. Marshe, happened to be, at the time, leasing Warwick Castle from its rightful owner. How that had happened, the story never said, so perhaps she did not know, though one imagines the wealthy American tycoon dealing with the slightly impoverished British aristocracy. But John Henry was able to arrange a private tour of the castle for the group, and someone who was in charge of it showed them all around the place. The other tour participants were suitably grateful and sent John Henry a postcard, a rather dull black and white depiction of the castle's inner yard, thanking him for the opportunity. Bee's Georgian Court College yearbook (she transferred there after Berkeley) quoted (in the manner of yearbooks) one of her favorite expressions: "My father is a big man," and she liked to tell how the nuns at the college were always impressed when he would bring her back to campus in his chauffeured Cadillac (he had never learned to drive and did not care to); as she liked to tell how his responsibility (and perk?) at his insurance company was to, after a board meeting, hand out the pay—a twenty-dollar gold piece—to each director who had participated, almost like paying off the help. He subscribed to the Theatre Guild, so the family had regular tickets to Broadway shows, and he escorted them periodically to the bright lights. Bee was most struck by and told the story of going to a Eugene O'Neill play—it must have been "Mourning Becomes Electra" or "Long Day's Journey into Night"—not only because O'Neill was celebrated but because they had to come to the theater early and then break for an intermission and go to dinner and then return for the end of the very lengthy play. Given her father's indiscretions, that led to terrible family ruptures, ultimately her feeling about her father must have been complicated indeed, though stories of his importance in the world would have added to her own sense of status and to her sense of who her family was.

As for her years at Georgian Court—located in Lakewood, New Jersey, and occupying an old estate that George Jay Gould willed to an order of nuns, perhaps in expiation of his father's robber baron sins, and which has such peculiar amenities as a sunken Italian garden and gigantic classical statuary—she mostly liked to recall stories that, again, emphasized her role as a mischievous rebel in a flapper world:

Her second-floor dormitory room at Georgian Court opened out onto a private terrace where other students liked to come to smoke, in defiance of college rules. So she always had plenty of company, letting her friends pass, going and coming, through her room.

Then, she and they were all required to wear white gloves when they went off campus, but there was a great urn by the campus gates where the gloves would be deposited on their way out, to be picked up on their return.

And one of their science professors was noted to be a boring lecturer, but he had an obsession with the common cold; so periodically, when they were tired of the usual class work, she or someone else would say, "Professor, could you possibly tell us about the common cold?" And he would drone on about his pet topic, and they wouldn't have to listen at all.

During these years, Myrtle Belle took Bee and two of her prospective daughters-in-law on a Caribbean cruise—in fact, one specifically to Haiti, and both of them talked about this cruise for the rest of their lives. Bee liked to tell the story of how she acquired a parrot and got it back to New York:

Bee decided somewhere along the line that she wanted to bring home a monkey from the tropics, and once they got to Haiti, she set out to find one on the island. There were none to be had but she *was* offered a parrot, and she decided that would do. It wasn't legal to just bring an exotic bird into the United States; nor for that matter could she just keep it in her cabin on the ship. Fortunately she'd charmed some young members of the crew who not only transported it in their quarters but also smuggled it ashore in New York. The bird did, however, both smell bad and make a racket, so it did not remain long in the Mulvehill household.

I heard most of these stories from my mother, so clearly they represent her desire to shape a vision of the past and pass that on to me. There is the larger narrative of the family's prosperity and importance: the cruise to the Caribbean, the grand tour of Europe, her father's ability to evoke popes and castles or take the family to a Broadway theater. This suggests the necessary background for the time period, something of the wealth that animated the Roaring Twenties. Then within that larger narrative, there is Bee's vision of herself as the mischievous flapper—someone who tarries with young men under ship smokestacks, passes up dinner invitations to set out on her own, meets a young man arrested by Mussolini, charms people into smuggling a parrot for her, allows her friends access through her dorm room to break college rules, breaks those rules herself, even learns how to send a professor's lecture off track. Although naturally, I knew my mother in many contexts, her stories about her past utterly shaped my sense of who she had been and what her family had been. Stories, of course, communicate far more than mere statements, giving us something more concrete to go on, emanating messages that, if indirect, convey a more powerful sense of the reality of things. We want to give particular credence to stories.

THE DE CAROS GO TO EUROPE TOO

Meanwhile, through the lake years, the de Caros continued to interact with the Mulvehills and carry on their own lives. Although my father, Frank E, never got very far from New York until the war, *his* father did like to travel. Although the family never told me about his trips, pictures exist attesting that he journeyed to Niagara Falls and Arizona, presumably to see the Grand Canyon, evidently without his beloved Anna, who was almost obsessively domestic and seldom went far from home. No doubt, having remade himself as an American, he wanted at least to see the iconic American sights.

The older Frank also journeyed to Italy on several occasions on business, but he likely also wanted to touch base with his origins and present himself as the successful Italian-American—someone who could temporarily reenter his old world in a more advantageous position.

He put together a scrapbook that held invitations and notices to show that in New York he interacted with Italian consuls and visiting admirals and Italian-American officials, and family oral history insisted that he received decorations from King Victor Emmanuel and Queen Margrethe for tapestries made in his workshops on Grand Street that were entered into international competitions in their names. Attested to by a certificate and a cartoon that had appeared in an Italian-American newspaper that had been pasted into the scrapbook: in the 1920s he was knighted as a member of an order in Montenegro, then within the Italian sphere of influence, thus achieving the *cavaliere* status sought by many, though the Montenegrins actually used the French *chevalier*.

He had used his wits to become successful in business, making and selling a wide variety of flags, banners, uniforms, and other merchandise mostly to the Italian-American community. According to one family story, he made a good business of tailoring uniforms for those who marched in the Columbus Day Parade in New York City who liked to wear very fancy Italian military dress for the occasion. When the Italian consul, outraged by this appropriation of military uniforms, issued a decree that no one could march in the parade in a uniform unless he had a certificate to prove he was entitled to wear it, Frank printed up certificates that declared that the individual named enjoyed full entitlement to some particular outfit; the certificate bore a picture of said uniform but as worn by someone without a head; the buyer of the uniform received a certificate and could attach a small photograph of his own head to the headless shoulders.

On one of his business trips to Italy, Frank had bought a lovely series of soft-color postcards depicting a range of Italian regiments in uniform; he used these to tailor actual designs, in catalogs that offered the uniforms for sale, and probably also for the certificates. But the story suggests the wit that must have underlay his success.

It was, however, his Italian journey of 1921 that stuck in my mind through family lore, when he took along his daughter Frances (also called Fran, Fay, and Francesca), the beauty whose good looks had knocked John Mulvehill for a loop. There were photographs taken along the way, and stories about this trip, plus, unlike the diary of Bee's trip that petered out after Day 3, Fran kept a journal of the whole excursion.

According to family lore, Frank took his daughter along because she had formed a romantic attachment to an unsuitable man who was prominent and well-to-do but married and also Jewish, though the family may have taken the multicultural composition of American society to heart and may not have been bothered by his religion; Frank and Anna had already started their own brand of cross-cultural marriage and family life. By getting her out of New York for awhile, they did hope she would forget him; besides, she could be married off to an Italian aristocrat.

The Italian aristocrats were probably Frank's idea. Such an arrangement would not only get her away from her unsuitable liaison but also advance *Frank's* dreams about rising further in the world. In her journal, Fran mentions several aristocrats dangled before her, but the story she actually liked to tell went something like this:

"I remember this one count, oddly enough named Count Moroni, though I suppose he was smart enough to know what he wanted. He took me to dinner, and he brought along his mistress so they could both look me over. I forget how I felt about that, but there she was.

"They said that they found me very beautiful, but then the talk pretty quickly turned to money. I told him that the family was prosperous but that there was no great wealth, and the count politely lost interest pretty fast."

She first told me that story when she thought I was "old enough" to hear it, so I suppose that in a way it signaled my own coming of age. It was also designed to say something about the strangely glamorous world of her European journey and a sophisticated society that she had gotten a look at. Fran did, of course, bring home other glamorous habits from England, Bee said, like how to smoke in a manner so sophisticated that all the younger folk envied her. She resumed her liaison, which in fact lasted many years, until her paramour's death. Everyone in the family knew about that liaison but almost never said anything about it. Two bits of narrative oral history, probably told to me by another aunt, were all I ever heard about it, other than the knowledge that the liaison had happened:

Figure 4.4. Frank De Caro and his daughter Frances, St. Mark's, Venice, 1921.

The paramour bought her a partnership in a firm that she operated until her death and of which I was very much aware, an agency for court reporters, which she took full control of when she discovered that her partner was embezzling company funds. The paramour also left her a sizeable bequest, but Fran chose to abandon it rather than engage in a lengthy legal battle with his still-alive wife.

These fragmentary stories gave me a hint of their relationship and stressed his devotion to Fran as well as her essential decency.

During my childhood, Fran occupied her own spacious two-room suite in Frank and Anna's Brooklyn house, took up art and painted some dreadful pictures, wrote poetry, and continued to present herself glamorously. She rather reminded me of Brenda Starr, the glam comic strip character. Well into her sixties, she returned from a cruise and told me this story after I had seen photos of a handsome gentleman who had been on the ship:

"Oh, he was a German diplomat who was on the cruise. One night we danced together and he asked if I always slept alone.

"'Always,' I told him."

Whatever really happened next, the story projected both her ongoing attractiveness to men and her moral probity, along with another hint of her having just returned from a more sophisticated existence.

The stories of European sojourns were meant to project, I think (or so it seemed to me when I was a child), existence in a more stylish and sophisticated world of the past, when only the more elite journeyed to Europe, at a time when both families had enjoyed a certain social level and panache. Both Fran and Bee were projected as tantalizingly deviant: Fran with her paramour and her aristocrats and their mistresses, Bee more schoolgirlish and prone to gentle rebellions. The European stories joined with those of the good times at the lake and the formidable Myrtle Belle, and collectively, the stories and other memories gave the family and some of its members (me, anyway) the patina of specialness that Elizabeth Stone says family stories are meant to provide. Certainly the stories speak of that quintessential American process of rising in the world, of stepping off the packet ship from Cork or the steamer from Salerno with only seventeen cents, then merging with the strands of America, whether with the prairie-born pioneer spirit or through a multicultural union with other immigrants, and winding up with summer houses at the lake and European sojourns in the lavish Roaring Twenties.

Bee graduated from Georgian Court in 1930 and told stories about several of her subsequent endeavors, which emphasized ongoing wealth despite the gathering clouds of the national depression:

She took a job, but not actually needing money, took one without pay, a sort of internship assisting a woman who wrote an advice column for the old *Brooklyn Eagle*. She made the job sound like great fun, and that was probably the point of the story. Once she and Frank E used the column to find a home for a stray cat, going around to interview people who read about and wanted to adopt it and wrote in to the paper. And sometimes they got to write the answers to "lovelorn" people who wrote in asking for advice.

THE GATHERING DEPRESSION

Then Bee decided that gainful employment in a profession would be desirable, and she entered the graduate program in social work at Fordham University, where one of the Jesuit chaplains at her college was a professor. She told several stories about this period in her life, and it's interesting to see that they're not about classroom experiences or accounts of visits to social agencies, but rather the edge of the sinister and dangerous.

One of the Fordham Jesuits was also a chaplain at Sing Sing, the infamous New York penitentiary "up the river" on the Hudson in Ossining, the town that gave the prison its nickname. She and her fellow students took a field trip there, and her narrative of the visit focused on sitting in the actual electric chair where murderers were regularly dispatched to their fates. This was a great thrill for her, a lifelong fan of Hollywood gangster movies.

She also was sent out into the field, working with local social service agencies. She once entered a gloomy, dilapidated tenement in Queens to try to find someone. Slowly making her way down the murky hallway, she suddenly heard a loud plop behind her. She turned around to see a very dead cat sprawled out on the floor; someone had dropped it down the stairwell from a higher floor to warn her that she wasn't welcome. She quickly exited.

She must have felt—and the stories were meant to convey—that again she had gotten into something a little edgy and daring, a world of dangerous criminals and stone-dead beasts that provided a rather exciting contrast to her usual comfortable and secure existence.

But, according to her final story from her social work days, she was safer than she imagined. Myrtle Belle, concerned for Bee's safety and unable to dissuade her to abandon her social work pursuits, had detailed Jack the chauffeur to follow Bee into the field at a discreet distance and look out for her. Evidently Bee never spotted him, though she did give up her quest for a degree after the first year, giving in to her mother's concerns. Meanwhile, her youngest brother, the rambunctious Urban, had moved on from Georgetown to Harvard Law School, where he shared an apartment with several other fellows. Bee's oral history of Urban's law school career told of the black manservant who tended to him and his roommates by cooking, cleaning, and otherwise taking care of them. The stories maintained a vision of ongoing prosperity: a chauffeur to protect them and a manservant to do something similar.

Frank E was, professedly, never much of student, though his sister, the arch-flapper Lil, earned a degree in art from Cooper Union while their brother Arthur worked on an engineering degree there. Arthur was the great tragedy of the time. Just prior to his college graduation, he had been operated on for appendicitis, and he was in the hospital. Being very popular, he had a great many visitors, and they let chilly air into his sickroom. He caught pneumonia and died not long before graduation.

The sad story of Arthur's death was passed on to me early, and though it called attention to his shining personality that attracted people and gave personal agency to his death, it was meant to prefigure difficult times to come. Yet it was the Mulvehills who would seem to be more affected in subsequent years by shifting social and economic tides. Their stories—or perhaps I should say, my mother's stories, as my accounts of the family's fortunes came from her—probably look back, in the face of change, to grander prosperities and rather carefree lives that would slowly disappear: taking an interesting unpaid job with a newspaper, no salary necessary; undertaking not only a graduate degree but one in social work, enabling adventures while allowing one to stand above those less fortunate (and even to be protected by a family retainer); giving up that degree (which, like the salary, wasn't really needed) for other considerations; even a servant for one family member as he attends Harvard, surely a luxury that will come to seem increasingly remote.

Whatever the import of these stories, Frank's letters to Bee from the early 1930s survive; many of them are addressed to her at the lake, for he was working now and could only be there on some weekends. The letters attest to their obvious attachment and are full of such protestations as "I love you very much," and in a show of the teasing that demonstrates the continuing fusion of American ethnic groups, he addressed one "To my dear Irish mick." He still talks about golf and tennis and horseback riding and going to boxing matches. After one such match, he winds up with a friend at a "whisper" on 168th Street, meets people there, drinks, finally wakes up in a taxi going through Prospect Park; his new friends have put him in the cab and paid his fare home, where he arrives at six a.m., soon to be hungover. There are mentions of the Penn Roof and the theater. He and his father see a show at the Paramount and then go to "the best speak I've ever been

Figure 4.5. Frank E. de Caro bustling about New York, 1920s or 1930s.

in—the beer was awfully good. My father knows more about Broadway than I thought he did." A letter on January 1, 1933, speaks of "this depression," and one from May 24, 1930, notes, "They are going to swing the axe to-night and get rid of about thirty of my fellow workers. I asked this morning whether I was one of the lucky thirty—but much to my surprise I'm not going to be a job seeker." A newspaper clipping about unemployed people selling apples is included in another letter. In September 1930 he notes going to work to find that "ten of the boys in the office were laid off" and mentions "forced vacations." In July 1931 he takes a quick lunch break and runs into someone who had lost his job at the office a year and a half before and who has not worked since. The man tries to avoid him, seems to be wearing the same suit he did the day he was let go, looks like he has not "shaved in a month." He is at odds with his family and has no place to live. Frank E feels bad that he himself has no money to give the guy, asks in the office whether they could give him even a menial job. They might be able to, but of course, they have no idea how to find him again. Work at the Wall Street brokerage where Frank E is employed is indeed slow, though it picks up from time to time in moments of optimism. He tells Bee that he makes twenty-three dollars a week. Although Bee still stays at the lake house from May until late October, clearly the earth and history are beginning to shift.

JOHN HENRY'S DISGRACE

In fact, they had shifted in a different way long before, and the elephant in this chapter's room is the story of what John Henry did over a period of years. As a child, I only knew that he was dead and seemed to have died around the time I was born. Bee obviously admired him; her mother, Myrtle Belle, never mentioned him. Myrtle Belle died in 1963, and just before or, more probably, just after that, my mother said that she had something she needed to tell me. We sat in the living room of the second ground-floor apartment at 7002 Ridge, and she told me the story of John Henry's wayward path. Apparently she had decided that, at some point in my life, I should receive the true family history—the story that would come to fascinate my generation and those that came after. The story involved a sudden shift in perspective, reconfiguring a recent ancestor who had always seemed to me a little shadowy, someone just beyond my own direct knowledge of the world.

My mother's narrative of her father's actions must have been fairly long, and I probably interrupted her with questions and exclamations, but the basic story went as follows:

It seemed that John Henry had had "another woman," virtually a second wife whom he had lived with off and on for many years. In fact, he had produced children with her, a boy and a girl. He had lived something of a double life. He had met this woman—her name was given but I do not include it here—when they were both members of a drama group at, of all ironic places, Our Lady of Perpetual Help Church. When the affair had become known—at least to some in the parish—Bee's oldest brothers, Edward and Vincent, had been expelled from the church school for the sins of their father. In his double life, John Henry had provided another residence for his other family in Brooklyn and eventually, a second summer residence for them at Candlewood Lake, which Frank E had in fact helped create, working one summer on building the dam that brought it into existence. This was also in Litchfield County, some few miles away from Lake Waramaug. According to Bee, this other family kept up with the doings of the Mulvehills and always wanted whatever the Mulvehills had. For his double identity he had rather unimaginatively assumed the name John Smith. When he died he was living with the other family and had been buried as John Smith; the Mulvehills really had little idea just where he was interred. After his death the Smith children had assumed the name Mulvehill.

I was rather flabbergasted by the story, and I confess I have little sense of its chronology or how and when his children learned about it all. Bee herself certainly must have been ignorant for a long time, since he impressed her and the nuns by appearing at the lake house or dutifully arranging her papal audience. As the family still lived in Our Lady of Perpetual Help parish and Edward and Vincent were in elementary school, the affair must have begun in the first two decades of the century and gone on for thirty or more years. I also have no idea how John Henry made his exits and re-entrances, how exactly he carried on his double existence, maintaining lives in two worlds. It must have been a terrible strain for him and others. Did the family move to the Seventy-Fourth Street house both because they were better off and because it was a place where they were less known?

I should have asked Bee more questions, though she did tell me a few more bits of oral history. Myrtle Belle threatened to go to the president of John Henry's company in the hope of pressuring him to abandon the affair, but John Henry persuaded her not to. He argued that he might just lose his job, and then the whole family would be disadvantaged. His son John was particularly outraged by the behavior of "the Governor," as he called his father, and confronted him repeatedly. Sometimes John Henry was on the town with the other family, and the Mulvehills feared they might run into him; once Frank E saw all of them at a theater district restaurant and barely managed to avoid them. Although he was very much alive, John Henry became a sort of ghost—seen by some in some circumstances and avoided by others—a presence that frequently must have been absent. That stories cast him as someone only "sighted" does suggest that my family viewed him as someone, for all intents and purposes, gone.

Other members of my generation heard this part of the family saga in other ways and at other times, and some didn't hear it at all, at least not from their own parents; Bee decided she had to tell some who remained unaware. It was a surprise to all—perhaps a bit of a shock—but the events had happened so long ago that by then we felt removed from the emotional wrenches of betrayal and duplicity experienced by our parents and grandparents. Indeed, the story intrigued later generations and provided a frisson of scandal; earlier generations appeared more interesting because of this grandfather engaged in a secret life, the sexual impropriety on a rather grand scale, and the turmoil all this had once created. Some cousins began to refer to John Henry, with a trace of amusement, as "the scoundrel." For me at least, if other stories told the very American tale of arrival and cultural interaction and the rise to quite respectable status, the story of John Henry provided a rather delectable counterpoint: the successful and upstanding ancestor, a Knight of Columbus, the man who handed out gold pieces to his company's directors, the father who could arrange for his daughter to meet the pope and tour Warwick Castle, had a hidden—or at least a partially hidden—existence, rather like those grand Victorian gentlemen who in private collected pornography or frequented dens of iniquity.

Of course his actions *had* created much turmoil and sorrow. No wonder Myrtle Belle learned to be formidable. Even Bee cut off contact with him. In the end, he lived only as John Smith, though he showed up to escort her down the aisle at her wedding. A story of reconciliation seemed particularly important to her:

Once after she was married, she was going home to her apartment in Flatbush and ran into him riding in the same subway car. She did not say whether she felt shock or continuing disapproval or joy, but they did get off at a station and talk, and she felt there had been a reconciliation, though she never saw him again. This was not exactly a family story, and certainly some of her siblings were never reconciled to him, but I think it was important for her to pass this story on as a sort of personal, faintly happy conclusion to traumatic events.

His other fortunes had declined by then. His wealth continued into the 1930s, but his investments foundered and his company went into bankruptcy. According to one story, this decline had political implications:

Though John Henry was a Democrat, his company's management had strongly supported Herbert Hoover in the presidential election against Al Smith. The losing Smith, still powerful in New York, had retaliated by getting banks to call in loans the company could not repay, and it was forced into failure. Smith's mother was named Mulvehill, and the family often maintained he was a distant cousin—something never actually documented—and the story itself sounds like a classic of what Stanley Brandes called the "why we're not rich" genre, a narrative that, if historical at all, provides a simple, dramatic account for what probably was a much more complicated, more gradual process.[8] But certainly John Henry "lost his money" and died in a kind of obscurity, even more of a ghost. My father, Frank F., not surprisingly, as the Depression continued, finally lost his Wall Street job and went into the food processing business in New Jersey and did modeling in his spare time for extra money. Bee still had her Sterns-Knight roadster and sometimes drove over to pick him up after work. They married in 1938. Their wedding photographs are marked "Proofs" because they couldn't afford to have regular prints made. Perhaps it was so important to have stories about the prosperity and carefree living of the Roaring Twenties precisely because that life had slithered to an end and another way of life now stared them in the face.

The de Caros continued to go to Lakeville in the summers, at least to the end of the 1950s. The lake house stayed in the Mulvehill family and retained a lively existence with some shifts in its resident cast of characters. For my mother, though, the place belonged to an era—a constant presence while she and her crowd ran around to speakeasies, paddled their canoes in the moonlight, or romanced each other on the Penn Roof back in Manhattan. In some ways, powerful, debilitating economic forces and the gathering anguish of a great war chipped away at the era. Certainly the stories suggest the slowness of the process. They linger on the good times and upon the prosperity—the trips to Europe, the servants, the carefree days when the grounded speedboat could be freed from the shoals or a parrot smuggled into the country from a cruise ship.

In other ways, maybe the era was always undermined from within, by John Henry's long-lasting infidelity that perhaps permeated everything and lent a weakness, an air of denied dysfunction, to the whole enterprise, as if his actions and the impending economic crisis were equally responsible for a slowly unfolding social collapse. But eras are artificial constructs, and time goes on without them, bringing forward new events and new narratives. Recollections and older stories keep that era alive in memory, providing a necessary patchwork of personal history, explaining something of where we came from and how we managed to get here, things we all desire to know.

NOTES

1. General historical information is drawn from Mary Harwood, *A History of Lake Waramaug* (Washington Depot, CT: Design to Printing for the Lake Waramaug Association, 1996). This book is actually related to a story of mine. When I was tracking down rights holders for material I wanted to reprint in my collection of Louisiana travel writings, I had difficulty locating the rights holders for a book about revisiting places associated with John James Audubon. I finally discovered that the person I wanted was none other than Mary Harwood, who had written the Audubon book as Mary Durant with her late husband,

Michael Harwood. Probably this became a story because I liked to complain about how difficult it could be to find rights holders, and this bit of tracking down spilled over into another part of my life.

2. Harwood, *History of Lake Waramaug*, 4–5.

3. Of course, family saga is often informed by the pictorial—particularly family photographs and, as technology has changed, by video "documents."

4. Another piece of oral history, from my cousin Barbara Mulvehill Gray, complicates the story. There was another store in town, run by a Mr. Lyman. At one point, perhaps picking up on suspicions of family financial difficulties during the Depression, they refused credit to Myrtle Belle. So it was expedient to switch over to a new retailer.

5. Today, after a merger with another, newer institution, it is called the Berkeley Carroll School.

6. My cousin Bea Mulvehill Palmer shares her story of staying at the lake in the late 1930s, when her parents had gone to the Chicago World's Fair and left her to visit Myrtle Belle and Aunt Bee. There was a little hole in the lawn that they warned her not to drop anything into, so of course, she immediately deposited into it a set of keys. She felt, she says, certain that her kind grandmother and aunt were so indulgent that she could do so with impunity. Although the story reflects a child's feeling of security in being beloved by family members, I can't help but think that it indirectly recognizes something else: that Bee (my mother) appreciated a mischievous strain in others that mirrored her own.

7. Whether he was related to (or might even have been the same person as) Cecil L'Estrange Malone, Britain's first communist member of the House of Commons, I have no idea.

8. Stanley H. Brandes, "Family Misfortune Stories in American Folklore," *Journal of the Folklore Institute* 12 (1975): 5–17.

Five

Beyond 7002

Growing up at 7002 Ridge I felt connected by stories and other knowledge, connected to forebears and a past, though I would not know the true story of John Henry for some years. Such a connection is not an inconsiderable thing: the places where you walk take on greater meaning; the people whom you see acquire added dimensions.

Some of the connection was tangible: many of the people from the past still surrounded me, inhabiting space that was also mine. I lived with my mother, Bee, and my grandmother Myrtle Belle; uncles and aunts walked around the neighborhood; Bee's youngest brother, Urban, lived in another apartment at 7002 until he took his family off to suburban Connecticut around 1950. The Seventy-Fourth Street house, though no longer in the family, still stood and great boats still blew their foghorns on The Narrows, where Great Uncle Harry had sailed with the wind.

On alternate Sundays, Bee and I would share a meal with the de Caros near Prospect Park, riding two buses or two trains to get there, sometimes huddling in the dark of night in a cold doorway waiting for the B34 bus to take us home. The trip to see them never lost its flavor of exoticism—the trains and stations of the IND subway were so different in design from the older, far-more-familiar-to-me BMT and promised some other reality (originally built by different, private companies, the transit authority still maintained the BMT and IRT as separate lines; the city-built IND ran as a separate line too). Or the buses would take me through neighborhoods of scrunched-up little houses with asbestos siding—so unlike the neat brick exteriors of my own Bay Ridge—or stores with signs in Hebrew letters, nearly another world. The Sunday meal itself would be festive, as though my father's death in the war had been forgotten; it seemed to me to take place in the distant past, for I had no recollection of him. We would start out in the double living room of the Greenwood Avenue house, where my mother had been staying when news of my father's death arrived, and the adults would slosh back a pitcher or two of Manhattans and talk and indulge me as I did imitations of the TV giants of the day, such as Milton Berle or Jackie Gleason. My grandmother, Anna, would be bustling in the kitchen while my grandfather, the original Frank, mostly sat by himself a little apart from the rest, by then mostly lost in a cocoon of deafness but always attired in a suit and silk tie. I might slip away to the dining room to filch slices of salami from a table gradually filling with condiments and utensils or upstairs to the rooms of my aunt Frances, who never appeared as soon as everyone else and would still be "getting ready"; an intriguing, slightly sensual Maxfield Parrish print hung over her mantel, a painting of hers in progress might be on her easel, the aroma of perfumes and powders hung in the air like unknown spices. I probably did not know the word *boudoir*, but her living space bespoke it, even the big, old Underwood typewriter she brought home from her office added to the mystique.

Back downstairs, in the afternoon, we would march (a total of eight or ten of us, including my grandparents, my aunts and their husbands, Bee and I) into the dining room for the elaborate meal, usually an Italian feast of antipasto and spaghetti and pasta shells with homemade tomato sauce and glasses of wine all around; although occasionally the menu would be more Germanic, with Sauerbraten as the centerpiece. The soups, often thickly delicious cream of chicken or a clear broth with floating peas and dumplings, echoed north European flavors. The heaping plates of dismembered roast chicken seemed more American, yet the meat had a wonderful oily moistness that I never tasted anywhere else. For dessert we usually ate American ice cream, sometimes served with long-handled, ice cream parlor spoons probably left over from the Menkhoff *konditorei*. How my German-born grandmother had learned to cook such exquisite Italian food I never wondered until much later. My mother told me that my grandfather had taught her. Did all Italian men walk around with this innate knowledge of their native cuisine? Were sex roles so rigid that they could not actually practice the art except to pass the knowledge on to foreign wives?

Then we would break into more desultory, postprandial life. Some would drift back through the little library into the living room for more conversation. My grandfather loved sitting at a cleared dining table, staying to play Italian card games like *scopo* with Aunt Lil's husband, John Santo, and, when he came, Aunt Elsa's husband, Ed Napolis. Ed, a lawyer, and Elsa were involved in Brooklyn Democratic politics; family lore tells that he once shared law offices with Fiorello LaGuardia. On one occasion, he did something that became a memory for me and a story I've told:

Once he performed a magic trick for me. It must have been Christmas, for I had received a toy milk wagon, complete with tiny glass milk bottles, for a present. I remembered horse-drawn milk wagons, which had disappeared from the scene not so long before, and milk delivery by truck was still common. Ed was sitting in an easy chair in my grandparents' living room and, in what seemed to me a spontaneous gesture, reached out and took one of the little bottles, passed it behind his back, and brought it out full of milk! I drank the milk. He did this several times, and then the trick was over. He never repeated it, and so far as I was aware, he had no other interest in magic tricks, so that this one became a strange anomaly which he would never explain and which continued to baffle me forever both as to the mechanics of the trick and to his motivations.

Sometimes my cousin John would come by in the afternoon, and we'd play in the house or the garden, which stretched out alongside and behind the house and had fig trees—my grandfather's great joy—where Fran liked to putter in the soil, coaxing up spring flowers. The house had a couple of toy guns that shot rubber darts and we both liked those.

On Christmas Day, visiting Greenwood Avenue became a somewhat heightened version of our regular Sunday visits. After I opened some presents at home, Bee and I would proceed to Greenwood Avenue, though often someone would pick us up and drive us there. But the living room at the house would be closed off; Santa Claus was said to be still operating in there and indeed, noises might emanate from behind the door. We would be ushered to the rear, closed-in porch—warmed by a hissing gas heater, a little wall of flame—for the usual drinks and chat before moving to the dining room for an even grander meal than usual, which always featured homemade lasagnas (one with meat, one without, both chockablock with marvelous fillings like hard-boiled eggs) as the centerpiece. We then feasted our eyes on the world of Christmas in the living room: a decorated tree, an old Italian crèche that looked like a grotto with tiny peasants and angels and the Holy Family climbing all over its rocks, a miniature grocery store with a scale and little glass jars containing real merchandise like raisins, and mountains of presents in areas assigned to each family member. Usually one person at a time slowly tore open his or her presents; we kids played with the grocery store; my grandfather would delight in slipping off to the basement from time to time, where he roasted chestnuts in the old coal furnace—alas, a practice that ceased when the family installed oil heat; aunts would leave the room to try on dresses they insisted on giving each other. Then we'd head back to 7002, where a bunch of Mulvehills would be gathering around our tree, providing the other half of a Christmas tradition that many

Americans share: taking part in the celebrations of the two families to whom they're connected.

At Christmas, but generally always, the Mulvehills seemed the gayer, more carefree bunch. The de Caros always showed a strain of emotional undercurrent, some deep nostalgia or longing, perhaps for former, better times; they also shared a propensity for trying to run each other's lives. Indeed, sometimes they frightened me just a little, when they tried to draw me close in ways I found uncomfortable or perhaps to insist that I should feel a certain way. I learned to write off their behavior in terms of ethnic stereotyping, maybe a very American process: Italian emotionalism joined to a certain German broodiness versus Irish insouciance.

But the Mulvehill Christmas extended into New Year's Day, when Bee and Myrtle Belle and I would sit at home, refreshments piled up and waiting, as men of the family and an occasional old friend would drop in over the course of the afternoon for a "New Year's call," which involved drinks and snacks and convivial talk, the men making a round of several houses. Although I wondered if this custom was an old Irish tradition, I later found it to be the last vestige of an old New York City ritual certainly well in place by the early nineteenth century but dying out. The old, carnivalesque Christmas season also included more raucous street revels, and some thought that even the decorous practice of calling on homes was a little too raucous. The editor of one New York newspaper in 1823 asked that New Year's Day callers replace the large quantities of alcohol they consumed with coffee; this would provide the "young ladies" who served as hostesses with "an opportunity for a contest of skill in making coffee."[1] His words went unheeded, and I always looked forward to New Year's Day as the fortuitous prolongation of a lovely season. The closed-up and unvisited parlor at the de Caro house on Christmas Day was, I later learned, evidently a vestige of German custom.

Because I was born in 1943, for me the world seemed to begin with the 1940s and 1950s. What came before was just vague hearsay that did not begin to mean much to me until later. I was aware, for example, that my father had "died in the war," but I had no memory of him and his former existence seemed an abstraction. The adults around me had a greater sense of the immediacy of the recent past, though they seemed not to dwell upon its tragedies and dislocations and difficulties, perhaps preferring to look to the better times of peace and prosperity that had dawned in an expanding, supremely self-confident America, or to look back to still earlier, idyllic days. And so I lived in a world of normalcy and good feeling, with the entertaining drone of the splendid novelty television and the soothing, smooth hum of big, powerful cars with names like Galaxie and New Yorker and a backdrop of familial tradition and cohesion. Is it surprising, then, that two of the stories I most often remember relate to the political turmoil of the era, with Joe McCarthy?

And once, at the height of the televised Joseph McCarthy hearings, John coaxed all of us into playing congressional hearings, making us witnesses sit on the piano bench while he asked if we were then or ever had been members of the Communist Party. I was virtually unaware of the actual hearings, so I did not know what to make of this new game except that it did not seem like much fun. I could tell that the adults felt disquieted.

On one occasion, as Bee and I were changing from the IND to the BMT at Ninth Street, a woman with a clipboard asked Bee to sign a petition urging the impeachment of McCarthy. She declined. She did not generally sign petitions but did remark to me afterwards that Senator McCarthy had, after all, exposed some communists. I suppose that that man had taken her in, like he had so many others.

Both these incidents became stories of mine, perhaps because a fear of Communism was in the air, fanned by the pages of the *New York Journal-American*, the Hearst paper that ironically used splashes of red ink on its front page, though it did have a wonderful assortment of comic strips to gladden my days. I remember the giant headline on the *Daily News* proclaiming that the Rosenbergs had been executed but had little idea of what that meant. We did not take the *News*, however, preferring the more sober *Herald-Tribune* in the mornings; *The New York Times*, we thought, was somehow too serious.

I can only assume that, though I understood practically nothing about McCarthy's doings, I somehow sensed their disquieting import, picked up on the unease people felt below the surface calm of the times, on the real or imagined dangers from which Jackie Gleason and Lucky Strike's *Your Hit Parade* distracted us. Perhaps that's why another story from these times that I remember and tell is about my uncle's never-explained magic trick. It suggests an incompleteness of understanding, as if even then I knew that I lacked a thorough understanding of what I was living through—of things that might never be explained—though that may be a feature of childhood and memory as much as a feature of 1950s oblivion.

Our neighborhood enforced our sense of normalcy and self-containedness for it was an outpost of conservatism in a city not noted for either. Bay Ridge sat literally on a low ridge above New York Harbor and above The Narrows, the slim body of water that joined Upper and Lower New York Bays. Although my mother remembered when much of the neighborhood had been open fields, by my time only a few tantalizingly vacant lots remained; it was a place of brick one-family houses; some fine brownstones and limestones, like the Mulvehills' residence on Seventy-Fourth Street; some quite stately, even grand structures; and an array of the architecturally monotonous brick apartment houses, usually six stories in height—six, it was said, being the maximum height water would rise to because of the elevation of the upstate reservoirs, without being pumped. Trees lined many of the streets—often old sycamores, though we found two or three isolated gingkoes as part of a classroom botanical assignment, identified by their distinctively shaped leaves. Our favorite outdoor activities consisted of walks down to the shore and along the concourse that stretched along the water for miles or across to Staten Island by the ferry that embarked from a pier at the foot of Bay Ridge Avenue—usually just called Sixty-Ninth Street—and which we thought of as the real Staten Island ferry, its vessels small and olive green compared to the bigger, red ones that sailed over to Manhattan. Bay Ridge was a gently hilly place swept by pleasant, water-sent breezes, though in the height of summer the air could seem deadly still, and in winter months chilly winds might rake the streets.

Perhaps because I enjoyed an innate appreciation for difference, as I grew up I sensed that Bay Ridge was set in its ways. Once I took a fancy to Tyrolean hats and insisted on getting one for Christmas; whenever I wore it, locals stared and bolder boys called out "Hey, Pinocchio!" I took a similar liking to Bermuda shorts and even got myself a pair directly from H. A. & E. Smith Ltd. of Hamilton; when I wore them on appropriately warm summer nights I might attract a following of wolf-whistling admirers stunned to see anyone—certainly any male—in such attire.

Mostly, however, I just blended in: riding my balloon-tired Schwinn bike down the hills toward the shore, intrigued by the cobblestones or bricks that underlay the asphalt and resurfaced here and there; or engaging in the myriad games acted out in playgrounds or in the streets with rubber balls, like I Declare War and Kings (both described in chapter 2) or Stoop Ball, which was a largely imaginary baseball game where one team threw the ball against the steps of a house stoop and the other team had to catch it on the initial bounce to effect an out, the number of ground bounces indicating he number of imaginary bases tagged.

Or I might roam the hills of Bliss Park, officially called Owl's Head Park. It was a place that connected me to the past and the other worlds that the past holds, for local oral history said that:

It had once been the sprawling estate of a man named Bliss whose long-gone mansion sat at the crest of the park's great mound of a hill. According to the local lore, he had been a German spy in the years leading up to World War I and used to signal from his mansion's high windows to German ships at anchor in the harbor; somehow in line with these nefarious activities, he had dug a tunnel from the house to the bottom of the hill, perhaps as an escape route; park employees had unexpectedly come upon it and dug it up.

In the winter this hill was prime sledding country and even attracted skiers, though as a ski slope, it was pretty pathetic.

On Halloween we took to the streets with pieces of chalk and chalked up each others' bodies or, if we were daring, filled old socks with flour and battered away at each other, though occasionally we heard rumors that the police would confiscate anything so deadly as a flour-filled sock. Trick-or-treating would take place entirely within 7002 (with eighty-plus families, it yielded enough candy and pennies), but Thanksgiving provided a second annual occasion for costuming and begging, though instead of the ritual cry of "Trick or treat!" our call was a more tentative "Anything for Thanksgiving?"

Ordinary life often satisfied me. There were hero sandwiches—great half-loaves of Italian bread stuffed with roast beef or sliced turkey or ham and cheese, made to order at the Scandinavian-owned delicatessens that dotted the neighborhood. Bay Ridge was a multiethnic place, and no one group predominated; there were enough Jews for one local synagogue, plenty of Irish and Italians, a sprinkling of Lebanese and Syrians, and a goodly assortment of Norwegians and Swedes whose pretty blond girls noticeably filled my school classes. The Scandinavians ran the delicatessens, except for one kosher deli that sat on the neighborhood's fringes; they and the Germans owned the ice cream parlors, a notable local establishment. I've told a story that calls attention to the social and personal importance of this little local institution, though I think it may be more about the slow development of time, of how gradually the postwar world enveloped me:

"Oddly enough I had my introduction to pizza, my first bite, at Horman's, a German-run ice cream parlor on Third Avenue. A pizzeria had opened up across the street from it, and one day some neighbors had bought a pie and brought it into the ice cream store, which we treated like the neighborhood gathering place. They were passing pieces around like samples. It was a great novelty. This was Brooklyn, but it wasn't Italian Brooklyn, and this was before ethnic foods began to take on general familiarity. Hard as it is to believe, most of us had never seen anything like it before."

I still feel like I was there at the birth of a great American culinary moment, circa 1950, as pizza passed into the general population.

There was life at PS 102, known as the Bay View School—though the bay could only be seen from one window in one corner of the structure, a giant hulk that consisted of old and new buildings joined by a central stairway—run by a cadre of dedicated if sometimes cranky teachers, many members of a leftover stratum of New York WASP society. I remember recess in the vast schoolyard, where the boys peeled off for punchball games while the girls puttered in the garden or learned dances in which the boys were supremely uninterested; the lower grades played ancient ring games while teachers in the upper grades felt compelled to teach us square dancing. Why square dancing, a form so seemingly removed from the city traditions of Brooklyn? Was it part of a national craze for a "national" form of dance that would teach us about our American roots in order to unify our disparate cultural elements? Did our WASP-y teachers see it as somehow "their" culture that they passed on as a precious legacy? Or was it just a dance form more charmingly innocent than the other social dances we learned, leading up to an eighth grade prom with dance cards full of promised partners' names, stepping back into an earlier formality?

Class pictures were always taken in the same shady courtyard. For a short while we had a mimeographed student newspaper. Years before, some teacher or principal had created an elaborate system of stairway and crossing guards, with lieutenants and captains and even a colonel at the head of it all—hierarchy to give structure to our childhood days. Occasionally we would pile into yellow buses and take field trips to places like the Rankin Dairy, so we could see where our milk came from and so the dairy company could give us sample packs of sweet flavored powder to add to our milk.

There was the plethora of local movie theaters, the Bay Ridge and the Alpine—both part of the Loews chain—the Dyker of RKO, and in the age before the multiplex, a host of independents, including the Electra, the Harbor, and the Stanley. At a time when television just started to become the great American mass media, the movie palaces still served as community focal points, providing cavernous, dark places—sporting huge "Air Conditioned" banners in summer—for projecting the magical expression of our fantasies and larger-than-life realities (the Bay Ridge even still offered vaudeville acts one night a week into the 1950s). The candy counter enabled us to stuff ourselves with Dots and Junior Mints and other treats. On Saturdays a crowd of kids overflowed the children's section while a matron regularly patrolled with a flashlight in hand, tamping down the rowdiness that periodically erupted. Trained by my mother to silently enjoy the pleasures of a good movie, I avoided the section whenever I could. The movie theater was such an important social center that the manager of the Bay

Ridge, for example, was something of a local celebrity and everybody knew him by name. My friend John claimed to actually know Mr. Rose through his uncle, a local bank manager. Once we saw Mr. Rose standing outside the theater as we passed by, and John gave him the effusive greeting, "Hello, Mr. Rose!" Instead of saying something like "Oh, hello, kid," Mr. Rose shot him a piercing stare and demanded to know "Who are you?" Chagrined, John had to explain his connection while another friend and I laughed almost uncontrollably. The three of us enjoyed the story ever after, perhaps just because it was about one of us being discomfited but perhaps because it did speak to the centrality of the movies in our lives.

But as much as I savored the pleasures of ordinary life, I looked for the things that transcended it, for the world beyond.

Some were within easy reach. In Bay Ridge itself, a few houses sprinkled amid the apartment houses and uninteresting brick homes emitted auras of mystery or majesty. One sat on the very crest of the ridge and looked like a fairytale castle, and local lore said it had been copied after a *schloss* on the Rhine. It appeared craggy and opulent and a bit forbidding. Its location at the edge of a street that dead-ended in a set of steps running steeply down the ridge—whereas most neighboring streets just kept going on down— and across the way from another house that to my thinking looked like a plantation house (in fact, it was one of Brooklyn's few surviving eighteenth-century structures), only added to the allure. My mother told me that she had once been inside the building when a group medical practice she had consulted occupied it, but she remembered maddeningly little about the interior. That her bit of personal oral history never formed into more of a story disappointed me, so I had to—just as well—imagine the building's recesses. Closer to the local high school—Fort Hamilton High, said to have one of the best school locations in the country because it overlooked the harbor—was an Arts and Crafts style house built around 1917 of rough stone and with a roof that simulated thatch, which approximated the cottage end of the fairytale spectrum.

And though, so far as I could tell, many of the neighborhood kids and their parents seldom ventured very far beyond the neighborhood, I often went to other places.

Those places might be close by. "Our" Staten Island ferry, coupled with a train or bus ride out of St. George, where the ferry came in, could take me to what was then—before the advent of the Verrazano-Narrows Bridge, which brought a mad building and paving-over boom—a much sleepier borough across the bay. The little island train, which often took my mother and me to visit one of her college friends, reminded me of a little toy that crawled along deserted tracks. Clove Lakes Park offered a small zoo with a marvelous collection of reptiles safely writhing behind glass; we would enter the park after passing through a cemetery to find a waterfall and a stream that connected the series of lakes; horseback riders thundered somewhere above us on the other hillside, making their way on a bridle path, mostly hidden by underbrush. The narrow, interconnected lakes seemed to stretch out forever, one tailing off as another one just like it began, as if one were in a dream of an endless, repeating landscape (and for years, I really did dream about the endless lakes and about a lone grave on the hillside below the actual cemetery that held some spiritual secret never revealed; this dream was always slightly disquieting).

Back in Brooklyn, the Sea Beach Express (today the less colorfully named N Train) usually took us to Manhattan, but sometimes we would take our faithful Fourth Avenue Local (now known as the R) to the express stop at Fifty-Ninth Street and change to the Sea Beach to go the *other* way to fabled Coney Island, the train's very endpoint where it reached the sea rather like westering pioneers bumping into the Pacific. There the Sea Beach and several other trains from other routes would disgorge great mobs of people down ramps and stairways that fed into streets lined with vendors of popcorn or hot dogs or corn on the cob and the great whirl of amusement rides—colliding bumper cars, dizzying, mirrored merry-go-rounds, roller coasters roaring with both track sounds and the screams of passengers—that filled the famed place. On our way out of town we passed through actual fields where some of New York's truck farmers still tilled dark-soiled small holdings, so that we encountered another world even before we rumbled across the murky, mucky waters of the creek, with its leaning, rotting pilings that cut off Coney from the rest of the city, and before being funneled into the thrills and garish flavors of Surf Avenue. The station and street filled with people of unfamiliar mien and colors who, being from *other*, less trustworthy neighborhoods, were suspicious and loud and vaguely threatening. So we would hustle uneasily the few blocks to within the sheltering walls of self-contained Steeplechase Park that, despite some carryover of Coney's carnival atmosphere, seemed safe and controlled.

My mother liked to tell us that she had gone to school with a member of the Tilyou family that owned Steeplechase, the last of Coney's giant, unified amusement parks, like the lost, lamented Luna Park. Although she had lost touch with her acquaintance over the years, this fragment of her personal oral history seemed to give us additional, special protection there. Years later I read that a young Tilyou grandson, wonderfully enough, had free rein among the rides all season. My high school friend Joe DeMott worked summers at the park taking ride tickets, and he liked to regale us with stories about his time there. He said that the employees considered the kid a great annoyance, always underfoot and of course, untouchable.

Inside Steeplechase, we waited in lines to mount favorite rides or try to walk through rolling barrels-of-fun or flip through the cards of ancient animated stereopticons to watch turn-of-the-century boxers fight or outdated ladies flaunt their bathing costumes. As I grew older I gradually tried more daring rides, like the giant slide that dropped you into a sort of bowl or the fast-moving mechanical horses that shot around the whole exterior of the main building, but never the iconic parachute jump or the whirlpool that spun riders off a central platform to sprawl hopelessly together in a spinning well. We went once or twice to the park every summer. Late in the day we would head back toward the station and, as if we had acclimated just a bit to the dangers of this spinning-out-of-control, festive world, we might stop for cotton candy or a frank at Nathan's Famous, though my grandmother, who never went with us but remembered earlier days at Coney, still spoke of the legendary Feltmans as the premier purveyor of Coney cuisine.

The Sea Beach Express more often took us into Manhattan. We called Manhattan The City, a usage suggesting both its remoteness from and its centrality to our lives. In my younger days these shopping trips mostly took us to Macy's, which for awhile displayed an actual motorboat for sale, to my constant fascination; the vast lengthiness of Macy's with its arcane levels haunts my memories. Or our beloved B. Altman, where my grandmother had a charge account that my mother and I continued to use forever, surely maintaining the longest-lived account in history, a multigenerational billing service. Or we might head to Grand Central Station for a train to Connecticut. Often my uncle John Mulvehill would drive us, pulling into a little alcove in the station (where today a passageway leads to the Campbell Apartment Bar) where a cop always seemed to be guarding a few parking spaces; a quarter tip put discreetly into his palm secured a space for a few minutes.

My early acquaintance with Manhattan was limited in scope, though I immediately perceived it as a place of glamour and excitement, where very well-dressed people rushed around doing interesting things. Alternatively, we did our serious shopping along Fulton Street in downtown Brooklyn, reached by an interminable ride on the Third Avenue bus. This lacked the pizzazz of going into Manhattan, though it did introduce me to black people, some of our fellow shoppers whose presence I have always remembered as a story:

I noticed that at the end of the day they got on buses quite different from ours to go home, and I was puzzled as to just who they were. I asked my mother, who explained that formerly these folk had lived in the South, where white people were quite mean to them. If they were walking along the street down there they had to step off the sidewalk to let white people pass and might have to doff their hats to the white folk to boot. They certainly did none of that on Fulton Street. Somehow, I thought, they seemed almost not to see us at all. But my mother's story, if I may call it that, served to situate them and give more context to my own existence and those who inhabited it.

Attending high school at St. Francis Prep, then located in Williamsburg, revealed new geographic insight. Not only did my classmates come from improbable neighborhoods all over Brooklyn and Queens, but athletic events and acting in the school play and social doings pulled me to a Brooklyn and a New York I'd never seen before: ramshackle parish halls, streets that huddled in the shadows of strange elevated train lines, stadiums reached by long bus rides over bridges. Greenwich Village opened itself to me, and I discovered cappuccino; sometimes I huddled in one of the darkish old coffee houses favored by the bohemian monde, more often I went to a place on West Fourth Street called the Pompeian Faun that had a little fountain and the ambience of a Roman villa shuttled through Little Italy. My friend John, who went to the public Fort Hamilton High and was an artist, started taking me to art museums like the Frick Collection, and I was bowled over by the intricate beauties of Renaissance and Impressionist art. His love of the movies—I used to "act" in his 8 mm feature films by running around his house costumed like some sort of gangster, and later he wrote a lot about film and pop culture—often took us to Times Square, and the old Marboro Book Store on Forty-Second Street beckoned with bargains so I could stock up on art books. St. Francis itself initiated me into local Catholicism, oddly foreign to me because I had gone to a public elementary school and missed much of the inculcation into that world, despite my "religious instruction" by nuns two afternoons a week.

My classmates knew the names and locations of what I considered obscure, far-flung parishes; knew what it was like to have been an altar boy; knew the words to "Tantum Ergo." In my freshman year I loaned a pen to a classmate, and he told me that I was "a gentleman and a scholar." Unaware of this time-honored Catholic schoolboy put-on, the compliment highly flattered me and I told my mother the story in that spirit; later it became a story of my naïveté, stumbling into this new Catholic world I did not understand. Medieval-seeming Franciscan brothers in brown robes with rope sashes and great dangling rosaries gently poked fun at the "good nuns" who had heretofore educated many of us, implying a greater world of male sophistication. Real football appeared. There was a glee club: "You glee or I'll club" was said to be what the brother in charge of it would say to impress the unwilling to join up and sing. There were regular masses, a school newspaper, a yearbook and literary magazine for writers and photographers, a library chock-full of books. At the lunch hour a hangdog-looking man at the schoolyard gate vended soft, salted pretzels—I had never seen these before—out of a big basket.

This man was altogether a novelty, and I described him to my mother and grandmother. I felt that by buying one of his pretzels I was helping him out of what I conceived to be his poverty. Then one day I was amused to see him load the basket into a very fancy convertible and drive off, and this became another story of my naïveté.

Visits to see my friend Joe DeMott at his house in Park Slope, an old brownstone, gave me a story I told for years, perhaps because this was all so new to me: how we would go up to his room and he would smoke a cigarette (!), and if his parents happened to come upon us, I was supposed to say that I had been smoking. I met my friend Vincenzo Barone, who had emigrated from Sicily and who, when classmates eagerly pressed him to teach them genuine curse words in Italian, would rather imperiously say things like, "I was not a child of the streets that I should know such things." I delighted repeating stories about this comment, since he read John Steinbeck and Mika Waltari and Giovanni Guareschi and was even writing a novel. I went to dances and endured infatuations as girls bobbed into the world and eventually snagged a girlfriend. My world was definitely enlarging. Stories of my own naïveté emphasize that, suggesting as they do my unpreparedness for even the small changes I encountered.

Some of the places beyond Bay Ridge were further afield. Bay Ridge overlooked a vast expanse of New York Harbor; from the roof at 7002, the concourse along the shore, and the little Staten Island ferries, we always could see the moored freighters, the coast-going tankers, the less frequent passenger liners—all glorious things. The local scene evoked wanderlust and dreams of international trade routes. At one point I discovered my father's old copies of Richard Halliburton's romantic travel books, like *The Royal Road to Romance*, and I was an immediate sucker for John Masefield's poem "Sea Fever." Jan Morris begins her book *Manhattan '45*, about New York City "at the zenith of its existence," with the *Queen Mary* steaming into the harbor, and that is very evocative for me—even though Morris's *Queen*

Mary is a gray-painted wartime vessel carrying home troops; the harbor and its shipping were both quintessentially New York and suggestive of bold things beyond.[2] Going to sailing parties on ships along the Hudson when my Uncle Edward would be traveling to England on business or one of my father's sisters would be taking a cruise was something of a family tradition: drinks and snacks and running about the ship followed by, after disembarking, tossing coils of streamers at the ship before it pulled out into the river. I personally longed for an ocean voyage and probably hounded my mother and grandmother into actually thinking about taking one. In the 1950s we went to Bermuda aboard the *Ocean Monarch*, the smaller and newer of two Furness Line cruise ships that sailed there regularly.

I basked in the glamour of this ocean voyage, ordered Cokes at the bar, won or lost money on the afternoon horse racing games in the lounge, flailed away in the tiny swimming pool perched on a rear deck. Not surprisingly, this cruise gave me two stories. One is a small tale of personal satisfaction:

The morning of our arrival in Bermuda, I was on deck to see us pull into St. George, and I was standing next to another lad and must have said I was waiting to see the palm trees. He informed me that there would be no such trees. Bermuda was not far south enough to be tropical. Palm trees suddenly began to appear on the land and I asked him what, then, were those? It was a pleasantly victorious moment.

Bermuda offered the perfect combination of semitropical and British colonial ambience and a glimpse into quite a different culture. It was the Easter season, and on a bus tour we came upon a group of Gombey dancers (the Bermuda variant of Bahamian Goombay) and were told of our luck in seeing them; they moved in their outlandish, mirrored costumes to powerful, energetic, scratchy rhythms, and I found it difficult to tear myself away from them and get back on the bus.

We took up with an elderly carriage driver who drove us around several times, even to his house. Our connection with him gave me the second story. In conversation with him, my grandmother kept referring to "colored people," and I piped up that they preferred to be called "Negro." He laughed and said he didn't care.

When we landed back in cooler New York, I knew that I had been somewhere.

Another Easter season, Bee and Myrtle Belle thought it would be good for us to see the nation's capital, and we took a train journey down to Washington, DC, booking seats in the parlor car that enabled us to swing around and have easy access to the bar and observation cars. I remembered plenty of train trips in the Northeast in crowded coaches, and the parlor car seemed a wonderful luxury. I suppose I had never seen a big city that wasn't New York, and it was a revelation to see one so different, as we toured around this rather majestic sprawl of monumentality. We met scientists at the Smithsonian Institution through a local cousin—I had the usual dinosaur fixation—and ate at local eateries we'd never have found on our own. Taxis without meters zipped us around, and one driver, a talkative white Virginian, explained to us that the southern accent, which he certainly had, came from the influence of black people on the way white people talked. The story of how I "learned" this ethnographic detail is one I told for years.

Then one summer Bee and I flew to the Southwest, which was, I suppose, the beginning for me of a lifelong infatuation with that region. Bee's college friend Muriel McNeil lived in Santa Fe, and I had been told the story of how she got there:

She was from Brooklyn and her father was an executive of the BMT, the then-private subway company. There was legal trouble following a subway wreck, and he found it expedient to leave New York and wound up in New Mexico, buying up large quantities of land in Santa Fe, worthless because water was so scarce. He drilled for water and prospered, becoming governor of the state and later, its representative in Congress.

I suppose that this backstory was meant to explain some history, though perhaps it also again suggested our family's past connections with people of consequence. But it also suggested to me how Brooklynites could indeed go off into the great world beyond the city where they lived.

Finally we went to New Mexico, taking Trans World Airlines out of LaGuardia at a time when people still went to the airport observation roof just to watch planes land and take off and flying was more of an epic journey: the rituals of buying trip insurance at a special airport desk, then boxed lunches at another; enduring the incessant landings and temporary disembarkations at airports from Chicago to Amarillo as we made our tiring if exhilarating ten-hour cross-country journey to Albuquerque.

We arrived in Santa Fe in the middle of the night and woke up to the otherworldliness of the Sangre de Cristo and Jemez and Sandia Mountains in all directions and the carefully cultivated adobe look of the town. Typical businesses of the time ringed the Plaza, as opposed to the tourist-dominated shops of today, and I was captivated by the Indians selling their jewelry under the Palace of the Governors portico; the constant, buzzing stream of motorbikes driven around the square by, I assumed, young Hispanic guys, a sort of ritual of exciting noise; and by the dark crannies of the bustling Hotel La Fonda. We experienced life as the locals did: Bee was whisked off to a never-ending round of parties in what was Fiesta season, or leading up to it; I palled around with the McNeil kids and some of their friends. We would go to a bookstore down a dirt alleyway near the "oldest church" in town to buy Tom Swift Jr. volumes and marched in the Fiesta pet parade dressed like chefs, the McNeils' dogs labeled "hot dogs," a fragment of life that became oral history for me, probably because I liked talking about this tiny integration into the rituals of local life.

We roamed the dry hills and drove to Gallup for the great Indian festival, and none other than Leo Carrillo, who played Pancho on *The Cisco Kid* television series, befriended us (and immediately became the subject of story). He let us sit with him in the dining room of the hotel and was awfully sweet and charming to us. He fully dressed his part, wearing an elaborate vaquero outfit that I suppose called attention to his identity as both a famous actor and scion of a prominent California Hispanic family.

Back in Santa Fe we watched Zozobra burn to initiate Fiesta, formed a "business" that made luminarias for our hosts' own Fiesta party, and—dressed in Navajo-like finery—tried to help guests park in reasonable array at the party itself. New Mexico was certainly indelibly stamped into my consciousness: the clean tang of the air, the puffiness of the clouds overhanging the mountains, the honest, rich chocolate color of the scrubby earth.

More habitual journeys took place too. When I was around five years old, we started going back to Beech Lake, Pennsylvania, where my grandparents had taken Uncle Vincent so he could row his broken arm back into shape. We reestablished contact with the Olvers, who welcomed us back to their still-operating boardinghouse like old friends, though no one in the family had stayed there for well over twenty years; and we kept going back—usually for three weeks or more each summer—for the next five or six years. We would rent a rowboat from the town boat rental; hike frequently to the village general store, which had a whole counter full of "American Indian" souvenirs like tiny birch bark canoes and little leather tepees; swim twice daily at the Olvers' private beach on the lake; and sit in rocking chairs on the wide porches of the main house before and after communal meals at big, long tables that each accommodated a dozen or more guests. They still operated the boardinghouse as a dairy farm of several hundred acres, and the many kids who were guests played at being farm kids—watching the milking, hanging on to the rear end of the tractor as it gathered hay, jumping around in the comforting dried-grass aromas of the barn lofts, getting covered with hay dust. Bee wrote, cast, and directed plays for the kids (she gave me the best parts) that we performed in the barn for the other guests, and some days we'd row across the lake to look at the beaver dams up a side creek or to a spot in the woods called the "Indian burial ground," which contained straight rows of what seemed to be grave mounds. This spot was well situated for some oral history that centered around a local character who was the subject of talk:

Not far from the burial ground, further back in the woods but also closer to a road, there was a resident recluse we just called The Hermit. We might occasionally see him passing on the road that passed the Olvers' front lawn. When he was a child, the story went, he and his parents, living out in the woods, had been attacked by the Indians, but the Indians had caught a plague at that very moment and all died, and he and his family had buried them in the burial ground.

This account, of course, could only have seemed absurd to anyone with the slightest historical sense, but it made everything dovetail neatly for me: the "Indian" graves, the local character, the "Indian" artifacts at the local general store. And it gave added meaning to the family story that earlier in the century, when they had been the ones at Beech Lake, my uncles had spent one night camping in the woods at the burial ground; there was even the remnant of a lean-to structure that I imagined they had left behind—a semipermanent connection I enjoyed to the landscape. The Hermit became the subject of one of my own stories too:

Once I went with some older boys, coming in from the lake past the burial ground up to see if we could rouse The Hermit. I was left behind on the trail to guard the rear, given a BB gun I could barely even hold, and told to shoot The Hermit if he crept up on us from that direction. Fortunately he didn't, but in a few minutes my older companions came tearing back down the trail, and we all ran back toward the boat, The Hermit in hot pursuit—whether real or imagined I never quite understood, for I never set eyes on him myself.

In seasons other than summer we would go to Atlantic City in New Jersey for a few days at a time. The town was probably already fading as a beach resort despite the Miss America pageant, but it still had plenty of vibrancy along the boardwalk, long before its reincarnation as the glitzy gambling mecca of the East Coast. The train would take us through the New Jersey Pine Barrens, which seemed to go on forever as I wondered how they could even be there. This was not my image of New Jersey with its freeways and industrial aromas; New Yorkers liked to insist that New Jersey sent all of its bad smells to the city. Then we'd be at the shore. We would stay at the Marlborough Blenheim Hotel on the beach, a rambling collection of buildings with commodious public areas and an elaborately tiled cupola. The White family owned the hotel and Mrs. White had been to college with Bee at Georgian Court, so we felt an added connection to the place. They were Quakers and Bee had been to their wedding, an event she liked to recount and that obviously had been a high point for her regarding religious curiosities: the bride and groom just sat in the church and waited until the spirit moved them to wed themselves.

Rather than go to Atlantic City one year, we went farther down the coast to Ocean Grove. Located next to lively Asbury Park, the town had been founded as a Methodist seaside encampment and was quiet and sedate to the nth degree. Bars and drinking were not tolerated and Sunday was really a Sabbath when life itself almost seemed to cease. What with that and tales of the Quaker Whites, perhaps on some level I came to associate the Jersey Shore with religious oddity. At any rate, it was, culturally, something new. I might not know what to make of it, but it was interesting. In Atlantic City we would deign to be pushed along in the cumbersome wheeled chairs that plied the boardwalk, bundling up in blankets against the cutting sea breezes if we had come in early spring, when the weather was still chilly; or go for horseback rides on the beach, hooves kicking up damp sand; or swim in an indoor pool heavy with the scent of chlorine, like an odd but comforting perfume.

And we continued to go to Lake Waramaug, which continued to be a focus, albeit a less central one, for the family as our house and family both passed into a new era.

My grandparents' marriage had long failed to be a functioning one, and that debacle mirrored, if not actually contributed to, my grandfather's financial decline. By the 1930s the family rarely saw him, except when he showed up in 1938 to give away my mother in marriage.

My cousins had a few fragmentary stories about him. He showed up at the office of his oldest son, Edward, and asked for a loan. Edward, like his other brothers, was so angry at the "old man" for his behavior that he turned him down. Some of my older cousins were dimly aware of his existence; one had seen him one Christmas and, because of his white hair, confused him with Santa Claus. She asked what had happened to him because he was so seldom seen. She was told that his business had collapsed and that he'd had to go away. She imagined the collapse of a literal building, so it made perfect sense to her that he went somewhere else.[3]

The lake house itself had hardly collapsed but had fallen into neglect. It was still humming along in the late Thirties.

A cousin tells the story of staying in the house with her sister and being in an upstairs bedroom at night, gazing out on to the back lawn while members of my mother's generation gaily played croquet in the gathering darkness, blithely hitting each others' balls into the rough and managing to stay on the course in the dim light by affixing lighted candles to the wickets.

But the loss of money began to take its toll, and then the disruptions and rationing during the war that made travel problematic added other difficulties. One year the noted pianist Alexander Brailowsky rented the house for the summer. He moved in his grand piano, shifted the existing furniture around, and, according to family recountings of the events, neighbors spoke of listening to him play from a distance at dusk. But if his presence added a note of new life, it also meant that the family was losing control of the house. And he enjoyed using lighted candles in the living room, which made permanent smoke marks on the old beams, a mark signaling both foreign occupation and physical decline.

The house passed into the ownership by my mother's oldest brother, Edward, who would own it for many years. After his death his widow, Lillian Firmbach Mulvehill, continued to operate the house, and she was throughout her tenure a second formidable chatelaine rather in the mold of Myrtle Belle. To save rationed gasoline during the war, Edward and Lillian would sometimes pick up Myrtle Belle at the end of a subway line in the city and drive up to the lake from there.

Once, according to a cousin's story, a policeman stopped Edward en route for some supposed infraction, and Lillian proceeded to lecture the officer on the difficulties of the times and the sacrifices the family was making—including having members in the armed services—and how it was an effort to even be on the road. He decided not to issue a ticket; being married to this woman, he said, was penalty enough.

In later years, Edward enjoyed working around the property dressed in his oldest clothes, and on one occasion, workmen appeared at the house and, apparently taking him for a fellow worker, asked where the boss was. She's in the kitchen, he would reply.

Although this last story can be seen as reflecting a husband's typical humorous recognition of his wife's position, and although the story about the policeman may be one that jokingly comments on assertive women generally, it is hard not to see them in the family context as subtly suggesting Lillian's steely personality and a recognition, albeit a humorous one, of her important role.

She would later say that by wartime the property had become a "wreck"—the lawn overgrown with snakes crawling through it—so that its reclamation was an arduous task. She wrote a brief, typescript history of the house, and it appears to be no coincidence that she filled much of this document with accounts of repairs and improvements, as though reclamation once begun was never ending (and they don't call it "historical *preservation*" for nothing). I certainly remember Uncle Ed on seemingly constant patrol against the moles that at some point invaded the lawns with their burrowing depredations. He would use a pitchfork to uproot the burrows and try to spear a mole, standing with great patience over where tunneling appeared to be going on, waiting for the right moment.

His son-in-law, Richard Gray, tells the story of one occasion when they stood together on the lawn. Ed picked up on some virtually imperceptible subterranean activity that only he could sense and finally plunged the pitchfork decisively into the earth. How did he know he'd gotten a mole? They dug up a little earth and, sure enough, one dead mole.

In story, Ed acquires an almost Zen-like sensibility for underground threats, an uncanny ability to detect them; he becomes the ultimate guardian. Everybody in the family seemed to know a story that I think acknowledged the delicacy of the lake house as a place:

There was always on the back lawn one of those glass silver balls on a pedestal that often decorate gardens. When he was a child, my cousin Jack was visiting the lake house and playing near it and managed to knock the silver ball from the pedestal, smashing it to pieces, a consequence that evoked the considerable wrath of his parents. It was an offense he never forgot, nor did others, who also continued to tell the story.

So there has been a subtle shift in emphasis; the house was no longer the scene of carefree, Roaring Twenties summer abandon—dancing at the club, speedboats and cars driven heedlessly into the lake or insouciantly on to ice—but a place of some fragility, in need of constant attention and restoration, a treasure to be preserved.[4]

Not that the good times ended; the house certainly continued to be a place of peacefulness and good times under new stewardship, though some family members came less frequently or seldom. Bee, Myrtle Belle, and I often spent a few weeks there in the summer, sometimes after our stay at Beech Lake, and it was for me a joyful time of swimming, canoeing, and occasionally going on drives around the Litchfield County countryside. Occasionally a glimmer of the past would occur, as when Paul Kraselt greeted my grandmother, or when we would visit the odd surviving friend of hers from the old days, like Mrs. Jackson, who had a big house across the lake with her husband, always called Colonel Jackson though he was in fact a brigadier general, whose body lay in state at a Brooklyn armory when he died.

Mrs. Jackson herself lived on, and I remember visiting her in her big house on the other side of the lake. Her death, probably because it signaled the end of an era, made a big impression on me and became part of my oral history of Lake Waramaug: She had decided to install a new furnace in her fine house, and the workmen left the resulting hole in the floor uncovered overnight. Evidently she forgot about this gaping danger zone, and she plunged through it in the night—to the basement and a broken neck.

New York City was good in the summer when a gentle heat laid down on the streets and, with school out, an air of urban possibilities. But it was good to get away and be reminded of green hills and dark lakes and family continuity.

Some of the stories from this period offer what I like to think of as local connectivity. They served to provide an important link to place and context by giving me a special, personal knowledge of the past and ties to that past, whether a local park through an account of its one-time owner, the German spy; or my mother's speaking of once visiting a local landmark that stood out in the landscape, the "German castle"; or even a vague story about a family connection to the owners of the amusement park that we favored. Such links expand one's sense of belonging and enlarge one's sense of knowing and understanding where one is, providing a psychic anchor. Even places not so much my own as Brooklyn—like New Mexico—became mine just a bit through stories: through knowing my connection to someone who developed the local water supply—someone, interestingly enough, originally from my own Brooklyn—or being able to tell the story of my involvement in a local festivity, or even having hung out with a vaquero TV star. Knowing the story of how the Indian burial ground in Pennsylvania came to be, however absurd the story's historicity, or that my uncles had once camped there, gave me understandings that I thought expanded my self. Stories help one to claim connection, and when you are a child, or an adult looking back on a certain childhood, such connections are important.

Yet other stories—naturally enough, for I was growing up in big ways in this time period just after the war—speak of discovering a wider world, and certainly I was very much aware of moving to a larger stage than that of a provincial Brooklyn neighborhood. Stories about being informed that you are a gentleman and a scholar, encountering the imperiousness of a friend asked to teach curse words, or even being asked to cover for a friend who smokes cigarettes may be stories about small things, but those small things seem indicative of larger processes. Perhaps that is why we specifically remember such stories and tell them. Although a story about spotting palm trees on a voyage to Bermuda in the face of someone's skepticism about their very existence may be an account of a tiny personal triumph, the story is a reminder of having voyaged, of having gone to a distant shore. My discovery of pizza in a German-run ice cream parlor in Bay Ridge puts me in the mainstream—perhaps in a very out-of-the-way corner of that mainstream—of momentous developments in American and world culinary history. A wider world indeed.

I am only somewhat surprised in retrospect to realize how many of the stories from this time period relate to politics, notably Joe McCarthy's flaming-meteor presence on the scene, and to—in its way, also political—race in America. My encounters with black people while shopping in downtown Brooklyn, my sensitivity in Bermuda to what black people should be called, even my astonishment at our cab driver's theories about the southern accent I heard for the first time on our trip to Washington, DC. Perhaps these mirror in some way the family story of my uncle at Harvard having a black servant, though today I tend to find this only a story about an astoundingly different time, or the story of my grandmother's first word in America. Surprised, because I would have said that I had little concept of the political or larger social currents of the 1950s, other than a vague sense that I liked Ike because he was a war hero and had a good rhyming slogan, and that communism greatly threatened our way of life. (One of my friends was a great fan of Senator Estes Kefauver, but I suspect it was the appeal of his strange-sounding name.) I can only assume that, of course, the political and social currents—fear of communism, the pervasive last days of American segregation, and the American preoccupation with race—were just so powerful that they entered my mind despite my lack of conscious awareness about them. That is the power of stories: sometimes they can encapsulate things of which we are only dimly aware. In the future, I would become more consciously aware, would, for example, become peripherally involved in the civil rights and antiwar movements of the 1960s; but some seeds of knowledge seem to have been there already.

As for the family stories in this chapter, some are not stories I ever told or even heard until recently when I began asking family members about such things. Yet they make perfect sense to me as reflecting a coherent picture of family concerns and developments: my grandfather's last years and the threats posed to a beloved family place—whether symbolized by burning candles or a broken glass ball—the vigilance required to maintain that place, and a new generation that rescued it.

As we move forward we keep memories; we also keep stories. The stories tell us where we've been, offering a web of narrative that supports and gives form to memory and sometimes helps us to pass on memory that is not literally our own. Sometimes stories draw us into that more collective memory: of family, place, and people whom we did not even know. And our knowledge of the past becomes both intimate and more expansive, personal and shared, anchored in a range of meanings both ours and others'.

NOTES

1. Stephen Nissenbaum, *The Battle for Christmas* (New York: Knopf, 1996), 90–91.

2. Jan Morris, *Manhattan '45* (London: Faber and Faber, 1987); the quotation is from the book's dust jacket.

3. These and some other stories in this chapter are from my cousin Barbara Mulvehill Gray; one is from her sister, Beatrice Mulvehill Palmer.

4. Laura Clapp, a member of the fifth generation to use the house, recalls this story:

> One evening at Lake Waramaug, all my aunts and uncles and my parents went out to dinner. My three cousins, their friend Sam, my sister, and I were left alone at the lake house. We all played together for a while, and then when I was alone in the living room I saw something flying around the house. It looked like a bird. Then the thing flew into the dining room, and I told my cousin Paul. We all gathered around the dining room and guessed that it was no bird—it was a bat! Then the bat flew upstairs, and my funny cousin Dennis put a shower cap on so the bat wouldn't bite his hair. By then the bat was in Caroline's room, and my oldest cousin, Paul, said, "Let's shut the door and let the grown-ups deal with it when they get home." Then Caroline said, "But I'm sleeping in there!" So their crazy but brave friend Sam took the wastebasket and a paper bag and trapped the bat, opened the door, and let the bat fly out. We never saw the bat again!

This is reminiscent of a story of mine. I was staying at the house with Aunt Lillian (no one else was there), when around bedtime a bat appeared on the second floor. We tried to shoo it out a window, with no success, and to catch it in a net that we found; finally we put out the lights, opened a window, and it managed to find its own way out.

These two, cognate stories may simply be tales of slightly dramatic, unusual happenings. But it's hard not to see them as stories of outside forces that threaten the tranquility of the house, as yet other dangers (like burrowing moles or snakes in the grass) that are reminders of the house's fragile state.

Certainly there are family stories that do "merely" recount events that struck some of us as memorable. One such enduring story: At the lake house, steps to the basement led down from a hall closet. My cousin Mary Jane was staying at the house, as were my mother, grandmother, and I. At one point we heard a sudden and fearsome thumping coming from the hall closet. Mary Jane had somehow managed to go into it and tumble down the stairs, banging at every step. Unlike poor Mrs. Jackson, she was unhurt, though the closet ever afterward became the Mary Jane Closet. And Laura Clapp tells this:

> One day at Lake Waramaug, my three cousins, Paul, Caroline, and Dennis, bought a watermelon. They brought it down to the boathouse. A few people threw the watermelon into the lake. It made a big splash and then it floated to the top. Then we were playing games in the water with the watermelon, and my cousin Caroline got the watermelon and swam to the dock with it. She ran up to the high porch with the watermelon and threw it back into the lake, and it made a big splash again. We played in the water with the watermelon for a long time. Finally the watermelon broke apart, and their friend Sam took a piece of the watermelon and ate it!

Six

Becoming the East Village

IN THE PHASE OF MY LIFE THAT TRANSPIRED from 1963 to 1966, I was most involved in two kinds of stories: the fictional kind that preoccupied many creative writers at Johns Hopkins University and later, when I worked for the New York Welfare Department, the carefully typed kind that made up our case files. While this was a period for written stories, those stories did not impinge upon my larger narrative sense, and I have remembered and told other, oral stories long after I've forgotten the fiction and the files.

For example, I still tell about how I first encountered Baltimore, well before I even arrived:

It was my last year of college and I knew I was going to be living in Baltimore because I got offered a place in the Johns Hopkins Writing Seminars along with a fellowship. So I went to the famous newsstand in Times Square where the out-of-town papers were available every day. They were set out folded up in long racks, and I bought a copy of *The Baltimore Sun*.

Mostly I wanted the classified ads to see what sort of apartment I could find. The ads turned out to be slightly puzzling because a number of them specified "white." I wondered whether the colors of the walls—that was the only thing I could think of—were so important to Baltimore renters because of a local rage for neutrality. Or what?

It took me more than a few minutes to remember I was plunging into what I thought of as the South, into a city where segregation still held and where apartments might be apportioned on the basis of race. So the story is one of suddenly realized disquiet, and indeed so are others from this time in my life tales of unease, turmoil and tension.

I was only surprised to learn later that my fellow Johns Hopkins grad students who came from the real South were under the impression that they were moving to the North.

BALTIMORE

What to make of Baltimore in its reality I never decided. I thought I was in the South but in what looked like a big, northeastern industrial city. I liked the town's urban-ness, though I could not find much urbaneness; it seemed a pale comparison to my beloved New York. Doubtless I was so infatuated with New York that I was unwilling to give any other city a chance, and I had no starting place for finding Baltimore's soul. For Boston or Philadelphia or Washington I had stereotypes, vague pictures of the typical. The little white stoops of "Ball-a-mer" (to approximate what we thought was a local pronunciation of the place-name) did not seem to be enough for an identity, nor did Edgar Allan Poe's grave or Fort McHenry. Baltimore was a blank, just a big city, and I never felt that I had uncovered it. Even today, after *Hairspray* and *Avalon* and *Diner*, and after years of reading Anne Tyler's wonderful dissections of the city's eccentric and complex characters, I am unable to come to terms with the place. Perhaps I passed through too quickly. Perhaps the city hides its soul more effectively than most.[1]

But I did find an apartment to live in, a confined but comfortable enough furnished space on the top floor of a row house, and a community in the Writing Seminars, the department that taught creative writing as well as modern literature, an area which the Department of English seemed to view somewhat suspiciously. I found Judy Stark, from the University of Chicago, where I imagined the intenseness had matched her own, though she had a wonderful sense of amusement, as when she confided something that I have endlessly repeated: growing up in Springfield, Massachusetts, she had seen American society as made up of a great conglomeration of Catholics and her fellow Jews with a tiny sprinkling of Protestants. Her short stories were wonderfully wrought complexities of social and psychological observation and her death in the early Seventies in a bizarre auto accident was such a terrible, obvious loss. I found Eleanor Wilner, who would become so well known as a poet, whose quiet life in a small, uncertain suburb did not hide that she was more urbane than all of us. I found Joe Beatty, who mostly wrote fiction then, but who later published much poetry and became an ethicist of note and who seemed to bring a whimsical brightness into the world.

And others, too, who would go on to medical school or became academics or a noted author of children's books or a well-known regional artist and writer or even a famous director of horror movies, who during their year in Baltimore retired to little apartments to scribble away with pleasure or anguish or meet to share work or have coffee or poke through the much-trafficked library stacks after obscure British poets and European novelists. Those of us who wrote stories often sat at home, staring out the window or at the wall, where writers traditionally gaze while working, trying to think up plots and create characters and craft fictions that evoked somebody's life or spoke of society's ironies. Stories—short stories and novels—were important currency for us, but I am hard-pressed to remember what stories I wrote while staring at my wall. It's not that they had no personal significance, but it might be that other kinds of stories ultimately overcame them.

Through high school my world had continued to expand: operas at the Manhattan School of Music, "strawberry beer" in little Yorkville restaurants, the vast Metropolitan Museum of Art. I felt like I was drifting through my time at St. Francis College, a bit stuck in a provincial world. At Hopkins, the expansion was intensely internal and intensely personal, as I met not only new but unprecedented people while poking away at fictional storytelling.

Courtly Elliott Coleman presided over the Writing Seminars, poet and critic and Episcopal deacon, a white-haired man in academic tweed who remained something of a cipher. What he sought to achieve with us I never understood. Perhaps he wanted to give us a venue for working and working things out on our own; certainly he seemed a paragon of the modern in a day long before the postmodern was even a glimmer—a man who might almost have walked with Joyce or shared Proust's cork-lined room. Richard Macksey, who would become a virtual Hopkins legend, had another hand on the helm, holding classes in his Georgian Revival house north of campus amidst book-stuffed shelves that I think literally took up every wall, practically every book in my imaginary recollection some leather-bound volume from another century. Macksey, of course, tended to overwhelm us with erudition such that I often felt lost in his presence, destabilized by the absence of what I knew.

And so we proceeded through the year, hammering away at stories or poems and critical papers, rather uncertain about where or even how it was all going. I appreciated the time to work, the company I kept, and being at an institution like Hopkins, a great red-brick Georgian mass of excellence and style and regal bearing.[2] But after a year's respite in the strangest of provinces, I was happy enough to get back to my New York, where, I felt sure, I was missing the real action. I looked for a job in publishing with no success and finally became a caseworker for the welfare department, a job that, it was well known, was always available to anyone with a B.A. in anything. The turnover rate in such jobs was said to be 40 percent a year, as various misfits found their ways in and out of the position—actors and artists and writers and others looking for a "day job" who stopped by and then moved on to something better or a sojourn in Europe or Mexico or grad school. I relocated to an apartment on East Third Street, in the part of Manhattan that I still thought of as the Upper Lower East Side, but which was well on its way to becoming the East Village.

THE EAST VILLAGE SCENE

I found the welfare department and the East Village on the same day, so the two are irrevocably twisted together in my mind. On a snowy day in late 1964, I somehow found my way to a meeting of the Social Service Employees Union at a union hall on Lower Broadway. I was early for this meeting. I had been thinking I might move to the Upper West Side. Judy Stark, who *did* find work in publishing, had moved there and we had spent time together there during the summer after Hopkins. But as the snow fell, I decided to kill time by wandering east, over to and along St. Mark's Place, into a neighborhood that was beginning to pick up a reputation as a new haven for the hip—especially those who could no longer afford the glories of Greenwich Village to the west—as a place with pleasures of its own that ranged from affordable walk-ups to cheap ethnic eateries to proximity to the iconic Village itself. I was instantly charmed by the cityscape past Cooper Union, though the falling snow—gentle puffs out of some classic Japanese print—must have added and hidden much, and though St. Mark's Place, where W. H. Auden still lived, is the impressive queen street of the neighborhood, winding up at Tompkins Square Park. Exactly when this upper part of the Lower East Side came to be called the East Village, I don't know, nor do I know who popularized the name—probably real estate interests looking for a less downscale appellation—though it was a natural segue, lying just to the east of the "real" Village and being settled by those who saw themselves as the spiritual descendants of the radicals, bohemians, and aesthetic pioneers who once populated Greenwich Village itself.[3] I fixed on the place and started looking there for my new, independent residence. I wound up on Third Street, between Avenues B and C, in the subregion known as Alphabet City. I was not far from Stuyvesant Town, the ambitious housing development above Fourteenth Street erected in the late 1940s to provide a huge block of middle-class housing in Manhattan and where my father's sister Lil and her husband lived. But the gritty East Village seemed a world away from Stuy Town's neat red brick, careful landscaping, and garages that tucked away residents' late-model cars like hidden hints of suburbia.

In his memoir of New York in the 1950s, Dan Wakefield, who left the city in 1963, just before I gravitated to the East Village, wrote, "In the fifties was the word. The word was everywhere. The image was yet to predominate."[4] Books, writing, and literature were big in this world, and the word still had a potent presence for us. And we read a lot and talked about books and thought about books, and sometimes, about writers and their exploits. So maybe I can be forgiven if this chapter contains some retrospective looks at the period and its adjacent years as occasional reference points: memoirs by Dan Wakefield, Bob Dylan, John Tytell, Robert Stone—all, big-time words guys in one way or another—and by Suze Rotolo, who was less a wordsmith and more of a visual artist.[5] True, Robert Crumb and Gilbert Shelton comics were soon as ubiquitous as the marijuana in our stash boxes and were even taken seriously as creative endeavors, as if to suggest that the image was moving in on us in a big way—but I certainly did not see it that way.

In reading in the first volume of Dylan's *Chronicles*, about his New York years in the 1960s—though he is notoriously hard to pin down for details like dates—I was struck by how often he notes the cold, as though he was living through a perpetual winter. "New York City was cold," he writes, "muffled and mysterious." Or, "It was freezing cold. I put my hands in my pockets and headed off towards 6th Avenue." He heads from the Folklore Center, where he had made the acquaintance of Moe Asch, a great fixture of the New York folk music scene, "into the ice-chopping weather"; "[o]utside the Mills Tavern the thermometer was creeping up to about ten degrees below."[6] When I think of pictures of Dylan from the period, perhaps album covers or perhaps pictures I've invented in my own head, I see him hunched up against a cold wind in a jacket not quite toasty-looking enough, maybe slouching down a lonesome, chilly street.[7]

And somehow it *was* a cold time, or it seemed that way to me then and now, though no one but Dylan would likely claim it ever hit ten degrees below zero in Manhattan. I seem to remember always pushing through snow and sleet or coming around corners with the wind whipping up the world or bundling in coats that never quite kept out the chill or nipping into coffee shops to grab a quick cup of the brew and warm up. It was a time of blowing dead leaves and iced people showing up on doorsteps at night perhaps needing a place to bed down and tenement buildings—not your own—where you feared that people might not have enough heat to make it through.

I think of Conrad Aiken's short story "Silent Snow, Secret Snow," wherein the extreme cold threatens delusion and death. But the New York cold I remember was not necessarily a bad thing; even Dylan seemed to like it sometimes. Sometimes, he writes, it had "snap and sparkle."[8] It kept one alert. It provided the pleasure of slipping into warmth and being grateful one had cozy shelter. Yet plenty of mirroring, metaphorical chills matched the time and place. Many people felt oppressed by domineering social and historical forces. These were not the best times for New York City. Things were falling apart, centers were not holding. The streets were edgy, the dark corners threatening, the infrastructure uncertain. John Tytell writes of stopping by his landlord's office to pay the rent and finding armed robbers who held him up and chained him to the heating system. When he lived on Avenue D—my own apartment was between B and C—he kept his radio behind bookshelves to foil burglars. By the end of the 1960s he was beginning to agree with Saul Bellow's assessment of New York as a place that made one think of "the collapse of civilization."[9] These "dangerous times" even gave me a story:

"One night I was coming home to Third Street from somewhere. I was walking down Avenue B, the streets were deserted, and these three black guys show up from out of nowhere.

"I figured I'd just pass them by, but they decided to get real aggressive, to accost me, in fact. They shoved me up against a wall of a building and reached into their jackets like they were groping for knives. Sometimes, often enough, there were cops around the neighborhood, and if I'd seen some I would have yelled. But there weren't any now.

"I thought maybe I could just offer them my wallet, but all that I could realize was that water was pouring down off my head and down the front of my face. I was like a cartoon character who suddenly actually starts to sweat with fear!

"Then they just let me pass. Apparently they just wanted to scare the white guy. And they succeeded, believe me. Anyway, I just stumbled on home."

And there was the turmoil brought on by such events as the transit strike that paralyzed the city for days and the great blackout that brought a terrible blanket of darkness, crippled the subways, and left thousands displaced.[10] The strike, called by the fiery ex-communist union leader Mike Quill, much quoted for his assertion that the judge who issued an injunction against the strike could "drop dead in his black robes" before the strike would be called off, started on New Year's Day 1966. The following day those of us who worked for Welfare were told to report to the nearest departmental office, and once there, no one knew what to do with us, so the whole time took on a sort of holiday air. We mostly belonged to our own union that had its many problems with the city—probably sympathetic to the transit workers—but the disruptions of normal life and the jailing of union leaders and the mounting political tensions in a city whose economy could no longer support it, added to the ill ease and sense of near-chaos that sometimes hung in the air. But instead of the judge dropping dead, Quill himself, in ill-health during the strike, died at the end of January, as if portending a more general collapse.

Not long before, in November, the blackout came when the electricity supply suddenly dried up over a vast swath of the Northeast and Canada: lights flickered then went out, electrified trains slowed to a halt, TV screens went blank. Eventually we learned that the failure stemmed from power stations in Canada and upstate New York, but that fact was irrelevant to the flow of personal stories ("Where were you when . . . ?") that follow in the wake of involvement in momentous events. I had my own:

I was riding home from work at the Borough Hall welfare office in downtown Brooklyn, swaying along in what was one of the IND trains, as I usually did. We stopped in the tunnel, not an unusual event; subway trains were always stopping in tunnels for shorter or longer waits—signals, other trains, whatever. This wait began to seem unusually long. A conductor came through the cars looking puzzled, suggesting that perhaps something was unusually wrong. Stories of needing to abandon a train and walk along tracks appeared in my head. The lights of the car began to look a little dimmer than usual. But then the train managed to make a little lurch forward. Maybe no hike on the tracks was in store for us. Not much progress, but some. Finally there was a further, more concerted lurch, and we realized we had pulled into a station, or at least the front part of the train had. Doors slid open and, realizing that the station was pitch black and that indeed Something Pretty Big Was Wrong and that the train was best abandoned, we sidled out into utter darkness. Or maybe there was still a little glow from the train's lights, but I remember virtually feeling my way toward the stairs. How the hell did we find them? Sensing the flow of people ahead of us? I groped my way up to the street, where outside there was no light either, except the faint remains of the day. The city, so far as anyone could see, had no artificial light except for vehicles—no street lamps, no warm glows from apartments, no shop signs. Fortunately, I was just a subway stop from my usual and could walk home.

Once there, I walked to my apartment without light and found my next-door neighbor, the husband of a young couple, a grad student in psychology. We speculated on what was going on, and perhaps he had a portable radio and we began to realize that this Thing was Big. We chatted and greeted a few other neighbors who passed by. He was afraid that his wife was stuck on the subway, and indeed, she appeared hours later; her own train never made it to a station. She finally had been extricated and had to walk along the track, like I had feared I might have to do. She had brought home a perfect stranger, a man from Brooklyn Heights who was now stuck in Manhattan.

He worked for Radio Liberty, which I had never heard of before—a counterpart to the Voice of America—and lived in a tiny room to help pay for a Manhattan apartment for his divorced wife and child. We combined food supplies and ate together, enjoying each other's company, and the stranger then spent the night on my couch. He left in the morning and I never saw him nor probably chatted with my neighbors at length again.

There had been that moment of unity begotten by crisis, and a sudden conviviality mixed in with the inconvenient wrenching from normalcy and the minor trauma, and I suppose the story reminds me of that found-and-lost moment. It's a story that recalls our feelings that the city we lived in was on the verge of crisis, but it offers a personal take on the crisis by telling about the personal encounters that made up the larger event and even offers the solace of humans getting together to take care of each other.

Of course, there was also the war—the war in Vietnam that increasingly hung over our heads and the American landscape, bringing bitterness and rebellion and angst. "America was wrapped in a blanket of rage," according to Dylan. Wakefield realized the changing of the guard out of the 1950s when he watched—from the Edwardian Room at the Plaza Hotel, no less—policemen hold back a mob of young people in 1964, thus ushering in the "counterdecade."[11]

Letters from friends a little later in time, when I was in India, reflect the fear of being drafted into jungle combat and the heady relief that came with figuring ways out. After getting his deferment, one friend wrote, "my acne cleared up, my hernia disappeared, and my hair returned . . . a 2-S baby!" Another anticipated his physical exam, indicating he was "not too worried; I'll never be able to get my wheelchair through their narrow doors." They joked, but the anxiety was real; the draft cut into the middle class, the Asian death toll mounted, and hostility to our own government's involvement intensified. One friend, who worked for the leftist *National Guardian* newspaper and later decamped for Cuba wrote, "This country wallows in corruption and no protest here seems to have any effect either . . . but there is a kind of desperation in the Establishment now." Another, a friend from Hopkins, apologized for not writing a "real letter" and said she couldn't or "I'll get all mad and start screaming about our despot President and fat white Kate Smith America." One college friend, a sweet, sincere guy who decided he was a pacifist and could not obey his summons to military service, was prosecuted for draft evasion. His case was in progress before my trip to India; later he went to jail.

But if the times produced anxiety, they also took on a certain headiness and excitement. When the term *counterculture* came into use I don't recall, but we sensed we were into Something New and felt a spirit of joy and protest and even great progress. Perhaps we knew that even the edgier bits of our lives were only temporary. A friend wrote to me in India about renting a new apartment in the old neighborhood: "There's no garbage in the halls. How middle class we've become"; her comments underscored the decay that sometimes surrounded us and our abilities to move beyond it as our lives improved. That same friend also wrote, "Then came the Be-Ins. These are gatherings of people who love, give each other flowers, paint their faces, plant flowers and grain, dance, etc., together." Although that phenomenon must have developed while I was out of the country, certainly we were all aware much earlier of the people who came to be called hippies. I first heard the term from a fellow Welfare caseworker who complained that a new guy at work was hitting on her; but by calling him a hippie she only meant that he thought he was terribly hip, with his goatskin wine bag that matched his attitude, so the later meaning of the term had not quite formed.

For Dan Wakefield, the end of the Fifties in New York came on a night in 1961 when Bob Dylan, "a gawky kid . . . in a floppy hat," to quote Michael Harrington, walked into the White Horse Tavern in the Village.[12] Perhaps he means a shift in spirit from not only word to image but from a particular intellectual intensity to a fervid embracing of vaguely conceived notions of love, peace, and brotherhood; from a politics with a pedigree of ideas and goals to a more amorphous form of casual anarchy; from people firmly grounded in the larger culture to those who formed their own subset with their unique ways of dress and speech and music and mores; and maybe from the read to the sung word. I doubt that I knew even one hippie; my friends and acquaintances simply remained more mainstream. Maybe they saw themselves as bohemians or activists or artists or leftists or, for that matter, nothing in particular or just slightly unconventional or just people living on the fringes in a city where that was an old tradition. Maybe hippiedom was more than just people or groups of people but a spirit that at that time was indeed blowin' in the wind.[13]

Surely the spirit of hedonism—eventually captured in the slogan "sex, drugs, and rock 'n' roll"—appealed to us. Of course, we thought of our peccadilloes not as mere hedonism but as a kind of liberation and free-spirited expression in contrast to the "dogged centrism" of our place and time.[14] New attitudes and mores flourished. John Tytell writes about "marathon coupling . . . coming together with a beautiful, uninhibited woman on every part of the sectional couch I had inherited from my step-grandmother, on the floor, on the round oak table we ate on, as well as the bed," and of "martinis in the summer, Brandy Alexanders in the winter, marijuana . . . the life of one of Henry Miller's characters."[15] Sexuality became more casual. Wakefield would say of the Fifties that the period was "heavy with romance and light on sex"; the sex in the Sixties may have become a good deal heavier, but perhaps we imagined some of it more than we experienced it.[16]

Illegal drugs moved more into the mainstream. I never personally became enamored with the mythos of marijuana or hallucinogens, but others were, and it was always easy to score. If you didn't want to buy anything, friends would always give you a little. Some friends from my St. Francis days set up an apartment on First Avenue near Third Street, and their place always seemed full of the heady smoke of joints and talk of more powerful things to come.

MUSIC, PROTEST, AND CIVIL RIGHTS

One of those St. Francis friends was a former Franciscan brother who had thrown over the religious life; interestingly enough, he retained the more euphonious name he assumed in the monastery as his first name. His interest in the era's fascinations extended from pot to rock music, and his apartment contained mostly LPs, stacked against every wall or piece of furniture. He would play his discs at piercingly high volume at any hour of the day or night, seemingly bound by principle to exercise his musical tastes whenever he pleased. Rather like Dylan himself, I continued to be enthralled by the current revival of quieter, traditional folk music. This fascination no doubt limited my exposure to the latest pop music, and I was aware that rock had become a sort of jazz for our times. People went to the Dom on St. Mark's Place to dance or to various cavernous rooms just to listen. In smaller venues, black light cast uncanny impressions and other lights flashed with hallucinogenic speed as music throbbed and the walls pulsed. People would just stand around, entranced, or lounge about on carpeted floors like sound-happy slugs.

The music itself came to be seen as a form of protest, something new and loud and vibrant, like the psychedelic colors that splashed across posters or the outrageous comic books and underground newspapers—like the East Village Other—that proliferated at newsstands. Song lyrics might express protest, though the music alone was usually enough. We favored the local band the Fugs, whose lyrics often mocked the Establishment or aimed to shock; their name alone was seen as a not too subtle statement of convention-breaking onomastics. Great songsters they were not, but we listened raptly to them on record and live onstage.

At one party, a member of the Fugs appeared as a fellow guest, and that impressed the hell out of the rest of us. Although he wasn't core member Ed Sanders or Tuli Kupferberg, he looked big and hulking. I chatted with him and learned that he too came from Bay Ridge in Brooklyn and still lived there with his parents!

So much for rebellious and degenerate rock 'n' roll protest musicians, I thought, and told this story maybe to make the point that I had managed to come a little further along than this icon.

Protest was all around us, however, particularly as the war escalated and the sons of the middle class fell into greater danger. I marched down Fifth Avenue in one giant antiwar parade, and I mostly remember shifting away from the safe center of the trekking throng to the very edges near where pro-war protesters viewing the parade shouted at and heckled us. I was reminded of marching in the St. Patrick's Day Parade in college but without the bands and flasks of alcohol to make it a gayer occasion. I showed up on Park Avenue across the street from a hotel where LBJ was appearing, and we yelled and made noise. I walked up and down in front of Representative Manny Sellers's refined Prospect Park West apartment building to protest his position on seating Mississippi Democrats and boarded a chartered bus to Washington, DC, to lobby other New York congressional members on the issue. Isolated incidents, such as the arrest of young artist and prankster Joey Skaggs for trying to plant a crucifix he had made on a pile of dirt in Tompkins Square, pointed to more general concerns. The spirit of protest was in the air, and it seemed a constructive thing.

I became more aware of the issue of race as the civil rights movement progressed across headlines and TV screens and began volunteering for an organization called the Charter Group for a Pledge of Conscience, which aimed to enlist white people to make other whites more aware of race problems. People liked the name Charter Group, although the moniker was at first only meant as temporary, and no one ever changed it. The group channeled its energies into the cause of the Harlem Six, a group of young black men the group thought had been falsely accused of murder. We eventually organized a benefit event at Town Hall, that venerable Theatre District magnet for rallies and politically tinged meetings, featuring comedian Dick Gregory and author Truman Nelson, who wrote a book about the case. I leafleted other Town Hall gatherings and stored copies of the book in my apartment; journeyed to grand and not-so-grand apartments—mostly on the Upper West Side—that housed old leftists or activists of various stripes; and expanded my network of friends and acquaintances as we supped after meetings in old Broadway delis heaped high with corned beef.

Eventually, years later, the Harlem Six were retried. Problems of race continued in our daily reality and our hearts. A friend, a fellow Welfare caseworker, wrote me the year after I'd left New York for India that an East Village landlord had refused her an apartment because of her status as a white single mother with a black child. A southern friend from Hopkins wrote to assure me that her fiancé was "*not* a segregationist."

WELFARE

Meanwhile, I labored bureaucratically among the poor as a social investigator for the New York City Department of Welfare, a title that soon changed to "caseworker" in accordance with a labor settlement; in fact, I started my training with the approval of the union because they wanted more caseworkers as soon as possible during an actual strike in late 1964 or early 1965. I was a civil servant among civil servants, and we pushed a great deal of paper around and consulted great manuals of rules and dictated our notes—which became the written stories of our "clients"—onto Dictaphone belts in a special room and tried to keep people happy within the bounds of a giant government system. Some of us saw what we did as just another safe city job, though *safe* was a somewhat relative term. Occasionally a caseworker would be mugged out in the field, and we held to the belief that the black notebooks we carried—that we thought identified us—generally protected us; not even muggers wanted to disrupt somebody's welfare payments. Some of us were more idealistic: we thought we were helping people, even if we were part of a giant bureaucracy that often was itself not very helpful.

For that matter, our clients were often less than helpful—getting evicted, coming to the office to yell and make grand scenes, paralyzed by their frustrations or failings. I had mixed feelings about the system. Obviously it kept people from starving, clothed and housed them, and thus maintained a sort of social peace, but it seemed to lead people nowhere and hold them in little regard. Our files were full of life stories—at least so far as people's origins, liaisons, progeny, and economic well-being were concerned. We might consult the thick folders full of forms and narratives, set out on special departmental paper, that traced people's existence and development. But it seemed to me that we saw these as mere documents, not stories at all, not accounts of humans working out their struggles against a backdrop of trouble and slippery fortunes.

My fellow workers composed an intriguing mix of middle-class civil servants and earnest radicals, actors and artists trying to maintain a day job, the occasional acidhead, and pretty young women who looked like cheerleaders or debutantes but who read *New Left Review* on their breaks. One of the supervisors ran a morning coffee and doughnuts operation out of the cloakroom that benefited some charity. One caseworker, a taciturn Irishman from Queens, seemed to spend the whole day in the cloakroom reading the newspaper; his actual assignment supposedly allowed for this, though he was very close-mouthed about just what that entailed along with anything else, as if he fronted a very secretive Irish Republican Army operation. Most days of the week we visited our clients, asking after their needs, urging them to keep infrequent appointments with prospective employers, keeping up with their living situations, trying to guess if they had income they were not admitting to or unauthorized residents—like boyfriends—living with them, listening to the personal histories, the stories that we would later dictate for typists. Although officially we were there to help them, we were supposed to keep an eye on them too; our title had only recently been changed from "investigator," after all, and the clients certainly understood we were some manifestation of The Man, albeit a rather benign one. If necessary, we could call in a special investigations unit that carried guns and could make dawn raids to roust out those boyfriends or others not supposed to be there.

Many of us were indeed actors and writers and musicians holding on to day jobs; many of us were college-degreed, middle-class white folk temporarily passing through another existence where many of the people whose stories we recorded and whose lives we influenced, were black or Hispanic. I was a middle-class white guy in the midst of a world I had only imagined. I wish I could say that I learned something even superficial about people's cultures, that I had stories that at least called attention to our differences. But all I remember is a vague sense that they saw me as an inconvenient overlord—someone they were forced to interact with occasionally to keep receiving money. Sometimes I would ring a doorbell, a child would come to the door, and an unseen adult would call out to ask who it was. The child would shout back, "It's The Man"—not with hostility so much as resignation and a recognition of my designation, my identity, my role in their lives.

Although confrontations occasionally occurred in clients' home spaces, our interviews were mostly innocuous. In fact, being in the field was one of the pleasures of the job. It provided plenty of fresh air and exercise, one's own schedule, a chance to talk to people, and a good look at parts of New York City I'd have been unlikely to see otherwise—in my case, mostly brownstone-filled Bedford-Stuyvesant and less stately Brownsville, with occasional forays to the bleak South Bronx, rubble-strewn East New York, or unfamiliar parts of Brooklyn. In the field one felt cleansing rain and cooling breezes. In the field multicolored spring wildflowers popped up in dumpy playgrounds and old squares with wooden benches to plunk down on and ravaged vacant lots. I liked the feel of pavement under my feet, the sounds of traffic in the background, the deep brick colors of apartment houses, even the emptiness of lonely hallways.

On one little field excursion I delivered a check for moving expenses to a moving company, which considered the relocated client unreliable and had requested direct payment. After taking the check from me, the company's owner tried to give me a folded-up twenty-dollar bill. I evaded it with some difficulty, finally agreeing that he could give me a bottle of gin sometime. I doubted he would try to chase me down in some vague future waving a sloshing bottle, though I probably did drink gin at the time. Indeed, I never saw him again. He probably thought I was some sort of down-at-the-heels alcoholic. He, of course, wanted more moving jobs steered his way. He kept saying that I was underpaid, what a lousy job I had, how I deserved a little something extra. I was offended. I liked my strange job with all its problems. I was in it for the adventure: the walks in odd neighborhoods, the people and situations I could barely once have imagined, the coworkers I'd be unlikely to meet elsewhere. Later on, a coworker taking a temporary leave took me to lunch along with another moving company owner; this person had actually engineered unnecessary moves for clients, signed up the movers, and taken a cut. They wanted someone to continue the tradition. To me it seemed not only dishonest but a rather pitiful way to garner a few dollars. By then I knew that I would soon be moving on myself, though I suppose I did let the mover buy my lunch.

I would tell these stories of proffered bribes reluctantly, for perhaps they took me too close to corruption as I tried to live within a world of purity in which I saw myself helping people and protesting injustice.

The welfare department also offered us the spirit of protest that pervaded the times. We might be cogs in a great bureaucracy and our position vis-à-vis the downtrodden might be an ambiguous one, but we could exercise our subversive sides. But while grumbling about this ambiguity, we could actually subvert the system from time to time in tiny ways. Our ally was the Social Service Employees Union (SSEU), which we saw as a maverick sort of union that fit in with the protest ethic of the day. The SSEU had been founded not long before by a caseworker named Joe Tepedino, who thought that the existing Local 371, an affiliate of the American Federation of State, County and Municipal Employees (AFL-CIO), was ineffective. The independent SSEU in effect won a weeks-long strike in early 1965 and was riding high when I joined the welfare department, though inevitably some bitterness remained between those who had gone out on strike and those who had not.

In the participatory spirit of the times, I found it easy to be a union activist. One of the local delegates assigned me to talk informally with others on my floor, keeping my ears out for their concerns. We also formed picket lines, as when a young caseworker named Iris Archer was fired for what we considered ridiculous reasons. In memory I see myself walking the line, shouting "Free Iris Archer." Of course, Iris did not need freeing from anything; in retrospect, it seems like we were always trying to free somebody in the Sixties: the Harlem Six or one of the Black Panthers or George Jackson of the Soledad Brothers. The union moved into new offices near Madison Square, and we all just sort of milled around there as if waiting for great things to happen. A newspaper, that *sine qua non* of any real organization, was published. When union elections rolled around, a new, dissident faction that thought the Tepedino group too timid ran a slate of officers against his barely installed "old guard," which stirred up a round of internal activism as candidates maneuvered and squared off. Perhaps the spirit of the times demanded a certain level of constant turmoil, and times of quietude went against the grain. In fact, the new group did take over, but by then I was moving on.

ON EAST THIRD STREET

My life in the East Village was also full of ordinary domestic doings and simple routines. On days off I liked walking over to the "real" Village or taking the First Avenue bus up to Midtown or the Upper East Side for a change of scenery. My friend Wendy, whom I'd met during college when I worked in the Housewares Department at the old B. Altman department store, moved from L.A. back to New York and lived on the Upper West Side and then just off Greenwich Avenue. We had parties and went to post-college hangouts together. I discovered in a Village bar something called the Scopitone—a French invention—a jukebox with a TV screen that offered precursors to music videos that cost a quarter. These short video vignettes of performers singing French songs made the whole thing seem more avant-garde, and I always introduced out-of-town visitors to this marvel of international pop culture.[17] When I felt wealthy I liked to have an occasional meal at an expensive restaurant. On less flush days I ate at a Chinese restaurant just up Avenue B and a pair of nameless eateries near Tompkins Square that we just called "the Polish places," leftover from the large numbers of East Europeans that used to live in the neighborhood. For awhile in 1964 Wendy worked at the World's Fair, and I visited it in Flushing once or twice.[18] My mother, Bee, had marvelous memories of the 1939 fair and glowed with excitement over the current one. But by then the popularity of such fairs was waning, and I never could get terribly interested in it; to me it offered a dated vision of the present and an amusement-park atmosphere less intriguing than anything Manhattan had to offer.

I moved into my Third Street apartment early in 1965, after going through *The New York Times* classified ads and then looking at several places. An abundance of places had too-small rooms or grimy hallways or unpromising kitchens, so I was delighted to find the railroad-style half floor on the unremarkable block between B and C, which seemed about as far east as was tolerable to go. The apartment sat in a building that from the outside looked like the rest on the block, worn down by time and semi-neglect. Its owner—a squat, tough-looking Italian American named Joe, whose last name was improbably the same as a type of pasta—had gut renovated the inside by himself, and it was still in progress. It was a walk-up with carpeted stairways and gleaming linoleum hall floors, well lit and freshly painted. It also had a nonworking but decorative fireplace, a bare brick wall in the living room, and a big, functional kitchen to the rear of the row of rooms, which also included a bedroom and a little study. The place seemed perfect and was even rent-controlled; I took it, beginning a minor role in something of a saga, from which stories came.

Joe, it turned out, was obsessively possessive of his building, his creation. Although evidently he lived on Avenue C with a woman who was his business partner (and possibly his wife), he kept a little apartment on the ground floor on East Third with a cot and kitchenette. His door was almost always open, and he stayed there much of the day and night; when someone entered the front door, he usually popped his head out to see who it was. Of course, lots of snazzier New York apartment buildings employed well-paid doormen to do the same, and this certainly provided a measure of security in a still dicey neighborhood. But I soon learned that many of my fellow tenants found him far too intrusive, perhaps even a bit creepy. Indeed, his manner was not necessarily reassuring. He maintained a rough demeanor and liked to tell about how in his youth he had killed somebody and was whisked away by mob connections to hide out for a long time in Pennsylvania.

One afternoon I came home from work and started up the stairs to my second-floor apartment and noticed that the stairway carpet—I somehow remember it as green—had splotches of what looked to me like tar on a number of steps. I avoided stepping in any of these, but as I went up, Joe came out to talk. A tenant had moved out, he told me, apparently after a long-running dispute with Joe. He had sprinkled acid on the carpet as his final farewell.

I immediately started telling this incident as a story—probably because it struck me as so bizarre—but as time went on, I came to realize that a number of tenants seemed to have sorely felt grievances over things like security deposits and leases, though mostly I think they resented Joe's looming, proprietary presence. This was New York, the city where people expect and perhaps seek anonymity.

I began to accumulate what I thought of as "Joe stories," little narratives about his interactions with the rest of us, maybe as a subgenre of "landlord stories," a story form familiar to all New Yorkers:

I became friendly with a sociologist named Peter Freund, who had his own dispute with Joe, though I do not recall over what. When Peter entered the building and Joe stuck out his head to see who was coming in, Peter liked to yell, "Get your head back in there, you animal!"

Clearly Joe touched off some nerves.

One afternoon I was laying on my couch—a sort of Danish modern thing I had bought at someplace like the Door Store—when the front door opened suddenly. Joe and several other people stepped into my apartment with a klieg-lighted movie camera rolling! "Oh, sorry," said Joe, "I thought nobody was home," though he had not knocked. The people with him were philanthropists of some sort who had bought a nearby building and wanted to rehab it for affordable housing. He was showing them the marvels that could be done with old tenements; they were recording the tour for their reference, or maybe to use in applying for grants.

Fortunately, I wasn't having sex, ingesting illegal substances, or lying about naked when the film crew burst in, though the apartment was particularly messy at the time. That, said the philanthropists, as they continued to film, was just what they wanted—the place would look lived-in.

So Joe certainly could intrude, and I could feel the tension between him and some of his tenants, who often did not stay long in residence. Personally, I got along with him well enough. Perhaps because one night I had come home late and saw him lying in the hallway face down outside his little cubbyhole. He seemed to be dead drunk, and I helped him to his cot, for which he later thanked me. But as time went on, he clearly resented the fact that I was friendly with tenants with whom he was on the outs. He continued as an uneasy but inevitable presence. Of course, looking for a new and better apartment has long been a New York preoccupation. Wakefield mentions using journalistic connections to get advance copies of the *Village*

Voice, with its rental ads, to beat out the competition in finding the best apartment deals. I well remember apartment-seeking folks lining up at a particular Village newsstand to buy the first available copies of the *Voice* for the same reason. People came and went from East Third Street, because of Joe's looming glower or not.

Peter found a place with a working fireplace down the street, but in true New Yorker spirit, he kept looking for something even better and preferably cheaper, which gave me one of my favorite stories:

One evening I went with him to look at a new place. He had an appointment with a building "super" for six p.m., and we pulled up at the door of the super's apartment on time (or so I thought). Peter knocked. A voice, with a pronounced German accent, came through the door: "Who is it?" "It's Peter Freund, come to look at the apartment as scheduled." "Mr. Freund," said the voice. "Our appointment was for six p.m. According to my watch it is still two minutes before six. Please wait."

And a scant two minutes later, at exactly six, the door opened and the man showed us the apartment. Peter and I both marveled at this man who seemed determined to fulfill our stereotype of German precision.

Daily life went on. Peter also acted, and I saw a play he was in, at a marvelous old neighborhood theater almost unrecognizable as such from the street, which the nutrition guru J. I. Rodale leased to produce plays he wrote himself, sort of Restoration-style period pieces. Some of the people I knew were fond of having "readings," where we'd get together and one of us writers would read our poetry or short stories or bits of novels to the assembled group. We might be at Judy Stark's on the Upper West Side or at my place, and we tried to make them convivial occasions.

Through my Hopkins friend Joe Beatty I met Carl and Lin Patrick, who lived in Philadelphia's Germantown, in an apartment that had enormous front and rear balconies, and I took to visiting them sometimes as a respite from New York in what seemed a quieter, more leisurely locale.

One morning—they told me this story, and while I did not experience it directly, the telling imprinted itself into my own narrative repertoire—their upstairs neighbor was found hanging by his neck from a rope attached to the railing of his rear balcony. Evidently despondent over life, he had put his affairs in order, arranged for his own funeral, and in the predawn hours dressed himself well, affixed a rope to the railing and a noose around his neck, and jumped, to be noticed after the quiet neighborhood awoke to discover him swinging in the wind.[19]

Lin was a genuine Lower East Sider, having grown up in Knickerbocker Village, a housing development that preceded Stuy Town, and I would bring them genuine New York bagels, at a time when the bagel was still a regional specialty. Later Carl and Lin moved back into the old family apartment in New York City.

I was saving up funds for an epic journey across Europe, though I had also applied for a Fulbright to India. I could see Europe on the return trip from India, if the US government first would pay my fare halfway around the world. Sometime in 1966 I got word that I was on a waiting list for the Fulbright. Two days later a notice came that I had been selected.

I have come to think of my journey to India as beginning that night, with the story that came out of what happened next, as I almost joined a group of earlier Indian sojourners from the West via film:

Jubilant over getting the Fulbright, I made my way over to the Village, consumed two whiskey sours in some bar, and saw that the film *Shakespeare Wallah* was playing at a Village cinema. That seemed like a perfect portent for the night, and I bought a ticket. Then as Merchant and Ivory's troupe of British actors arrived at the hill station to play their plays, the whiskey sours and the remains of the day kicked in and I fell fast asleep in the darkness of the theater. When I woke up I had missed most of the movie, only to see it many years later via a borrowed DVD.

Although on one level, this is just a slightly amusing story about inconveniently nodding off, it is tempting to see it in more symbolic terms: falling asleep in one time of life, waking up in the next; literally falling asleep in New York, waking up in a cinematic Indian hill station—where I would be in reality in a matter of weeks. Also, I was suddenly in transition. I had expected to be moving on shortly and had booked passage to Europe for a few months hence. But the offer of a Fulbright advanced the schedule, and before long I was in full moving-on mode, leaving the East Village behind to mount a more international stage. An older woman who worked at Welfare, an American married to an Indian cleric, invited me to dinner to tell me about India, to which they themselves planned to return in a few years. They lived in a vast if crumbling apartment in an old hotel near Madison Square and her husband fell asleep during dinner. But I felt like I was being launched to another world.

I remember my Baltimore and East Village periods rather fondly, as times of excitement and interesting people and new places and aspects of life. Yet the actual stories I've told about my time there suggest something rather different, as though providing a variant backdrop, which is something that stories can do—revealing things that we may otherwise not acknowledge. The stories suggest turmoil and tension. Those set against my living arrangements on East Third Street, where I thought my apartment actually quite pleasant, involve intrusion, destruction of property—even murder—whether or not we accept the literal truth of landlord Joe killing somebody and hiding out in another state. New York could be a place of danger and intimidation; I was "held up" on the street in the dark of night. It could be a place of tenuous existence or disaster—a nightmare of being trapped by a power failure in its subterranean bowels—though I personally managed to get to safety and even enjoyed communing with neighbors and taking in a stranded stranger. I actually liked working for the Welfare department, tramping around the city and hobnobbing with unlikely people—both colleagues and clients. I also found an undercurrent of corruption, of movers who wanted to offer petty bribes. The one story that sticks in my mind from my occasional respites in "quieter" Philadelphia is about suicide; the unfortunate specter of American race relations comes through too. In going to Baltimore I suddenly found real, out-in-the-open segregation. The guys who held me up on Avenue B were black and obviously disgruntled. Perhaps even Judy Stark's amusing story about her naïve childhood sociology—in which Catholics and Jews vastly outnumbered the Protestants—comments on social division.

If it was a time of expansion and excitement, both personal and collective, the stories remind me that it was also one of uneasiness, turmoil, and disquieting change.[20]

NOTES

1. But I'm still trying. Madison Smartt Bell's *Charm City: A Walk through Baltimore* (New York: Crown Journeys, 2007) was a good read but concerned mostly with his reaction to the city's physical layout and hence only somewhat helpful. And I asked Laura Lippman, at her Garden District Books appearance in New Orleans, if she could explain Baltimore. She kindly took a stab at it, to some avail.

2. My old high school and college friend Joseph Skerrett, who went to Hopkins the year after I did, tells this story: Elliott Coleman was also the translator for the Belgian critic and theoretician Georges Poulet. Poulet came to speak and a Hopkins professor of history asked him a question. When Poulet seemed to misunderstand, the historian asked again in perfect French. Hopkins was that kind of place.

3. The Wikipedia entry on the neighborhood gives credit to "newcomers and real estate brokers," noting that by the mid-1960s the media had adopted the name. "East Village, Manhattan," *Wikipedia*, last modified 22 February 2013, http://en.wikipedia.org/wiki/East_Village_Manhattan.

4. Dan Wakefield, *New York in the 50s* (New York: St. Martin's Griffin, 1999), 275.

5. Wakefield; Bob Dylan, *Chronicles*: Volume 1 (New York: Simon & Schuster, 2004); John Tytell, *Reading New York* (New York: Knopf, 2003); Robert Stone, *Prime Green: Remembering the Sixties* (New York: Harper Perennial, 2008); Suze Rotolo, *A Freewheelin' Time: A Memoir*

of *Greenwich Village in the Sixties* (New York: Broadway Books, 2008). Although Stone spent time in New York, he was in California as well as elsewhere, and he concentrates less on New York than the other writers. Rotolo was romantically involved with Dylan, and much of her memoir concentrates on that relationship and upon various other individuals she knew; she has a lot to say about the world of revivalist folk singers, which she observed partly because of her connection with Dylan.

6. Dylan, *Chronicles*, 103, 72, 22.

7. Probably I did not invent these but am indeed thinking about the cover photo for Dylan's second album, *The Freewheelin' Bob Dylan*, which Rotolo discusses in *A Freewheelin' Time* (214ff); her book includes additional photos taken on the same occasion on Jones Street. She notes that Dylan grabbed a suede jacket for the photo shoot quickly and that "It was an 'image' choice because that jacket was not remotely suited for the weather . . . he was bound to freeze going out in that" (215). I suppose that the image made a big impression on me. Rotolo also recalls that "it was one of those damp New York City winter days that chill to the bone" (214).

8. Dylan, *Chronicles*, 54.

9. Tytell, *Reading New York*, 301.

10. Which Rotolo writes about in *A Freewheelin' Time* (349, 342–44); she suggests that the blackout was "controlled chaos." She also writes (361) how, as time went on, New York seemed to be "getting grittier and more dangerous . . . The counterculture was imploding; chaos lurked along the edges," and suggests being "mired in Vietnam" as a root cause.

11. Wakefield, *New York in the 50s*, 1.

12. Ibid., 158. It is interesting to note how differently Wakefield and Dylan look at the White Horse (where I went only occasionally, mostly because it was a sort of shrine; everybody seemed to know the macabre "fact" that Dylan Thomas had died in the gutter after an epic drunk there). Wakefield saw it as a central gathering spot, the locus for intense intellectual and political discussion and a close-knit camaraderie, inhabited nightly by a great mixture of American writers and talkers and local workers and Irish rebels. For Dylan, who was fascinated by and writes fervidly in *Chronicles* of the power of folk music (whatever exactly he means by that), it's just a place where the Irish folk singer Liam Clancy happened to hang out: "mainly an Irish bar frequented mostly by guys from the old country" (83). In *A Freewheelin' Time*, Rotolo, who has much to say about the New York "folk scene," writes that she hung out at the White Horse "for many years" (147) and mostly discusses Liam Clancy, his brothers, and their fellow singer Tommy Makem ("they sang and told stories and had a good time along with everyone else who ended their evenings at the White Horse" [147]); she thought they were actors who sang rather than singers.

13. Stone suggests in *Prime Green* (92) that people in the 1960s "believed ourselves in a time of our own making." The earlier world that he at any rate had known "simply disappeared" (83). Echoing Dylan's famous lyrics, Rotolo, in *A Freewheelin' Time* (213), notes that "times would soon be a-changin'."

14. Wakefield, *New York in the 50s*, 6.

15. Tytell, *Reading New York*, 251–52.

16. Wakefield, *New York in the 50s*, 196.

17. Rotolo, in *A Freewheelin' Time* (360), recalls the place as the Riviera at Sheridan Square and Seventh Avenue, though she does not refer to the video jukebox as a Scopitone.

18. Rotolo mentions the World's Fair, but Stone reminds us in *Prime Green* (119ff) that the destination of Ken Kesey's famous cross-country bus trip was the fair.

19. Recently Carl Patrick reminded me that it had not been the upstairs neighbor but the building superintendent who had hung himself and that he had done so in the building's stairwell, not from a balcony outside. Narrative memory, obviously, is fallible.

Two of Carl's stories are embedded in my own memory, both relating to later years when he lived by himself or sometimes with his son, Matt, in Brooklyn Heights. On one occasion, he was walking home from the subway stop that opens into the old St. George Hotel (where I would go as a child to swim in their vast, mirror-ceilinged pool). At the time, New York universities used part of the old hotel building (in fact, a complex of accretions) as dorm space. As Carl strolled along an air conditioning unit from one of the rooms suddenly plunged below, smashing onto the sidewalk inches away, a mass of very heavy, very deadly metal. Feeling himself the nonchalant New Yorker, he shrugged to witnesses across the street and continued on his way. For a time Carl's upstairs neighbor in his mid-size apartment building was a young broker. One day Carl heard great hammering noises and water seeped from above into his small kitchen area. He also smelled an aroma he could not place wafting down from the upstairs apartment, but which his hip son immediately identified as marijuana. Carl and the building super decided that the neighbor had cobbled together a hydroponic pot farm. They climbed the fire escape to see what could be seen from outside, but the neighbor, suspiciously enough, had also completely taped over his windows so that nothing in his apartment was visible from outside. They dropped hints and allusions to the neighbor, but he never admitted to anything and eventually moved out.

Why some stories of friends stick with us I'm not certain. Perhaps these stories focus on striking incidents that highlight something that seems notable (here the vagaries and dangers of city life maybe, or the pervasiveness of a drug culture such that even brokers grow marijuana, or the astonishing ingenuity of urban agriculture). Or perhaps such stories, whatever may be their meaning and significance to the original tellers, help us to fill out our pictures of our friends' lives, giving them a fuller existence in our own. For example, I certainly internalized, to some degree, stories told by friends Anna Nardo and Neal Cronin, who came to LSU in the early 1970s, about their graduate school days at Emory in Atlanta (about, say, a colleague who set John Donne's poetry to country-western tunes) or their families (a psychiatrist relative who, for reasons of his own, had only a single valid license plate for all of his vehicles and had to constantly detach it from and reattach it to various cars in order to drive without being stopped by the police). Such stories—we may eventually forget them or we may retell them, or perhaps reinvent them—amplify our friends' existence in our lives and thus amplify our own lives too. I am still puzzling out—something we should always do with stories—the possible significance of whether two of Carl's stories that I well remember involve upstairs neighbors (and the third something hurtling *from above*), though it is a funny coincidence, especially as I seem to have reinvented the suicide as an upstairs neighbor; all do suggest disquieting "things" that are somehow "over" us or perhaps just very close to us.

20. And a time that seemed to throw a lasting fear into a more conservative America. The threat of a decade that ran counter to some conventional mores and ideas terrified some. Decades later the right wing still seemed obsessed by the idea that hippies and dangerous radicals, leftover from the Sixties, were somehow undermining American life. (Stone suggests in *Prime Green* [81] that the public was particularly disturbed by student demonstrations: "things that happened in Trieste, as far as most Americans were concerned.") In retrospect, though the Sixties did bring about some lasting and important cultural and social shifts, the idea that some sort of radical transformation was taking place seems ludicrous. We are simply too adept as a society at adapting and changing and absorbing new ideas and conditions and comfortably accommodating them. Suze Rotolo, however, ends her memoir with this capsule summary of the time: "The sixties were an era that spoke a language of inquiry and curiosity and rebelliousness . . . The new generation

causing all the fuss was not driven by the market: we had something to say, not something to sell" (*A Freewheelin' Time*, 367).

Seven

Tinkly Temple Bells

Before I even arrived in 1966, India had already entered my consciousness in many ways. Thanks in part to the Beatles and their maharishi, the country was enjoying a resurgence as a place of mysticism and mystery. Sitars and tablas could be heard in Western pop and rock music. In the East Village, Beat poet Allen Ginsberg—both influenced by and a propagator of tropes of the Asian East and its mysticism—was a major presence, writing, chanting, being. And the more mobile hipsters who traveled abroad in increasing numbers often made India their endpoint, where they could trip out on saddhus and ganja. As someone who had just passed through the East Village, I was not immune to these influences. Yet I had not been able to shake my childhood book- and movie-inspired images of dashing English sahibs striding through the Khyber Pass to quell native mutinies or play the "Great Game" of British and Russian rivalry on the fabled North West Frontier; so I was also aware of India as a once-colonial place. I set out under the sober auspices of the US government as one of a band of ultra-respectable Fulbright exchange scholars, not a seeker after gurus.

If a colonial past and mysticism loomed large in my mind, so did other quite secular stereotypes. I was going to an overpopulated country. In 1966 India ranked as the world's second most populated country, with nearly half a billion people. I was not aware of the actual statistics—498,883,000 people, to be exact—but expected a land of teeming masses where great crowds would be jostling for places. India was also an impoverished county. In 1966 its gross domestic product was barely more than 3 percent of America's—another statistic I did not actually know. Jawaharlal Nehru, the first prime minister of independent India, who died in 1964, still stood in my mind as a key postwar world leader. I knew I was going to a land of five-year plans and some sort of nationalistic socialism as well as fakirs and many-armed gods.

Indeed, I was headed for a place where ancient-looking holy men and a unique sort of modernism lived side by side. I knew that India was also a land of great stories and was, according to some older theories, the home of the folktale; the great myths of Shiva and Vishnu and Krishna stood out vaguely in my head. Surely I might evolve some stories of my own. Of those stories that I came away with, several relate to the traveling itself and suggest that to me this trip was indeed a serious journey into another world and other modes of life—by no means a casual jaunt. Other stories foreground the nature of that other world.

THE JOURNEY AND ARRIVAL

The journey seemed an arduous one, perhaps more so than in the days of the P & O passenger liners with their leisurely deck games, long stops at Port Said, and comfortable cabins. Prior to the trip, my plane tickets were lost, and this incident became one of my first stories—a story that stressed this Eastern journey as a difficult one, even before I literally left on it. American Express handled Fulbright travel, and although they had been informed that I had shifted back to 7002 Ridge, they insisted on sending my tickets to my East Village apartment. There they were marked "Return to Sender" and sent back to Amex. I spent a day running around to various Amex offices—seemingly all over Manhattan—tracking them down. I explained my problem multiple times to multiple clerks and executives. Finally someone thought to come up with duplicate tickets, but it was little comfort for the anguished day I expended on the eve of my departure worrying over documents that would enable me to go!

Days later, when I finally flew there, the open-air terminals at the New Delhi airport, thick with flying insects—threw up a wall of amazingly hot and sticky air (I thought I knew heat from those hot, muggy New York summers) before an air-conditioned bus whisked the Fulbright group to the YMCA Tourist Hostel, where we had rooms to bathe and change.

But not before I picked up another story about my first encounter with the corrupt bureaucrats who I assumed filled the Third World. I suppose it's a story of transitions into that world as well as another story about the difficulties of the journey, and I liked to tell it something like this (probably after noting how the airport seemed like it was out of an old movie):

"So anyway, we got to Indian customs and this inspector asked me if I had this or that. Finally he asked if I had any medicines, and I told him I had a bottle of rhubarb and soda for indigestion.

"Rhubarb and soda was an old remedy long used by my family. At the time any Brooklyn drug store could whip it up. It was a sort of tasty brown liquid, and it always seemed to soothe the stomach.

"'Do you suffer from this indigestion?' he asked.

"'Well, sometimes. It's just a precaution, really.'

"Then he asked to see the bottle, and I fished around in my luggage until I found it and handed it to him, and he looked at it carefully like he was examining it for secret compartments. He asked if it came from Germany, as if all modern marvels came from there. 'No,' I told him, 'it's American.' I guess I would have said 'Brooklyn,' but I figured that wouldn't mean anything to him.

"'I also sometimes suffer from this,' he said back. 'I think I will take this.' And he did, before waving me through. Just grabbed my bottle of rhubarb and soda! I think I was too dumbfounded to protest."

Then we took an Indian Airlines flight to Kashmir for an orientation. The sudden transition from New York to India—the astonishing heat, the virtual theft of my property by a uniformed official, the equally sudden hop to a place where the Himalayas towered above us and transportation consisted of little watercraft moving through canals overhung by old houses made of ancient timbers and muddy bricks—was enough to induce culture shock. We were lodged on moored houseboats in Dal Lake, and though I appreciated the romance of this, and the magnificent scenery, and—after the brief passage through the oven of the Indian plains—the cool air, I felt unsettled. No wonder that my stories of getting here are about unsettling events, about lost tickets and stolen medications, about the difficulties of this whole journey to the other side of the earth.

Back in Delhi after a couple of weeks in the mountains, waiting for trains to our final destinations, bowled over by the heat, we ventured out a little to look over the capital. The Fulbright people took us to their headquarters and on an overnight side trip to Agra for the age-old obligatory visit to the Taj Mahal and out to Fatehpur Sikri, the Mughal city that had faded into a splendid ruin when the water ran out. Later I found myself telling two stories about Agra and Fatehpur Sikri. One expressed our changing attitudes about our bodies and our adaptation to new environments and situations; the other concerned my own attempt to retain my blasé attitude only to be overwhelmed by India:

As we pulled up to Fatehpur Sikri, one of our "Fulbright girls" jumped out of the bus and ran off to a nearby but isolated hillside. We all understood that nature called. "Memsahib, memsahib," a local warned her. "Cobra, cobra." But she needed the nearest place to squat in the privacy afforded by a bush to relieve her bowels; this was a condition we were learning to live with.

At first I tried to avoid the Taj and spend the visit in the bar at Hotel Clarks Shiraz, which did have a distant view of the white tomb, but I couldn't maintain my cynicism and gave in and took a taxi out to the famous site. Of course, I'd seen pictures and knew what to expect, but of course, I didn't. Its ethereal beauty—and only on a later trip would I see it in its fabled moonlight incarnation—overwhelmed me: the tomb's perfect proportions, its unearthly white color suggesting moonlight even in the daytime, its undulating lines and shapes, the peacefulness of the pools that led up to its front.

Only by finally circling around it and taking in the beautiful but earthly red stone structures that flank the tomb and by seeing the lazy, muddy river that flows below could I feel that I had been brought back to the real world and thus move on. On the trip back to Delhi the antiquated bus broke down, and we danced on its roof while waiting for repairs.

These two stories are, appropriately, about acculturation, about being taken in by India and adapting to its new realities—whether the astonishing beauty of a great tomb or newly discovered ways of coping with bodily needs. As the previous stories of lost tickets and stolen medicines laid out the problems of getting to this new world, so do these latter two stories speak of adaptation to discovery. But the discovery period continued, and I soon picked up another story for my repertoire.

Fellow Fulbright Paul Cravath and I eventually found ourselves on our way to Indore, the city where we would spend the year, and changing trains at a place called Ratlam Junction. While Paul and I waited on the platform next to our new train we looked at the next car down and watched as an old man was being loaded into a compartment, his chair being literally lifted into the train with him in it. Somebody told us that the man was the "old" Maharaja of Indore, father of the last maharaja, Yeshwant Rao. We heard plenty of stories about how the old man had ordered his rival, a wealthy Bombay businessman, murdered for the love of a mistress; the body had been found on a Bombay golf course. He was clearly the perpetrator, but a ruling prince could not be prosecuted. The British overlords could only have him deposed, and he still lived out his long life in one of the family palaces in Indore. His son, who succeeded him and had a serious problem with alcohol, was long dead by then.

This little encounter and its background became for me a story I'd tell, probably because the incident—really just a quick glance—took me into a world long since past at the same time I was going there in the present; our city, Indore, had been a royal capital until a few years before, and we would live with the remnants of that. The British had sometimes thought of the culturally conservative "princely states" as the "real India." Although that bit of easy romanticism was questionable at best, I was about to make further discoveries in that context.

It took another seven or eight hours from Ratlam Junction to reach Indore, but somewhere along the way, cool, damp air began to filter in and we looked out and saw rain; we had run into the monsoon that Delhi and the North Indian plain had been waiting for eagerly. It came as an incredible respite, as though a relief column had arrived at our besieged fortress; suddenly we were sharing feelings that had pervaded this land for thousands of years: the quickening of life's tempo when the rains came, when joyous songs are sung in villages as maidens sway on ribbon-bedecked swings. Years later I'd listen to old British sahibs speak of these times of blessed release—when the searing heat and incessant dryness would break—although the rains could also wash cobras out of their holes. So it could be a time of peril too.

INDORE

We might have slept through Indore, but someone woke us up, and two professors from our college met the train, took us in hand, and helped us settle into a small flat in a pleasantly suburban part of the city over an establishment called the Ratnadeep Nursing Home. We never really understood its function, which was certainly not to house the sick or elderly; rather, it seemed to be a not-very-busy obstetrician's office. So our living over a nursing home—or whatever it was—had a certain whimsical appeal. Just down the street stood Nath Mandir, a temple that served as a guidepost in directing rickshaw wallahs to our house and where little ever seemed to happen. I kept hoping for Kipling's tinkly temple bells, but that was Mandalay in Burma, not India; never were there noisy ceremonies or splashy processions, perhaps in keeping with the rather quiet, suburban character of the neighborhood. Our little place had been furnished with surplus college equipment, and we were taken to buy mosquito netting for our metal cots and I acquired gum boots and a genuine Calcutta Duckback raincoat, for the rain continued to fall for weeks—seldom very heavy but constant. When the rains stopped, we moved into the delightful Northern India winter, a time of agreeably temperate weather.

And we moved into a routine of teaching at the prosaically named Government College of Arts & Commerce, across the street from the older, more euphoniously named Holkar College. Holkar was the family name for the local ruling family of maharajas; we had come to what had been the capital of one of the old princely states, which the imperial British had pretended were independent kingdoms until independent India absorbed these entities after 1947. This gave the place a certain air of royal antiquity and we would encounter leftover courtiers and have stories to tell about minor princes.

One of Paul's students, Jogdapendra Singh Holkar, for example, was said to be discontented that the "throne" of Indore, such as it was, had gone to a branch of the family not his own. Once Paul was chatting with a group of students that included Jogdapendra Singh and another student said something about how he himself wanted to be a lawyer. To keep the conversation going, Paul asked Jogdapendra Singh if he too wanted to be a lawyer. A third student, dumbstruck at such a question, blurted out, "Oh no, sir, he's a prince!"

A student who attended the English MA program at the college was the actual Maharaja of Arma Nagar, a tiny and unimportant former princely state that was by his own admission just a collection of villages. He drove two ancient American cars with the distinctive red license plates that Indian royals received with the names of "their" states emblazoned on them. Indore was full of HSC license plates—meaning "Holkar State Car"—and plates of other, lesser royals who had gravitated to comparatively lively Indore. The "ruling" Maharani of Indore herself lived mostly in Bombay. Mr. Samatwala, as Arma Nagar was generally known, invited Paul and me to dinner and was known locally for being "simple," evidently a praiseworthy trait implying modesty and simplicity of spirit.

My stories of Jogdapendra Singh and Mr. Samatwala, like that of the old maharaja at the station, briefly connect me to the last days of a world we lived amidst. I do think that the princeliness of Indore, though clearly something ignored by the world and which modern India was fast forgetting, added to my sense of otherworldliness, to my discovery of, if not mystic saddhus or mythic tales, a reality very different from anything I had hitherto known, with many ramifications yet to be discovered.

Our students seemed to us sweet and unacquainted with much beyond their local world. Indeed, India seemed cut off in these days, with no TV and few foreign publications, with travel to foreign countries severely limited. Intrigued by young, foreign professors, some students would visit us at our flat, and we would do our best to enlighten them.

Some were, as I would tell the story later, shocked that we "ate flesh of cow." One told us a story about passing a Christian church while a service was going on and, though Hindu, he went in and blithely took communion in hopes that this might help him pass his exams. In telling us the story he suddenly wondered if his actions had offended anyone, but we assured him that what he had done was just fine.

Their geographic knowledge seemed woeful. Several thought that as Americans we were from the Soviet Union. Paul asked his mother in Minnesota to send a globe or map of the world so that he could at least point out where America was, and she eventually did send an inflatable globe. All Paul ever received, however, was a note from Indian Customs saying that the globe had been seized at the port of entry! Its offense had been in depicting Kashmir as disputed territory and the state of Goa as still Portuguese.

This story of the seized globe has appealed to me, I think, because it explained something about how isolated we were—and felt—at the time, so much in another world that not even maps that might situate us could get through to us; we were in a place with quite a different perspective than our own: where eating beef could shock people and certain cartographic realities might be forbidden.

I lost weight, drifting ever further into thinness, so food seemed increasingly important. So often what we got seemed meager or unnourishing (or by my cultural norms, too spicy). It's probably not surprising that several of my stories of this period relate to food—whether students' remarks about eating cow flesh or even one student's consumption of communion—both stories that also tie food to religion. There are other food stories:

My own mother regularly sent food parcels, including, to my amazement, Lipton tea bags, the very concept of which puzzled the students in this, the original home of tea—of course, loose tea. Among the things she sent was packets of Jell-O, a food I would normally have turned up my nose at, but it became a beloved comfort food here. One day, I offered some, strawberry flavored, to a visiting student, in fact, a Brahmin by caste. He expressed some doubt about it, asking if it contained meat. Of course not, I said, it's *Jell-O*. I could only think of Jell-O as fruity, and he sampled it. Only much later did I realize that the gelatin which allows Jell-O to form comes from animal—probably cattle—marrow, and I earnestly hoped that my negligent ignorance has not caused him to be born again incarnated as some loathsome insect or worse.

We did eat "flesh of cow," though in Indore it was evidently water buffalo, the real stuff simply was not available. Even the buffalo was hard to come by, and we resorted to the services of a man we took to calling our "beef pusher" when we told his story—a man who got the meat in Mhow, where a government-run slaughterhouse was located; soldiers needed beef to keep up their strength, and the "pusher" brought it into Indore by bus.

Then one day he was busted—as we thought of it; what he was doing was, of course, illegal in this sacred-cow-revering land—even if his beef was buffalo—and the supply dried up for awhile.

I would tell other stories about things sent to us (like rupee notes my generous mother bought at a currency exchange place near Rockefeller Center for what seemed to her to be next to nothing) because they stress the otherworldliness of where we found ourselves: a place so off the map that not only could we not get maps but our needs had to be met by virtual airdrops from America. Our local sources of food were prey to the vagaries of culture.

When we first arrived in Indore we were unable to locate a cook. A sweeper, whom we never actually saw, came with the flat and slipped in while we were still asleep to clean the toilet, which was a hole in the floor to be squatted over. The college had also hired for us a man who came early and drew water from the pump downstairs and carted it up to our storage tank; there was a local water shortage, and the water was turned on only an hour a day. But before long, we found Maden Lal, a young man from the Himalayan foothills who had been brought down by one of the resident Canadian missionaries as a cook for some Dutch well drillers who were in Indore to help with the local water supply. Since they had already found a cook, we hired him as our *khansamah* (cook and majordomo). He spoke English and came with a repertoire of meals; he recorded recipes in a little notebook he titled "The Joy of Cooking." He managed credible French toast for breakfast and several regular lunch or dinner offerings, which gave us another food story:

One day, he suggested that for dinner he could make peach pie. We demurred; he kept bringing the subject up; we tried to explain that peach pie was a dessert, not a proper meal. Then it became clear that he was not saying "peach" but "pizza" pie, and we were delighted to go ahead. What he made was an odd sort of pizza, a deep-dish pie with an array of tossed-on toppings like hard-boiled eggs along with the tomato sauce and cheese. It became a great favorite with us, maybe the more so as he couldn't make it often because some ingredients were expensive and hard to come by, or so he said.

Our landlord was an elderly gentleman who liked to be called Baba-ji, a title of great respect, though in his case self-applied. He lived in a large house next to our compound of flats and nursing home, and he became the subject of one of my stories: One day he invited us in to show us his art, of which he seemed inordinately proud. This turned out to be a couple of touristy African carvings. "These are by those African niggers," he told us matter-of-factly and went on to tell us a few other details of his life, like how he had once worked for the railroads but was passed over for promotion in favor of a Britisher and had duly resigned.

This little encounter became a story because of the disconnect I perceived between him being discriminated against and his use of a racist word for others, though perhaps he admired Africans—he did seem to value their art.

Baba-ji ("honored father") had no job since resigning from the railroad. He claimed to be some sort of a relative of the woman doctor who actually owned the house and our compound and who lived somewhere else. Others snickered at this claim and seemed to imply—they were always veiled in their attitude—that he was, in fact, her old lover. A similar attitude of slight amusement applied to a professor of English who taught at another Indore college and who was a son of the late Maharaja of Dewas (Senior). E. M. Forster had been his secretary: Forster's *The Hill of Devi* recounts his experiences in Dewas, and parts of *A Passage to India* are based on things he saw there. The professor said he remembered Forster padding about the palace, but people smiled about his being the raja's son; and we gathered that perhaps he was the child of a royal concubine, though he was wealthy and had certainly been well provided for.

We lived quiet lives in Indore, falling into routines like meals and sitting on our flat's little balcony in the evening watching flocks of wild parrots soar over our heads in flashing green blurs, smoking a little ganja—when we had it—or just tobacco in our pipes, and playing cribbage. A student did take me to see Bollywood's *Love in Tokyo* and translated for me, even the parts already in English. Sometimes we danced at the Yeshwant Club, a grand private establishment.

In addition to some Peace Corps folks—we met a number of them—the Canadian missionaries were sweet to us, though only one was single and young and whom we saw from time to time.[1] An American-Indian couple, Judy and Fred Issacs, ran the local School of Social Work; the college was called a "school" on the American model, causing Fred to complain that the word *school* confused salesmen, who were always sending him ads for playground equipment. And there were other Indians, like Naren, an older, portly man who lived in a mansion in another part of town, across the street from an even larger family mansion and who obviously needed no visible means of support. Perhaps his very opulence made him the subject of several of my stories:

He claimed that there was a family cobra in his own garden and that he made regular offerings of milk to it, a fact—if it was fact—that made me a little nervous about stepping into his garden.

One evening, we did indeed drop in on him. Why we just dropped in I cannot recall, especially as we would have had to cross part of the supposedly cobra-infested garden to get to his front door in semi-darkness, but we did, several of us Americans. Naren, who was not expecting us, was eating from a gigantic *thalli*, (a metal tray with compartments for food) piled high with rice and curries, a sort of nighttime snack. I didn't mind not being offered any, but I was startled that in the course of our conversation, he chose the moment to hold forth on how ascetic Jains were—he was a Jain—as he stuffed whopping handfuls into his mouth!

He had taken up oil painting—had a passionate enthusiasm for it in fact—and produced a number of canvases, each in quite slavish and recognizable imitation of the style of some notable European artist like Monet or Van Gogh, whose work he knew only from books. He was evidently surprised to be told that such obvious imitation wasn't thought to be such a good thing, but through his influence, got himself an exhibition at the local museum, which was at least another diversion for us.

But if living in Indore was mostly a routine existence, from time to time we found ourselves siphoned off into encounters with something beyond our everyday lives—experiences that seemed to come from another world. Once our friend Bana pointed out a band of *hijras* (transvestite performers) passing through, their large forms moving darkly under saris and heavy makeup. And two Peace Corps friends became friends with the members of a traveling tent show—mostly members of the same family who did rather clumsy acrobatics or hootchy-kootchy dances à la Little Egypt—who performed in costumes that would hardly have drawn a breath of scandal at Minsky's.

What became a favorite story of mine, however, emerged out of one of Paul's strange passions:

Paul, inspired by a rediscovery of T. E. Lawrence's *Seven Pillars of Wisdom*, decided that he really, really wanted a camel. Of course, though we did see an occasional camel in Indore, we were hardly in camel country, so Paul considered going up to Rajasthan to bring one back in a lorry. He did not pursue that particular plan but did send out the word that he was interested in having a humpbacked beast. Before too long Siru Namli, a local with connections to the old royal court, found a man with a camel who was supposedly willing to rent it. He brought it by our compound, and Paul mounted the critter and rode back and forth, swaying on a kind of saddle, in the street, a small mob of us following along, the camel's owner leading his camel. Paul proposed to rent the camel for several hundred rupees a month—not an inconsiderable sum—and proposed tethering it in the little backyard behind the compound. The camel's owner agreed and said he'd return but he went away, and neither he nor the camel ever came back. Perhaps he was just being polite or humoring a crazy sahib or a powerful person like Siru. Paul's interest faded, though his one ride had been a high point for us.

And one evening in that little yard behind the compound, where Paul would have stabled his camel, a group of men showed up blowing on a conch shell and playing a harmonium and chanting right under our windows. It was some sort of religious ritual and they kept it up much of the night, though who exactly they were or why they were there we never learned. Like the man with the camel, they never returned after that one appearance. The event turned into a story for me, probably because of its very mysteriousness: their sudden, unexplained presence; their definitive disappearance; their enactment of a ritual that seemed to drip with Indian-ness.

Sometimes slightly untoward events or more comical encounters interrupted our routines, and some of them became fodder for stories.

One day, for example, an Indian man came to our door with a small girl in tow. She never spoke but he explained that he worked for an American agency in Hyderabad and had taken his family to see their extended family in the north. They had traveled on the railway pass of a brother-in-law who worked for the railroad and had just been caught out using this pass against regulations. The pass had been confiscated, and now the family was stuck in Indore. He needed money to get them home, had heard at the station about the Americans living nearby, and came to ask us for some money. He worked for Americans and knew we would understand. We could phone the agency he worked for. Of course, we had virtually no access to a phone; the entire Indore phone "book" consisted of three pages—seventeen of the phones listed to the Holkar palace. Or we could come to the station and meet the rest of his family. We chatted a bit, though we didn't think to ask him how his family happened to be stuck in a town not exactly on the main railway lines. We gave him eighty rupees, and he went happily on his way, blessing us and promising to send us repayment.

A few weeks later our Fulbright supervisor, Mr. Sharma, whom we called Sharma-ji, came by to see how we were doing. In the course of lunch he said, almost as an afterthought, that he had to warn us about a con man going around to Americans with a story about being stranded with his family. Of course, that was precisely the story we had heard. Obviously, we too had been swindled. "Oh, my God," I said. "He was here, and we gave him twenty rupees!" Sharma-ji looked grave. "Not one rupee, not a few rupees, but twenty rupees," he said in shocked tones. What a fortune. What a disaster! Of course, we never saw the eighty rupees (which I minimized to twenty for Sharma's benefit) again or heard anything further, so we wrote the incident off, though it made for a good story.

Our guy was evidently not the only con man going about India, where wandering holy men were both revered and suspect and where the words *fakir* and *faker* were sometimes conflated.[2]

Sometime later a Peace Corps volunteer whom Paul had known in college visited us, and he told us much of the story, which fascinated me enough to become one of my own. This PC volunteer was stationed in a small place in the state of Madhya Pradesh, somewhere south of Indore, and he had, it seemed, played a big role in apprehending another con man. This one called himself Wayne Dunning Farmer along with, as it turned out, several other names, including the inimitable Wynograd Smeltzer. He called on Americans and seemed to be an American who claimed he was stranded in India without funds and needed financial help. He had gone to see Paul's acquaintance who, whether alerted by reports of the man or just suspicious, stalled him until he could get the police. Smeltzer was now languishing in jail. The Peace Corps guy who had turned him in was feeling proud of himself. Smeltzer still claimed to be a wandering American, thus evincing some embassy concern, though the police were absolutely unable to determine his identity; they thought he might be an Anglo-Indian.

He intrigued me because he could pass himself off as one of us; the aliases he used just seemed so American that I couldn't imagine some Anglo-Indian coming up with them. Who was he? It was a time when odd Americans had taken to wandering into strange places around the globe, and in Cambodia some time later I met a Canadian who was sort of conning his way around the world. The idea that he might just be a missing fellow countryman—a Westerner lost indefinitely in an Asian land, a traveler without papers caught out of place and just trying to survive—was unsettling. I later wrote a letter or two of inquiry, but I have no idea what happened to Smeltzer, whoever or whatever he was.

But the untoward could have more comic dimensions, and comic incidents inevitably become stories.

A few weeks after we slung up our mosquito nets to the metal poles on our cots, we began to notice little bugs living in the upper corners of the netting. It looked difficult to get at them to dislodge or kill them. Besides, this was India, where all life was respected; and orthodox Jains, it was said, actually wore surgical masks lest they breathe in and inadvertently kill some hapless insect. These bugs looked innocuous enough, so we let them be. We also noticed little bite marks appearing on our bodies and wondered how the mosquitoes were getting us despite our precautions. Only eventually, with some input from students, did we put two and two together: those little bugs were bedbugs (*katmal*). Bedbugs were so far removed from even being a possibility in our American middle-class existence that the thought had never occurred to us. Could we deal with the problem? Of course, that was simple—just sprinkle bedbug powder around the mattress, and they would soon be gone. Someone bought some in the bazaar, we sprinkled, they disappeared. Our ignorance had its comic side, but we felt foolish, misled by our cultural assumptions and our previous existence in a world where bedbugs seemed like a nearly imaginary holdover from long-gone Victorian squalor.

Vicious *katmal* were not the only pests, however, to plague us (and give me one of the stories that suggested my presence here in another world, pestilence that was unimaginable to a twentieth-century urban American).

Again, early in our Indore tenure, scuffling sounds kept waking us in the night, which seemed to come from the college-provided almirah where we stored our worldly goods. We thought we might have mice, and one night I jumped out from under my netting—well-placed mosquito netting certainly can impede swift rising—flicked on the light, grabbed at the suitcases we'd stored atop the almirah, and dislodged a rat that fell to the floor and scurried under a door into an adjacent flat. We realized that the rat had chewed great holes in my fine leather suitcase—purchased recently in New York for some princely sum—and some of our clothes, mostly mine. We plugged the space under the door and never saw the rat again, but my clothes looked ruined. I threw them out, but Maden Lal took them to be repaired and wound up wearing them—notably, a fairly elegant polo shirt. Every time I saw him in it, I felt a pang of regret; I should have realized that this was India and that there was always someone who could expertly patch anything.

Later someone reported that our *dhoby*, the laundryman, was seen wearing more of my nice polo shirts around town. This young fellow, taken with fashionable dress, was not what I thought of even then—before I had read *Behind the Bungalow* or encountered the old servant postcards the Brits seemed to love—as fitting the traditional image of the local washerman: old and dressed only in a simple *dhoti*, or loincloth. I never caught him wearing my clothes, but we did change washermen, and sometimes I grafted this story onto the story of the rat and Maden Lal's taking over my repaired shirt, for discrete stories do become tied together.

There were other minor, story-worthy comedies. For awhile a street vendor came into our compound every afternoon selling the sort of spicy trail mix snack he called—or so it sounded to us—*dal safe mixture*. He would stop under our balcony and yell out, "Dal safe mixture wallah, dal safe mixture wallah" in a singsong street-vendor chant and keep this up until we bought some, though we found it too spicy for our own casual snacking. One day, when the mixture wallah arrived and set about his chant, actor Paul took a tiny rug and our teakettle downstairs, spread out the rug, squatted on it, and began to chant, "Chai, garam chai, chai, garam chai," as if he were the seller of hot tea. A few of our neighbors guffawed. The mixture wallah seemed to enjoy the joke by grinning through broken teeth, and the frequency of his visits fell off.

TRAVELS

But one of our great joys in being in India was being able to leave Indore frequently and travel over the great subcontinent. Think speeding old trains to the strains of sitar music in *Gandhi*. One of my later sahib informants spoke of it thusly: you might wake up in the most *improbable* places. Trains had a certain leisurely pace and people to chat with and stops for meals. The college scheduled frequent vacations and closed down for a cooling-off period during periods of student unrest—another time when ample warning allowed us to get away, though the unrest flared up suddenly and violently on one occasion, and the principal hustled us home in his car and advised us to stay indoors; on the way we saw the police charge a group of students with their *lathis*—a kind of staff lead-weighted for a good, stiff swing.

So we took short, sometimes weekend trips to nearby places.

The remoteness of some parts of Central India particularly fascinated me. On a trip to the ancient Buddhist Bagh Caves our bus passed Bhil tribesmen walking along carrying bows and arrows or huge, old shotguns. The caves themselves were literally out in the jungle—no habitations anywhere near, a single watchman on guard to collect our entrance fee. We had to ford a river that ran at the base of the bluff where the caves stood to even get to them. A lot of Central India was indeed *jungle*: an English word derived from an Indian word meaning some sort of wild place. The tribesmen we saw might be referred to as *jungli*—that is, wild—though in Central India, the jungle was wild, scrubby open space, not anything like a tropical rain forest. Peace Corps women told stories of village women they knew who were held up by *dacoits*—bandits who hid out in the jungle—who might rip the gold-bangle earrings right out of the women's earlobes. Shades of *Bandit Queen*, the movie![3] It was hardly surprising that the Bhils carried bows or shotguns.

Figure 7.1. The ruins at Mandu, from a nineteenth-century print.

Mandu was another "local" place. The city had been the ancient capital of Malwa—the plateau region in which Indore was situated—as far back as the 1400s, but it had become little more than a collection of ruins stretching across one low crest of the Vindhya Mountains. Mandu was now a rural expanse of vegetation broken up by the remains of ancient fortifications.

Everybody in Indore seemed to know the story of the love its sixteenth-century Muslim ruler Baz Bahadur had borne for his lovely Hindu mistress, Rupmati, which had been the subject of a book translated into English by a British Indian Civil Service man, an amateur scholar.[4] To get there, Paul and I changed buses in Dhar, and after a day of travel we reached the former city by going up a long, defensible ramp that stretched up the side of a great hill: defensible, that is, by fifteenth-century standards. Clearly this was an amazing place, yet the stories I came away with seem to be about more mundane matters. I would tell, for example, how

"We got out of the bus at a little plaza area. So suddenly we found ourselves standing by the bus. Night about to fall; you know, it was heavy twilight. We had no idea whatsoever about where to go, and no obvious destination presented itself. Obviously we hadn't planned very far ahead. We hadn't asked anybody what exactly to do once we got there. Or we thought there'd be an obvious hotel or something, but there seemed to be nothing around. We were in the middle of this ancient city, but a lot of it had reverted to countryside. A lot of it had just disappeared and there were fields all around.

"But thank goodness, a student at the college in Dhar was home in Mandu for the weekend, and he took us in hand, managed to get a bicycle rented for us, and led us to the government tourist bungalow on his own bike. By then it was dark, and we pitched through the near-blackness on the bike. Paul was perched on the bike's carrier, an Indian style of riding as a passenger that he had adopted. I was driving like a blind demon, but somehow we reached the bungalow and got a room for the night.

"The next day the student—I don't remember his name, but he was a pleasant guy—was obviously angling for a tip. At the end we gave him something like ten rupees, which seemed to overjoy him—he came back and showed us around the sprawling ruins."

I love ruins, and these were indeed amazing: numerous, virtually deserted, offering vast views of the Central India countryside, ready to be clambered over and poked about in, which I certainly did. But another story concerned our accommodations: We ate well at the bungalow, though when it came time to leave, we thought that the khansamah was trying to charge us too much. We tried to bargain, aided by our student friend, along with a friendly Indian Army major who was taking a little holiday at Mandu with his family. But the khansamah refused to budge on the price. We thought that by then we had a firm grasp of how not to taken over by the locals, and we just refused to pay. Finally we stalked off, stopping at the district engineer's office—the tourist bungalow was under the charge of the office—to explain in writing what we did. This brouhaha was over a matter of about five rupees—less than fifty cents—and later we felt foolish and unreasonable and eventually tried to send the money to the khansamah.

The first night of our stay, we fell in with some family planning officials who stopped at the bungalow. They told us about encouraging a local Bhil chief who had a dozen children to start using contraceptives; he was so incensed that he chased them out of his house with his bow and arrow. Ah, we thought knowingly: India. I adopted this story because it did seem to say something about India and how hard it is to change cultural attitudes and the possible futility of our attempts to be "modern."

Bhopal had been the capital of another princely state like Indore—one founded by an Afghan Muslim dynasty in the late seventeenth century—and the last nawab to actually rule the place had been a famous polo or cricket player. Buses traveled regularly from Indore to Bhopal—a trip of four or five hours. The place initially attracted us because a Peace Corps contingent lived there (e.g., new Peace Corps women). It contained a regional Peace Corps office too, and we visited somewhat regularly, becoming familiar with the towns where the bus stopped, with their highway tea stalls and cesspool toilets. Bhopal was built on hills around a lovely lake, and I found it a rather enchanting place. It was also handy stopover for a visit to Sanchi just north, an important Buddhist site with a great rounded stupa, where I once I met some fellow Fulbrights who lived in Lucknow; together we marveled at the place—like Mandu, it was virtually deserted. Bhopal ultimately became a household name years later, in 1984, when the American-owned Union Carbide plant there exploded and the release of toxic gases killed thousands. I could never reconcile the reality of what was probably the greatest industrial accident in history with my memories of the idyllic little Muslim city on the hills above the lake where water buffalo swam at dusk, twining out in the water like a great serpent.

Khajuraho, visited these days by hordes of tourists in search of its erotic sculptures, was in MP State but in a far-off corner, and Paul and a Peace Corps friend and I got there by train through Jhansi. What can I say about the carvings? They are indeed erotic—stone apsaras and their consorts hanging off the sides of temples in a profusion of improbable positions and poses. John Murray's handbook for Indian travelers calls them "obscene," though this book figures more in a story of mine:

Just before leaving for India, I had gone in New York to Orientalia, the specialist bookstore, and bought a copy of Murray's, which had gone through numerous editions since the nineteenth century. Mine was published in 1965 and must have been the last edition before modern guidebooks more suited for the tourists of today took over. It still contained advice on hiring "travelling servants," suggesting that friends 'up country" might engage one for you, as "'Up-country' servants are often cheaper and more trustworthy."[5]

I'm sure that this snippet of bibliographic memory became a story because it appealed to me as such a relic: of a time so very different from the one I found myself traveling in, a time when an Indian journey was even more of an expedition, maybe a time that mirrored the Indore of the recent past with its princes and courtiers and inhabited palaces. Telling the story of buying the book—then and now—has provided a neat fulcrum where I can stand poised on the brink of the other world I entered.

But from this journey to Khajuraho, I remember more vividly the Central Indian countryside. We had trouble with train connections back to Indore, and even spent the night locked in a station waiting for a morning train that seemed promising but wasn't. We finally did some backtracking and caught a bus out of somewhere, which bumped interminably toward Bhopal, where we could change for Indore, hot and dust-grimed and tired. Again, Central India screamed remoteness, mile after mile of empty, scrubby, jungly country punctuated every now and again by ancient hill forts crumbling up on a ridge or a town like Nowgong, which suddenly appeared with its ghostly old British cantonment in the middle, looking spacious and serene and thoroughly abandoned.

I traveled further afield than Central India, even if in many ways Central India—off the beaten track of fame and tourism—remains most vividly in my mind.

We passed through the fabled places of Rajasthan, to the north, and I came away with stories:

"In Udaipur we wanted to see the Lake Palace, which is set on an island in the middle of a lake, but it covers the island in a way that the building appears to be actually floating on the water. It had become a hotel, though it was one we certainly couldn't afford to stay in. But we did book dinner in their dining room so we could see the place. On the phone they told us to go to a landing to pick up a launch that would take us out, and we got there just as darkness was falling. We took a *tonga*, which is a sort of clunky one-horse carriage, and it obviously dropped us off in the wrong place. Probably not too many hotel guests traveled by tonga, and the driver didn't really know where the hell to go.

"So we found ourselves stumbling around steps leading down to the lake, trying to make our way in the shadow of the City Palace, and it was getting darker by the minute. I managed to find an open side door in the City Palace wall, and we pushed through, stumbled some more, and then somehow came out at the right dock. I couldn't believe we could actually get through the wall and to the right place—it was like fate had smiled. Someone there made a phone call, and in a few minutes a launch steered its way across from the Lake Palace toward us, like a smuggler's boat slipping through the blackness in a 1930s movie. Then as we headed out across the lake in the launch, someone at the top of the City Palace flashed a light, probably to give the launch a reference point, but it seemed like something out a Hardy Boys story, like a signal sent out from some craggy coast.

"So we had dinner (it was okay, nothing special) and went back in the launch—same beacon light from the top of the City Palace—and found another tonga. We shared this one with somebody else, and when we were dropped off, we refused to pay the tonga wallah any more than we thought the ride was worth; he chased us back to the entrance of our own cheap hotel, and he would have chased us inside except that he was stopped by the *chowkidar*, the night watchman, at the gate."

We had definitely conceived our own ideas about what to pay for things in a land where bargaining was king, though whether we were being fair or just stubborn is hard to say.

Paul, who was studying Indian cinema, went off to do that, and at one point I found myself alone in Delhi. The hotels were full, and I wound up back at the YMCA hostel, where a Peace Corps guy had a spare bed in his room and took me in. He had been in the family business in Westchester and worked in India with a retail co-op and was plugged into the Peace Corps's more business-oriented types, one of whom was also at the hostel: a guy who had worked in New York for Brooks Brothers. He told me a story that became one of my own, probably because it evoked my far-off home:

Brooks Brothers, it seemed, had been caught off guard by the craze for the polo shirts with little alligators on them made by the French company Lacoste. I was probably wearing one, which probably occasioned the story. But Brooks, despite the huge sales potential, wouldn't carry Lacoste shirts because they only sold their own brands. However, they came up with the plan to produce polos with their own little golden-fleece emblem instead of the alligator. All went well until one day the chairman of the company saw the pool boy at his country club wearing a golden-fleece polo. He was so chagrined to see it on someone so lowly that he cancelled the whole shirt design, though it was later revived as all sorts of little polo shirt emblems hit the market.

Then I flew on to Bombay and enjoyed its cosmopolitan atmosphere. Delhi always seemed to wear a more utilitarian air—a modern capital, but one based on an artificial British one superimposed on a faded Mughal one. Bombay became a locus for stories in a way that Delhi never did:

At one restaurant, I ate Tournedos Rossini while a foursome sang Beatles songs in close imitation of the then-riding-high Fab Four. One member of the group bore an uncanny resemblance to my friend Carl Patrick, so that he was both distracting and a homey reminder of my life elsewhere.

I acquired a liquor license because in order to buy booze in Bombay, individuals had to obtain a license (Prohibition existed in Maharashtra State); foreigners could automatically get one and Indians could with a doctor's note confirming they were alcoholics! The license allotted only a certain amount per month, and in a bar the waiter or bartender would inscribe a careful record of consumption on the document. Of course, Prohibition did dim the cosmopolitan light of Bombay. I got my license by going to a faceless office and bribing an orderly with a rupee to expedite my request.

I also made the acquaintance of an American man in his sixties who was staying at my hotel near Arthur Bunder Road and the Gate of India. He was a retired farm equipment salesman whose wife had died and who was undertaking a venturesome trip around the world, staying at second-string hotels like ours. He wanted to see Bombay's "cages," where the cheap prostitutes showed themselves off in little cubicles, row after row, street after street. They were infamous, though at the time, I'm not sure I had ever heard of them. I was dubious about going to a place that sounded so squalid, but he said he'd pay for the taxi and was insistent that this was a sight to see. The taxi driver tried to dissuade us, insisting that the hotel could find us better girls than the cages offered, but my companion insisted we just wanted to see the place—I hoped he was being honest about that. I had no intention of getting out of the cab or, for that matter, leaving him off somewhere, defenseless. So we set off. I don't know just where the cages were, but our driver found them with no difficulty, and they were as squalid as I could have imagined—little barred enclosures full of women who looked simultaneously dark and wan. As our taxi slowed to practically a halt, we were suddenly spotted—two wealthy sahibs looking for action—and girls and pimps vying for business mobbed us, yelling. I thought for an alarmed instant they would pull us out of the car, but the driver saw an opening and picked up speed and moved on. It had been a horrendous experience, though I had to admire my companion's spirit: he not only set off around the world late in life but went looking for the world's more offbeat attractions, however dubious.

I went back to Bombay at Christmas, and Paul came along—mostly because he couldn't get to Nepal and back as he'd wanted, a happenstance that became one of his stories and, because I kept hearing it, one of my own:

With our particular visas, to leave India and return required a special exit visa, and he set out one day to obtain one because he did want to get up to Nepal and return to India for the rest of his Fulbright tour. Hours later he came home, utterly defeated in his attempt. He had gone across the breadth of Indore, in rickshaws and afoot, from this office to that. Each office sent him somewhere else. Finally some bureaucrat sent him to a convent that housed European nuns, whose very existence had been unknown to us, on the theory that the nuns sometimes needed such visas and would know how to obtain one. It had been a reasonable enough suggestion. His last stop had been this convent, where the nuns were very kind and gave him a chocolate bar. But they had no more idea than anybody else where to apply for the right visa; they'd been trying to get some for themselves for months without success!

So instead we set out for Bombay, traveling third-class-reserved, our usual mode of travel, with our Peace Corps friend Jackie, who actually had a Sindhi fiancé in Bombay she'd become acquainted with in the States. He met her at Victoria Terminus while we went on to the harbor and another story:

We got over to Elephanta Island on the regular tour boat that left from near the Gate of India, but then we stayed behind on the island when the return boat left, spending the night in the little dak (literally, "mail"; by extension, "government-run") bungalow there. Then in the morning we went with the bungalow manager, who was getting supplies, back to Bombay. We took a *matchwa*, one of the dhow-like sailboats that plied the harbor. Its rigging creaked as we slowly went across, disappearing into a world invisible to tourists, landing at a lumber yard somewhere along the shore from the Gate of India and the Royal Bombay Yacht Club.

We had slipped away from the world of tourists into the "real India," reinforcing our sense of being more than casual outsiders, relishing our "native" mode of transport that took us behind the scenes. No doubt this is why this memory became for me a story; many of my India stories seem to be about living a life that made me, however tangentially, part of another culture.

Once back in Bombay proper we met up with another Fulbright or two and decided that since it was Christmas Eve, we'd go to church and maybe hear some familiar carols to remind us of home and other lives.

The church service we chose—maybe the only one we could find—was at the old Anglican cathedral, an appropriately pseudo-Gothic structure filled with worshippers. As we waited for the service to begin, the sweat poured off our faces from the Bombay heat as a phalanx of ceiling fans whirled heroically at full speed to keep us all from fainting. Finally the officiants processed in, looking for all the world as if they had just made their entrance straight from some parish church in Devon, arrayed in the usual ecclesiastical robes that looked far more uncomfortable than what anyone else wore as they soldiered along, dripping. Old familiar carols were duly sung, a place on the other side of the world was duly re-created, all seemed disjointed and thoroughly unreal under the valiantly turning ceiling fans as the temperature and humidity rose in the night to levels that hit new highs of tropical perfection. We slipped out hoping for just a breath of fresh air, and the incident, with its powerful mixing of tropes from opposite sides of the earth, became another of my stories.

A day or two later several of us embarked for Goa, which had gotten quite a rep as a place of good beaches and a laid-back style, on a little coastal steamer that regularly plied the waters south of Bombay down the Malabar Coast. By the time we'd booked passage all the cabins were taken, and we got deck passage, which suited us fine, this being more appropriate for our wallets and our sense of ourselves as young adventurers. When night came we lay on the deck and gazed up at the stars.

We arrived at Panjim in the morning and found ourselves a hotel on the beach, a collection of cottages with a bar in the middle. Up until an Indian invasion a few years earlier, Goa had been a Portuguese colony and still had a European colonial flavor, with a Latin aftertaste. One of its many baroque churches held the mummified body of St. Francis Xavier, the Jesuit saint who had died in in the town, and which was trotted out for veneration every few years, something which must not have seemed odd to saint-revering, devout India; the body had reportedly been pulled out of storage at the time of the Indian invasion to help repel the heathens—to no avail. We soaked up the sun, swam in warm, surf-lapped Indian Ocean waters, and downed large quantities of rum drinks, no liquor license needed.

At one point on the return voyage, a huge liner with gleaming lights traveling a bit further off the coast passed us; I imagined it to be a powerful P & O ship—at that time it might still have been—coming up from Australia to put in at Bombay. The liner quickly overtook us and was soon gone from sight—a giant, moving resort leaving our bobbing little boardinghouse in its wake. It was a sight I would often describe, evoking as it did thoughts of distant sea lanes, leisurely deck games, and a wondrous—if dying—mode of travel.

Back in Bombay, Paul and I found it impossible to get reservations on the train we wanted, so we tried to bluff our way onto a third-class-reserved car by just squatting in an empty space and trusting we'd be taken for sahibs too ignorant to understand the system. In fact, we were summarily tossed off the train as it was starting to move out of the station. I stalked off to the railway office and filed a complaint against the conductor. This became a story, perhaps because of our very foolishness. The fault had been entirely ours, but India seemed to induce in us a strange mind-set; perhaps owing to the intense, mind-numbing heat, or a sense of entitlement—because people were often indulgent to foreigners, especially white foreigners—or maybe just the disorientation of being in a distinctive place where the rules either shifted in unexpected ways or just were maddeningly different. Maybe the story expressed such speculations.

THE END

One of my final trips in India took me to a remote place called Bastar because of my interest in the folk sculpture made there. My curiosity may have been piqued by the fact that the newspapers had been full of a recently issued report about the death of Bastar's former maharaja a year or two before. He had been killed at his palace in the midst of rioting by local tribal people. A few from the old royal set in Indore remembered the man from Daly College, the local school for princes and nobles; even then, I gathered, he had been considered a bit barmy. So an Indian friend and I made our way to Jagdalpur, the capital of Bastar District, via a thin ribbon of road that connected the place to the rest of the world through Raipur.[6]

Bastar was all I could have asked for in the way of a final dose of Central Indian remoteness. Old silver rupees with the image of the last King Emperor, George VI, still circulated, as though their local coinage had been caught in a time warp. At the dak bungalow, a horde of tribal dancers suddenly showed up to drum away and gyrate in unison and collect baksheesh from a visitor. The holiday of Holi transpired as I passed through, and the multi-colored water people tossed at all and sundry soaked me. The old palace at Bastar was appropriately brooding and seemed deserted. I found some *kasers* (metalsmiths), who made my sculpture—fashioned of bell metal and brass through the lost wax casting process—as well as a government-sponsored center to promote the craft through a training program. I was instructed in some of the ways of making the sculpture and its local, ritual uses. At a riverside temple we ran into a traveling saddhu carrying a pitchfork trident who was happy to chat with us between his cigarette-induced coughs. Then we boarded the Raipur bus and slowly proceeded back to the rest of the world.

Fulbrighters were already gathering in Madras to head up to a final conference in a hill station called Kodaikanal, and we gravitated to the same cheap hotel. When we got to Kodai—as we quickly took to calling it—the Fulbright director appeared and reminisced about going there as a child with her missionary parents, and about the trip up into the hills then, with the baggage carried separately by porters. The ascent of our luggage was more prosaic, for it went with us on a public bus that met our train and then snaked up to higher altitudes. But her story seemed to bring back, as stories do, an earlier time frame when this other world was even more otherworldly.

Then we were in Kodai itself, savoring the pleasures that had made hill stations irresistible to generations of Brits: cool, clear air, neat little bungalows, manicured flower gardens, a club where a European child on a swing could be gently pushed by a servant. Indeed, I saw one of these kids, all by herself, as if she were the last European child in India. The Carleton Hotel, where we stayed, was right next to the boat club, so I could hire a craft and row around the little lake, and its servants would haul firewood to your room and start up a fire in your fireplace, and you could feel the delicious thrill of being warmed from a mountain chill in the middle of a land of oppressive heat.

I hadn't seen much of south India, and Fulbright friend Buzz Poverman and I traveled around there for a few days. My Anglo-Indian friend from Indore, Alderick, had invited me to stay at his plantation at Kotagiri, and we stayed there a night or two. His cousin showed us a tea factory; we also went to Ootacamund—the queen hill station of the South, with its race course and smart little club—in part because I'd read about the Toda tribal people who were centered there and wanted to see some.[7] In tiny Kotagiri we strolled a little, and Europeans seemed to appear on the streets in surprising numbers—local planters still doing tea, we supposed. Then we pushed on to Kerala to travel by boat through the Backwaters, a network of streams and canals and lagoons that interlaced a part of the coast. Boats regularly serviced numerous destinations, and the dock looked like a bus station, with dozens of people waiting for the right boat to pull up. An obviously hostile man deliberately pushed against a leaning Buzz (Kerala was a communist stronghold; maybe there was lots of anti-Western sentiment), and I thought we'd have a fight on our hands. But both eased off, though I would tell this story because Indian hostility had been so rare. And then we floated for a whole day through tropical waterways to some destination where we could get a bus to someplace else.

At a rest house on a beach we ate fresh-caught lobsters while lines of nearby fishermen hauled in nets from the sea, singing monotonous work shanties. At Madurai we gazed up at the amazing tiered temples that had once been painted in dazzling colors. In Trivandrum the local maharaja's special license plate bore no numbers or letters, just his conch shell coat of arms; and the landlady at our guesthouse thought that the shorts Buzz wore were the height of indecency—like going out in his underwear. I played a round of golf at Cochin, at the Bolgatty Island Palace—once the British residency and now a splendid government guesthouse decorated with old prints and surrounded by a ratty golf course—and we hired rowers who plied the harbor, taxi-like, to take us to places like the posh Malabar Hotel. We paid a visit to the synagogue of the famed "white Jews" of Cochin, remnants of a long and complicated history of Jewish settlement along the Malabar Coast, though even in 1967, many local Jews had immigrated to Israel.

Then I flew out of Cochin, caught a train somewhere, and traveled by rail for literally three days. Worn out by the very monotony of the journey, so thirsty from the growing heat and my failure to provide myself an adequate supply of water, I leapt off at one station and drank from a public fountain, knowing that might be suicidal. I seemed to suffer no ill effects, but the incident did become a story featuring my recklessness and desperation. I reached Benares—called Varanasi by then—and found a room at the gracious, colonial Hotel Clarks. Another Fulbrighter I met simplified my visit by renting a boat that rowed us to see the ghats—the phalanx of steps along the Ganges River—and sacred Benares did seem to be that quintessential India of book and film and popular image: a place of temple bells and row upon row of begging religious mendicants lined up in narrow lanes and holy men covered in ashes sitting on nails or with spikes through their tongues.

Calcutta, my last stop, teemed with the Indian masses of stereotypical visions, far more than any other place I'd been: Howrah Bridge jammed to the point of madness, chockablock sidewalks, high levels of grime, ranks of beaten-down-looking people. In a couple of days I set out for Dum Dum Airport and left India, heading for Burma (not yet called Myanmar).

In trying to characterize Kipling's Indian short stories, Randall Jarrell says that "behind most of these stories is Kipling's conviction that he and his Anglo-Indians knew life as the English in England could never know it— knew, that is, the wild, varied, and terrible existence of the planet Earth, and not the tame and restricted existence of a Victorian island."[8] Although it would be madness to suggest that the far safer, post-colonial world of the 1960s allowed me to experience India as a "wild, varied, and terrible existence"—I encountered no phantom rickshaws and never found myself, like Morrowbie Jukes, trapped in a sand crater among the living dead—I do think that some of my stories claim a little something in that vein: a life unlike anything I'd had before and which people who stayed "home"— though home for me was not England—did not have the opportunity to experience nor probably imagine.[9] I certainly knew India very differently from how increasing numbers of tourists did. I glimpsed at least a few realities that challenged my perceptions of how the world was put together. Venal or stupid customs officials grabbed medicines or seized politically incorrect globes. Riots, replete with police lathi charges, might interrupt daily life. Bandits ripped earrings from women's bodies. The strange illnesses that wracked our bodies forced us to brave cobras and dash off into the bush to suddenly relieve ourselves. Hitherto unknown pests like bedbugs and gnawing rats appeared regularly while con men used the byways to take us in. Women were displayed in cages. We had to buy personal liquor licenses just to carry on a normal, everyday activity like drinking or relied upon a beef pusher to supply basic food needs. Men blowing on conch shells might show up in the backyard. Sweetly naïve students might show up to take communion or confuse America with Russia or feel a need to translate English into English. Princes drove around with special license plates and had once dispatched inconvenient rivals. One acquired a strange self-image and a strange social position that caused one to fight with khansamahs and tonga wallahs over pennies while giving in to the con men or trying to bluff one's way onto an overcrowded train.

In some measure, these stories are about cultural differences and are the kinds of stories that always emerge when people from one culture find themselves in another, less familiar one—the kinds of stories that are a staple of travel books in which an American or English person, say, settles down for awhile in Provence or Tuscany or Mexico. A humorous edge often accompanies such stories, whether to point out one's own cultural ignorance or patronize the strange natives, whoever they may be. Pizza and Jell-O take on new meanings. One may try to rent a camel. Bureaucracy may foil one's best attempts to secure an exit visa, though sympathetic nuns may offer solace. One may be tempted to parody local ways by pretending to be a street vendor. The natives may take one's own ways to be peculiar—or even scandalous—choosing to be puzzled that one eats beef. Linguistic confusion abounds, and so a school of social work needs playground equipment. And there are those perennial living-abroad stories: the servants who may secretly wear your clothes or confuse the names of pies. But humorous or not, these stories are also statements of feeling off-balanced in unfamiliar cultural territory, in a place where you may behave strangely or have your expectations thwarted or meet up with unexpected reactions. You are living where your understanding may falter; where those insulated by tourism's institutional supports do not venture; where those who never came in the first place will never get to have their smug assumptions challenged.

Those challenges, however much they may in the moment concern or threaten or make us uncomfortable, are a good thing in the long run; they show us things we would not otherwise see, expanding our conceptions of reality and life, though we may particularly remember (and retell) the discomforts and threats. And of course, the stories also remind us of the sublime moments too: being dazzled by the Taj after momentarily trying to give it up in favor of a gin and tonic; of feeling the haze of schoolboy romance floating out to the Lake Palace as mysterious beacons flash; of watching a giant ocean liner lit up like a Christmas tree pass your own little scow in the night; of floating across Bombay Harbor in the dawn on an ancient, working sailboat.

Ultimately many of the stories—though their meanings may be multivalent—remind one of becoming a bit of an insider to a different cultural reality, enduring the local illnesses and other plagues, listening to familiar Christmas carols under utterly unfamiliar circumstances, finally acclimated enough to jump off a train to drink from a trickling public fountain. And I am reminded of sitting in the little living room of the Indore flat, reading the newspaper, looking up and saying to Paul, "I see they've blown up the 46 Down again." And we understand that Indian trains that don't have grand names like Frontier Mail or Deccan Queen have numbers and are Up or Down depending on their direction, and that rebels up in Nagaland have been able to blow the same train off its tracks time after time. This is familiar local news. We can both nod knowingly.

The journey home from India was hardly anticlimactic, but the stories from that return trip seem mostly stories of those chance encounters and random adventures and incidents that happen in the course of casual travel. You are going around the world and one or another thing that happens to you sticks in narrative. Although I think that many of the stories we tell or remember fit patterns and themes that illuminate our memory and our lives in a larger sense, probably not all do; and it's hard to say why stories from casual journeying become stories, other than that something striking or amusing or compelling made an impression on us. Traveling induces liminality, and perhaps the stories that I remember from my return from India to the States are just an expression of that—of transition salted by events. There is a story in which Prince Sihanouk of Cambodia appears and one about sharing a room in Angkor with a US Army man from Saigon who was writing a book on the birds of Southeast Asia, so that the Vietnam War—surely a defining concern for these times—does intrude a little into these stories. And in Phnom Penh I met a Canadian who was a bit of a con man, so perhaps the reemergence of a Wynograd Smeltzer-like figure suggests my very fascination with the liminalities of travelers themselves, with those who seem so much on the edges that they become emblematic of the marginal status of all travelers. But if those are my narrative themes, they are faint ones; and the stories that emerged from my Return Home from India seem random, and I will not repeat them here except for the very last story of that return, because it adds a perfect—if not particularly welcome—symmetry: an encounter with another customs inspector, when my journey virtually began with the inspector who pinched my rhubarb and soda. It may also mark the end of my own liminality, providing a return to my old, familiar world, a safe return despite a last-minute problem:

 The last leg of my journey was aboard the SS *United States* out of Southampton and into New York. I was up early on the last day to watch us slip under the Verrazano-Narrows Bridge, so familiar to me from quite different shore perspectives, and we docked along the Hudson. On the chaotic pier you were expected to somehow personally grab the services of a harried customs inspector. Maybe this was leftover from the days when many travelers had servants who could perform this duty or when there were fewer travelers and more inspectors to go around, but I finally managed to snag one to look at my luggage, which mostly consisted of an embroidered leather bag that I'd bought in MP [Madhya Pradesh] from a traveling Kashmiri merchant. The top had a drawstring and everything got tossed in as I traveled. It was literally a holdall for a not very meticulous traveler, me. The inspector's hands started to rummage through my worldly possessions, but only for an instant. Almost at once his hand pulled out, streaming blood. He had found my razor, carelessly tossed in with the rest. An unassuming man, he told me, holding on to his bleeding hand, that he'd go onto the ship and get patched up, please wait for him. Oh, God, I thought, I'm never going to get off this pier, except maybe in chains. I've almost made it home; I'm a hair's breadth from familiar territory; and I'm not going to make it. I had begun the journey having my rhubarb and soda pinched; now I'd end it with another customs man having me arrested or sued. There was my symmetry; and this story does indeed seem to mirror my earlier one, as if one is a story of entry into another world, this one a story of my reentry home. This inspector came back surprisingly quickly, his hand swathed in a bandage, told me that these things happened, and calmly finished his inspection.

Five minutes later I was on the street, the all-too-familiar honks of New York traffic welling up, exhaust fumes filling my nostrils with a good sense of my having made it home.

NOTES

1. Two of them invited us to stay in their village, where I collected a story that became one of my first publications in folklore. F. A. de Caro, "A Hindu Religious Anecdote," *Journal of Popular Culture* 4 (1970): 240–43.

2. *Fakir*, which is found in English sources from the early seventeenth century, is from an Arabic word meaning "a poor man" and originally referred to a Muslim religious mendicant, though it came to loosely refer to a holy man. It is not linguistically related to the English word *fake*, though skepticism about the virtue of religious mendicants might lead to a conflation of the two words.

3. *Bandit Queen*, directed by Shekhar Kapur, came out in 1994.

4. L. M. Crump, trans., *The Lady of the Lotus: Rupmati, Queen of Mandu; A Strange Tale of Faithfulness* (Oxford, UK: Oxford University Press, 1926).

5. L. F. Rushbrook Williams, ed., *A Handbook for Travellers in India, Pakistan, Burma, and Ceylon* (London: John Murray, 1965), 143, xv.

6. Years later one of my informants for the sahib project (see chapter 10) would be Kate Smith-Pearse, whose late husband had been principal of a college for Indian princes at Raipur.

7. Subject of Mollie Panter-Downes's book *Ooty Preserved: A Victorian Hill Station in India* (London: Hamish Hamilton, 1967), much of which originally appeared in *The New Yorker*, and which had just come out when I reached London. India's "tribals" included not only the Todas but also the Bhils, who we sometimes saw along the road in the wilder parts of Central India, and groups living around Jagdalpur, where I went to investigate the local folk sculpture. Of their cultural identity within India, Ramachandra Guha asks, "Who, exactly, are the Indian tribals? There is a long-running dispute on this question. Some, like the great French anthropologist Marcel Mauss, merely saw them as 'Hindus lost in the forest'; others, like the British ethnographer Verrier Elwin, insisted that they could not be so easily assimilated into the mainstream of Indic civilization . . . the arguments about their cultural distinctiveness (or lack thereof) continue." "A War in the Heart of India," *Nation* 285, no. 3 (July 16/23, 2007): 28–29.

8. Rudyard Kipling, *In the Vernacular: The English in India*, ed. Randall Jarrell (Garden City, NY: Doubleday, 1963), xix.

9. Kipling's short stories "The Phantom Rickshaw" and "The Strange Ride of Morrowbie Jukes" were first published in 1885 in the Christmas annual of the British Indian newspaper *Quartette*.

Eight

Life in a Cornfield

A COUPLE OF YEARS LATER, IN BLOOMINGTON, INDIANA, I met my future wife, Rosan Augusta Jordan, probably first while she put in a few hours staffing the desk at the Indiana University Folklore Library (the folklore collection was housed separately at that time). She had finished her coursework and doctoral exams, completed her dissertation fieldwork in Texas and Mexico, and came back to work on the diss in Bloomington's familiar atmosphere. She came into my life with her own set of stories that helped to give her a past and identity to me. I cannot say that stories played a key role in our getting together, but in retrospect, her stories seem important. Stories are one of the chief ways that we know others, whether friends or lovers or even acquaintances: who they and their families are, where they have been, what they have experienced, how they got to where they are now. If "they" are a potential mate, stories can shed light on a background as well as fill in the blanks of a larger whole. Stories—narrative blocks that amplify and call special attention to personal meanings and memories—are crucial to understanding another person.

Rosan's stories include how faithful slaves used wheelbarrows to carry the bodies of family members killed in The War home to Georgia; how ancestor Joseph Jefferson Carson, during the beginning of Reconstruction when carpetbaggers encouraged ex-slaves to sit in church in the downstairs pews with the white folk, would thump the floor with his gold-handled cane and thunder, "Get back upstairs where you belong, you black bastards!"; being refused service in a Texas cafeteria during a drive home from IU with several fellow students because one was black; and leaving at dusk on family trips west and driving through the night, not stopping until they saw the oil-field flare burning off gas in Hobbs, New Mexico. Or about working at the Pentagon after living in DC following college, in the operation that was just becoming involved in Vietnam, and where she had to have a Top Secret clearance and took her turn in shutting sensitive material away in a safe at night. In one story that didn't directly involve her, several members of her office went to Japan on a mission and decided to take along a lowly GS–5 to do the scut work. The folks in Japan assumed he was a GS–15 to go on such a trip and assigned him to the officers' mess until his true rank was discovered, whereupon he was relegated to the outer darkness and the officials who brought him got fussed at. More stories include going to the Five Spot in New York with a Brooklyn-born, jazz-fan boyfriend to hear Monk and running into a drunken Jack Kerouac who asked her boyfriend if he could kiss her and did. And after growing up with the idea that the South and Texas were primitive and the North was civilized and modern, her shock at Bloomington and the primitive state of some people's lives there—with shacks and outside privies. She once took me on a tour of areas of Bloomington that I would otherwise have never seen; outhouses were still in place.

People's stories—personal narratives, family saga—take us into their lives, and these stories took me into hers. As for the Bloomington stories I've told over the years, I suppose that they served to highlight my own passing, like some of my ancestors, into the world of the American heartland; although by the 1960s it was less a heartland of hardy pioneers and romantic Indians and more an uneasy one of distrust of the bearded or protesting students.

Arriving in Bloomington by plane after a couple of post-India weeks in New York in 1967, landing in what must have been a little puddle-jumper out of Indianapolis, I seemed to alight in the middle of a cornfield. I know that corn grew alongside the airfield, though perhaps my expectations put it there or increased its extent. I was going to the Midwest—the land of waves of corn—so naturally, it greeted me there and informed me of where I was: a place where the hicks were called "Hoosiers" and corn was the coin of the realm.

Years later—I love to tell this as a story—my mother, Bee, flew to Indiana for my and Rosan's wedding, and we picked her up in Indianapolis. I asked her what she thought of the landscape, after we'd gotten to Bloomington. "Flat," she said. "Very flat." Southern Indiana, a sort of extension of the Kentucky mountain country, is a hilly place, so her reaction startled me. But she was quite determined to have fulfilled her own vision of the Middle West—perhaps her mother's Kansas—and I made a story out of the incident because it seemed to so perfectly say something about preconceptions, though most of my stories from this time have other themes.

I soon forgot about corn because I seldom went outside the Bloomington city limits and my sights shifted to life in small-town America. I found myself in a place of neat little houses and slightly uneasy town-gown relations—although the movie *Breaking Away*, which explored that very thing, was still in the future—as well as a shortage of restaurants and vestiges of earlier college culture, like malt shops and hints of arcane traditions in the Indiana Memorial Union. One of my stories from the period focuses on what I saw as Hoosier provincialism—even here in the heart of higher learning:

When I went to buy a new typewriter in a shop just off the IU campus, I was asked for a picture ID because I had given them a check. I still had my India-grown beard but the ID, whatever it was, had some image of me clean-shaven. "Oh," said the clerk, visibly surprised. "You were a good looking fellah." I feigned pleasantness, but, fresh from the pulsing Lower East Side, fresh from India and the wider world, grandly bohemian in my hirsuteness, I felt oppressed by heartland provincialism and normalcy.

Bloomington had a town square with a statue of a Union soldier and a drab sort of charm and a place down along the railroad tracks that ran not far from the square called The Levee, where freight trains were loaded or once had been. This levee terminology was inexplicable but seemed vaguely sinister, as though the town secretly longed to be part of the Mississippi Delta. This was long before Bloomington, like a lot of other college towns, became one of the latest hip places with boutiques and J. Crew and quiche.

I found the university campus to be a different story. It squatted quite majestically in the middle of town, a mass of massive buildings, both old and new, crafted out of bright Indiana limestone. I had been assigned a room in Memorial Hall—a seasoned, older building—and settled in for my first-ever experience of dormitory living. I enjoyed having a little monk's cell and used its isolation to become a folklore scholar, shutting myself away for the year to intensively read my way into the field, usually taking my meals alone in the Union cafeteria.

Virtually my first destination after checking in at Memorial Hall was the Folklore Institute, located just north of the campus in a leafy residential neighborhood that the university was beginning to encroach. The Institute, which was actually an academic department, occupied what had once been a large residence, giving it a homey feel. Later I would occupy a pleasant, sunny, enclosed side porch as an editorial assistant. I waited on the ground floor for my first meeting with the man in charge—Richard Mercer Dorson—whose office was a flight up. I don't really recall my first impressions of him, though it did not take long to realize how he dominated the study of folklore at Indiana through his outsized personality. He doled out financial assistance, directed everybody's dissertations, and invited scholars from elsewhere to speak at IU, which was especially known for its folklore program, an admittedly offbeat area of knowledge. My interest probably went back to the folksong revival that had swept over us during my late high school and college years. We middle-class, urban youth felt a strange, perhaps nationalistic pull toward traditions that seemed to come from and bind us to some past that mostly still existed—or so we thought—in rurally remote places. As I studied medieval literature in college, it fascinated me to learn that in remote reaches as close as New Jersey and upstate New York people still sang songs like "Lord Randall" that had come down to them by word of mouth from—or so I thought—the Middle Ages. This fact promised strange connections through time and space.

In my years at Indiana I would learn much else and much different about folklore, and I learned much about told stories, though what I learned would mostly percolate for years inside my head, to be resurrected later. In Bloomington we studied stories—rather intensively at that. We looked at traditional stories, folktales and legends, ballad narratives and myths; the day when personal narratives and anecdotes became subjects for examination had not yet dawned. Yet I think that our intense interest in certain kinds of stories gave us a sensitivity to the potency and importance of oral narrative; and years later, I would come to recognize the power in my own stories and those told by my friends and family to reveal memory and meaning in our life passages. Perhaps I would have come to see that perspective whatever my life had been, but my studies in Bloomington, and my residence there among people aware of the possibilities of oral narrative, no doubt hastened my focus.

For virtually all of us grad students coming out of majors like English or anthropology or maybe history or American studies, much of being inculcated into the field of folklore—and it was an inculcation—meant immersing oneself in Richard Dorson's perspectives. The type and motif indexes invented or perfected by Dorson's IU predecessor, Stith Thompson, were invaluable tools that virtually defined our subject matter. Any confusion of genuine folklore with fakelore—cultural products like Paul Bunyan tales passed off as folklore by unscrupulous commercial interests or ignorant writers—was to be avoided at all costs.

The folksong revival of the 1960s brought many students to recognize their interest in folklore, and music making was popular and widespread among students at the Institute; but this activity, too, was, if tolerated, a trifle suspect because it took folklore out of its usual, "natural" social context. The folklore faculty consisted of brilliant and talented people, but it was left to Dorson to exercise a powerful command; and indeed, when he passed from the scene a few years later—collapsing from a stroke on one of

Courtesy, The Lilly Library, Indiana University, Bloomington, Indiana, and the Dorson Estate

Figure 8.1. Richard M. Dorson.

his beloved tennis courts, then vegetating in a coma for months—a terrible leadership vacuum plagued the IU Folklore Program.

Yet, though Dorson's presence was pervasive and an academic culture that bore his stamp sucked us in, the student culture of both folklore and the times pulled at us further. These were still the days of Sixties radicalism and flower power and the antiwar movement, and the IU campus, though hardly a fiery hotbed like we presumed Berkeley to be, shared in the spirit

Figure 8.2. The author, Indiana University campus, Bloomington, 1970.

of the times. Picket lines went up around hulking Ballantine Hall, rallies formed in sylvan Dunn Meadow, and such a backdrop formed my stories about these times:

As various fiery speakers in Dunn Meadow excoriated the war in Vietnam and the government, one day billows of smoke shot up from the nearby main University Library, rising into the sky like a bomb blast. The library was indeed aflame, though the fire was quickly put out. Then, astonishingly enough, it burned again the following day. Again the flames were extinguished. The damage was relatively minor. Lost mostly were some books in a distant sort of basement area I had found my way down to once or twice where, amazingly, the place had dirt floors. But campus and town also flamed with theories about the cause of the fire because arson was suspected. The culprits were theorized to be the Klan, which was active in Southern Indiana, and as an earlier fire in an off-campus African American center had been laid to their door. Or the culprits who set the fire might have been—the other theory—leftist radicals. Your conclusions about who had set the fires depended on your politics.

Months later they discovered the perpetrator to be a library stacks supervisor with pyromaniacal tendencies whose hands, it was said, were scarred from other fires he'd set that had gone awry. Supposedly his identity as the arsonist had been discovered soon after the fires, but his arrest was delayed for several months until after the completion of a long-planned move to a grand new library. He was apparently the only one who knew where all the books were supposed to go.

A less well-known but certainly more delicious moment came when a small group of students picketed the university administration building, which stood not on campus but across a public street just outside it. The police told the students to move along. A Canadian grad student named George Farkas—I knew him through somebody else, and he told me the story himself soon after—told an officer, "Go fuck yourself." They promptly arrested him and hauled him off to the station house. When he asked what the charge was, he was told "blasphemy." Being a student of philosophy, he asked for a definition of blasphemy and was informed that it meant "taking God's name in vain." He said that he wanted to point out that "go fuck yourself" was not one of the names of the Lord but remained discreet and was eventually released.

The initial division of opinion over who set the fires—and for that matter, the hasty blasphemy arrest—were indicative of the tensions of the moment (and hence became my stories), and from time to time the campus bristled over this thing or that, like a teaching assistant who had supposedly been fired because of his radical views or some new development in Southeast Asia.

Occasionally a humorous story would develop out of these times. When student demands for US troops to leave Vietnam were directed at the university, our folklore colleague Elliott Oring—whose brother, Mark, was a leading leftist politician on campus, so that Elliott was always being assumed to know more about the campus political situation than he cared to know—suggested that if he were the president of IU, he'd just issue a declaration ordering all Indiana University troops out of 'Nam! His was a reaction and later a story that addressed the tensions of the time—the seriousness of our demonstrations and what we perceived as our conflicts with the university—and poked fun at our pretensions and imaginings of the university being more than just a convenient target. The ultimately humorous tone of George Farkas's arrest for blasphemy also served to cut the tensions a bit, revealing the absurdity, ultimately, of the concerns of the day, though those concerns were based in important issues.

Bloomington saw protests, but the city was hardly a seething cauldron. Often a sweet sense of collectivity filled and animated us, maybe also in the spirit of the times of Be-Ins and Diggers and Woodstock wannabes, maybe just part of the camaraderie that often pervades a campus. Dunn Meadow sometimes just swarmed with sunbathers, and on the occasion of a solar eclipse, we all spilled into the place to observe the heavenly phenomenon, carefully

Life in a Cornfield   149

warned not to look at the sun itself but to observe the eclipse indirectly via shadows cast on pieces of cardboard. A few of the musical giants of the time, like Gracie Slick and Jefferson Airplane (or was it Jefferson Starship by then?) came and went, and once—in a more neutral vein but in a spirit of being taken care of by the university—the whole student body turned out to troop through the Union to be treated en masse with whatever wonderful ingredient the IU Dental School had developed and Crest toothpaste was using to miraculously protect teeth; we scrubbed it on our teeth with little rubber finger coverings and went away confident of never needing to see a dentist again.

The folklore students themselves developed an easy congeniality and entered into a life of parties, occasionally fueled by Barbara Kirshenblatt-Gimblett's homemade beer; Richard Dorson might show up with his own joke glass—a plastic one with a yellow, beer-like liquid inside sealed off by a clear plastic top—and we assumed he had given up drinking but wanted to hold some jolly-looking glass in his hand as a substitute for the real thing. We engaged in stimulating conversations. And there was the occasional tragedy, as when a fellow grad student—a gruff but likable guy from Massachusetts—was killed by a passing car while changing a tire by the side of a highway. Barbara K-G amazed us with her frugal genius; she taught us how to find the perfectly-good-but-discarded day-old produce tossed out by the local supermarket while her artist husband, Max G, cut lawns to make an occasional buck and showed us how money sometimes just seemed to show up in the mail, as his painting flourished and his art career slowly moved along.[1]

One grad school folklore colleague, beset by an array of health problems and perennially short of funds—though he managed to maintain a Ford Thunderbird throughout—drove a taxi and later discovered he was able to cheaply rent a huge apartment with rooms he could rent out to other grad students for a tidy profit; his relationship with credit cards became one of my stories. Credit card companies kept sending him cards unsolicited, and he would run them up to their limit while developing the philosophy of "Just send 'em five dollars a month, that keeps 'em happy"; he would also say, whether about credit card companies or humanity in general, "Frank, the world is full of assholes, Frank."

Another colleague, who had nearly finished a PhD in German before moving into folklore, impressed us with his keen mind and broad knowledge while we worked on parodying his singular way of speaking and shuddered a bit at his social skills, which seemed to consist mostly of incessantly talking at you, to the extent that I had a story about him:

In the final days of a shaky romance, my Canadian girlfriend, Carla, came to visit me in Bloomington, and we drank with some folklore students at Nick's bar before heading back to her hotel in a worsening snowstorm. Unwilling to abandon whatever he was talking about, this colleague followed us, clearly going out of his way, keeping us standing in the storm outside the hotel, talking on, until we practically had to push him away.

He disappeared from the world of folklore before too long, as did John Lair, a Kentuckian whose singular obsession was to found a bread museum—we discussed ways of preserving and displaying loaves. A few more had been repelled by Dorson or found the study of folklore not what they expected—Joseph Campbell or plinking a banjo, say—or just found paths that went somewhere else. A few banjos did get plinked and Neil Rosenberg even found time to manage Bill Monroe's little Bluegrass operation over in Bean Blossom in Brown County for awhile; we used to go on Sundays, sit in the tent, and listen to the bands passing through town. Elliott and grad student Jim Durham founded a student journal, the *Folklore Forum*, after they decided that folklore students needed their own journal and just mimeographed it up; I became involved shortly after that, telling them they needed book reviews and a reviews editor, and others got behind it. On occasion a whole group would put the finishing touches to an issue, marching around a table, collating. The folklore students' organization huffed along, not necessarily developing a lot of activities, though we toured the Kinsey Institute, conducted by director Paul Gebhard himself, where we saw boxes and boxes of shoes donated by a fetishist and heard the tale of how the Kinsey had imported pornography with the help of a sympathetic US Customs inspector at the Indianapolis International Airport until one day someone else on duty was horrified by what was coming in to corrupt America. This did give us a sense of being together and of being "organized" according to the feelings of these times when The Movement seemed to be surging ahead with locomotive power.

It was a context inducive of close friendships, further forged by our ongoing involvement in studying folklore, which Richard Dorson had turned into something of a crusade, an attitude that rubbed off on us however much we resisted it. I made many close friends in Bloomington. Barbara and Elliott were maid of honor and best man, respectively, at my wedding, held in nearby Columbus, Indiana, because my cousin Joan Beattie lived there and her husband, an Episcopal rector, performed the ceremony. Elliott and I had become close through some odd natural affinities and the *Folklore Forum*. If Elliott joked that he loved to quote himself, he was usually worth quoting. His quick mind and quicker wit made him a fixture on the IU folklore scene. Once:

As we gyrated to thumping, jungly sounds at a noisy party given by Neyde Alexander—a Brazilian married to an American who had shown up in Bloomington with a small pet jaguar that sometimes sat high on her kitchen cabinets and looked down on us as though contemplating dinner—Elliott and I got separated on opposite sides of a dancing conga line, drums thumping on the stereo; across this jumping mass of humanity, he mock-shouted to me, "Try to get word to the district commissioner," and his joke on the cliché of colonial fiction embedded itself into a story.

A few others ushered at or came as guests to my and Rosan's wedding, and many of us have kept up with each other since, though a few also wandered off to seemingly disappear from my purview at any rate, including Mike Mullarky, an Icelander who had wound up drafted by the US Army, thus obtaining American citizenship, and who took up for awhile with Neyde, separated from her husband by then, and who wound up getting pounced on or peed on from time to time by the jealous jaguar until the cat ran off one day and—unaccustomed to the dangers of the American jungle—promptly got flattened by a truck. Mike did at least go to a known place—Canada's National Museum—and I remember him in the story about the jaguar.

As for the Bloomington stories I've told over the years, I suppose that they served to highlight my own passing, like some of my ancestors, into the American heartland. They serve to highlight, too, my involvement—if only peripherally—in a world of exciting if problematic turmoil: of fires and arrests and discomfort over a foreign war that divided the nation, an issue that was on center stage nationally. Other Bloomington stories tell of our student-days poverty—of collecting day-old produce or expecting money to arrive in the mail or manipulating the newfangled credit card revolution to our advantage—times we moved beyond into greater prosperity, but which defined us then. Or about our clever quips at parties, our intellectual intensity, our eccentricities—like maintaining jaguars or touring collections of fetishists' shoes. In story, someone like Richard Dorson, who inspired a whole range of ambivalent feelings, becomes an odd, perhaps beloved, eccentric presence grasping his fake plastic beer glass while his students party around him. The stories simplify a time, as of course stories do; but they also make it more vivid and foreground some of the ways in which we seemed to define ourselves and experience that time and place as beginning folklorists, as radical students, as a community inevitably made ephemeral by the terms of its temporary existence.

NOTE

1. We savored this related story: One slightly confused grad student colleague did not catch on to the system, which did involve a minor degree of surreptitiousness in finding the tossed-out food. She simply strode up to the store manager and asked where the store kept the produce that would be thrown out; she received a less than helpful response.

Nine

Mexico

When I left Bloomington, I took a job at Louisiana State University in Baton Rouge and settled into academia. Although I do not mean to slight the many years I spent there, I do not intend to drone on about them. LSU and Baton Rouge turned out to be a bit of the Old South where I found the material for stories about white-coated black men who served coffee to university administrators or took your tray to your table at the local cafeteria and of new neighbors who took us to Natchez for the Pilgrimage, which likened the Old South to divinity and visiting its relics to a religious journey, and of other black men who would come only to your back door or who mowed your lawn for years and then simply disappeared. But though older parts of Baton Rouge did drip a certain graciousness, with canopies of thick, shady trees, by and large the town seemed to be transitioning from an old-time provincialism to a newfound blandness, neither terribly attractive; and LSU seemed to be moving a bit painfully from the stodgy to the modern and trying to do it on the cheap.

It is not surprising, then, that my stories fix on the elements of life that seemed unusual—even odd—and culturally unique, on eccentric personalities or strange encounters and incongruous signs in the very landscape. The stories transmit a taste of bizarreries reassuring us that all was not the football and malls and fast food joints that did seem to loom large in our consciousness. That is, the stories pose a vision in opposition to what I possibly perceived, perhaps unfairly and inaccurately, as the blandness of everyday reality.

In these stories:

On the larger stage strode Governor Edwin Edwards, who would become nationally famous for declaring that he couldn't lose an election unless he was found in bed with a dead woman or a live boy. In my own stories about him, he shimmers with rhinestones embedded all over his pantsuit or gives an electoral victory party with Cajun, blues, and country-western bands to cannily cover the state's voting blocs. In a friend's story Edwin makes his bodyguard hold his wallet because it would, in his own pocket, spoil his profile. In general accounts he sends his minions to the LSU campus to pick up willing coeds for amorous trysts.

On the more local story stage, a man called Colonel Emerson devotes his property to weekly occult activities like pyramid power and telepathy.

At LSU one colleague displays noted extravagances: he loves first-class air travel, buys $200-dollar bottles of champagne, and trades in his cars when minor things misfunction. Another colleague obsessively collects holy cards, is devoted to his plastic dipping bird, and hates Stalin sufficiently to hang the dictator's picture upside-down. Yet another raves about the dean as a "fat pimp" while others forge the department chair's initials to play pranks with fake memos. The chair himself utilizes an office chair that automatically puts faculty visitors at a lower level and stories from other times tell of departed professors who raved in the hallways or how the chair's innate stinginess drove a famous poet professor away. In stories about the Louisiana Folklore Society, one noted member engages in tirades against the Swiss, picks up lounge lizards to bring to official parties, and offers to take a distinguished visiting folklorist out to the swamps for nude photo sessions. Another has countless stories of his Creole ancestors while the ability to chatter a few phrases in French is a mark of the right stuff for this mostly southern Louisiana crowd—rather like wearing a Stetson and boots at Texas Folklore Society gatherings. The first state folklorist pokes around cemeteries, disappoints informants who want their traffic tickets "fixed" because he is a state official, and coinvents the "Creole meter," which detects levels of Louisiana-ness. As we visit local plantation houses—a significant local pastime—we discover faded chatelaines and movie sets where governors have bit parts, and we tell stories about this too.

Obviously stories do not form around the most ordinary or the most routine levels of existence but around things that seem unusual, if not actually extraordinary (though what is unusual to a teller may not always seem so to others). The very nature of stories suggests that they contrast with the ordinary even if the ordinary remains unstated. Although I have suggested that Baton Rouge may have been less than maximally congenial for me, probably anywhere that I settled into "normal" adult life would have seemed a bit humdrum, such that I would reach for stories that offered a contrast. My years in Baton Rouge were filled with many pleasures and enjoyable things, so that again one wonders a bit about the precise roles played by one's narratives. Do they reveal inner conceptions, do they hide as much as they convey, are they a terribly partial view of things? My Baton Rouge stories foreground eccentricity and the unusual not because everyday reality was somehow unbearable, but because they are stories; although these stories may partially reassure me that these years sparkled with some out-of-the-ordinary experiences, whatever else may have been happening.

It is probably no coincidence that my years in Baton Rouge coincide with some of my trips to Mexico, another place that provided me with a number of stories that highlight the unusual.

I grew up with an image of The Exotic that included a prologue—an approach, so to speak. In its purest form, this prologue required the stuff of old movies, like a steamboat slipping into a surf-washed harbor at the foot of a half-dormant volcano. In a more realistic incarnation, it required a plane, hours in the air stuffed into a knee-cramping seat, followed by indifferent, swarthy or ebony or high-cheekboned officials in brown, unfamiliar uniforms. That is, The Exotic was a matter of distance and to be reached by modes of transit that bespoke distance and a kind of stretched-out *en route*dness.

That is why Mexico—sometimes as strange as India, easily stranger than Lebanon or Greece—is an absurdity. You *drive* there—in your own car, with its familiar smells and bland floor mats and only a *turista* sticker with stylized pre-Columbian glyphs on the side window to mark the fact that you have passed into that place with the half-dormant volcano. And, though *La Frontera* is not a simple, thin, imaginary line but a swath that stretches indistinctly into Texas or New Mexico or Arizona: the change is sudden. One minute you are among safe landmarks—the smooth blacktop, a Holiday Inn, a rangy Anglo with an Immigration Service patch on his shoulder. The next a small, low-slung porter is intoning suggestively, "Por el capitan"—hitting you up for the first *mordida*, the bribe for the nearby, vaguely sinister, uniformed man who has just allowed your vehicle to pass through.

It is disorienting to make such a sea change without the sea, to make it by slipping behind the wheel and steering as if only bound for Cleveland or Roanoke. So Mexico, because it was the place next door, became the gringo hip-pocket Other, the place where writers headed for cheap, prose-enhancing thrills and the despondent lovers of country-western songs found sanctuary in margaritas and the solace of the sun.

One June in the 1980s we headed our gray Ford Granada toward Mexico City, where Rosan would be teaching in LSU's summer program, which actually started in Havana in 1937, long before Castro made Cuba unsafe for Louisianans. With us we took Bee, my mother, who would fly home after the drive down.

But this was hardly our first encounter with Mexico, and our encounters over the years produced stories.

As a teenager—and earlier, probably as early as 1950—Rosan had traveled to Mexico with her Texan parents. Those were the last days when the mountains that ring Mexico City stood out with a beautiful clarity since obscured by the polluting haze of too many people, too many cars, too many dreams of industrial glory. A time that, to me, gave her travels a venerable antiquity, like a linen postcard of the Tijuana bus depot we bought years later—in London. And a time later, with her Brazilian friend Celina—the result of an abortive attempt to reach Rio from Miami by somebody's private plane—and which filled her dreams since of Uxmal and patios and buses belching exhaust fumes and chicken feathers.

Our first trip together was in a Pan Am plane, which set us down in Mérida in the Yucatan and left us for the mosquitoes, the Flit ladies, and the German tourists.

It was 1971, our first year in Baton Rouge; our psychological proximity to Mexico and our temporal proximity to spring break made the journey seem irresistible. On a map, the Yucatan humped cozily up toward New Orleans, as though we could almost skip across that stretch of the Gulf with the ease of Quetzalcoatl returning home. Indeed, it was a short flight, and the three of us—including our newly acquired friend Dixie, then turning out stories and poems for the *North American Review*—taxied up to the Gran Hotel in nothing flat.

This Gran Hotel—how did we find it?—was a statuesque relic, a great squarish hulk beribboned with Victorian trimming. Statuary nymphs holding electrically lit globes lighted guests' first few steps up a grand central staircase to tiers of broad terraces that surrounded a grand open courtyard.[1] Corinthian columns held up everything—Mexico does not enjoy an ionic culture—and painted varying shades of time-faded orange and peeling cream. A vastness and openness made the place impervious to crowding, and indeed, it always seemed empty, even as people constantly came and went.

I immediately liked the Gran Hotel, and it should have been a propitious beginning. Yet this was not the happiest of trips. In part I was—despite India—unprepared for the tropical essence that we encountered: the pure, undistilled humidity and heat and sunlight, the Graham Greene seediness, the unrelenting hot cement in the towns and uncertain arrangements in the country. At night in our room at the Gran, I, who cringe at skin creams and emollients, learned to soak myself with OFF! after five minutes of lying down in the dark, as mosquitoes rampaged every part of my skin not covered by the sheet. I learned at siesta time to welcome the intruding knock of the maids who offered "Flit, señor?" with its greasy, chemical smell. As the only Spanish speaker, Rosan felt the oppressive pressure of constantly having to negotiate for us when the food was wrong, when the luggage needed storing, when transportation needed arranging. Dixie became ill at nearly the moment we landed and languished off and on. Perhaps we were already too old for what we were attempting, this sort of roughing-it on buses and sleeping in hotels that lacked even ceiling fans.

But neither was it a trip without pleasures, though I best remember the awe-inspiring intensity of the humid heat. I had felt nothing like it before except in those few days in Delhi when I had come down from Kashmir and was waiting to go on to Indore, where the rains met us and the heat broke—a scorching but dry heat. I have felt nothing like it except on another trip to Mexico years later, when we dipped out of Mexico City one weekend to visit Papantla in the coastal state of Veracruz in search of ruins, vanilla, banana trees, and coffee, and then we drove an air-conditioned car. In the Yucatan the heat surrounded everything, engulfed us in stewpot air, made us seek out patches of shade like dogs sniffing after lush, unseemly smells.

The Mayan ruins did give our minor sufferings meaning—giant obelisks pushing out of the earth, tops soaring out of the jungle like mountain peaks poking through cloud cover. On our second day at the Gran Hotel, we pushed off for Chichen Itza by public bus—Dixie remaining behind, illness already upon her—bought ourselves straw hats on the road at the edge of the archaeological zone, and plunged ahead to pyramids and ball courts and thoughts of human sacrifice. The great pyramid called El Castillo—The Castle—dominated the flat expanse of the site, and we climbed it using a chain that dribbled down the steep front steps that was the original handrail that the Empress Carlotta used to help her mount this pinnacle of her shaky domain. That no other Mexican pyramid I've seen has a similar climbing aid, and that it was still there a hundred years later said something about both power and inertia; but whoever climbs to the top of El Castillo, queen or tourist, is a fortunate one and given a perspective that intrigues the imagination: the carpet of low, green jungle under broad, blue skies, and the dots and humps and circles and obelisks of the ancients visible all around to remind us of time and glory and decay and pre-Columbian life and modern obsessions.[2]

I knew it must have been obsession that unearthed all this, though then I knew nothing about Edward Herbert Thompson and how—this seemed

Mexico

Figure 9.1. The ruins of Chichen Itza, from a nineteenth-century print.

to me a great story, when I did hear it and adopt it, about how research could be done in another age of American wealth and power—how he got himself appointed American consul in the Yucatan because that simplified his presence here while he excavated and how he bought the whole damn hacienda upon which the ruins sat so there could be no questions as to who owned and controlled the site. I knew only vaguely of John Lloyd Stephens's explorations in the 1830s and 1840s and nothing of Frederick Catherwood's fine engravings, with their intimations of discovery and lost beauty uncovered. I did know of Richard Halliburton, however, and we came down from El Castillo to proceed through the jungle to the well, the sacred *cenote* that Halliburton, in one of his books, claimed to have dived into on a sudden whim. I don't know what I was expecting—something more man-made and well-like, a neat cylinder of stonework perhaps—but not what was there, a giant cavity in the limestone, as though the surface had just given way and crumbled inward, a peaceful little pond at the bottom to belie the tales of maidens tossed in to hit the surface and sink, propitiating the divine. These wells, more like water holes, dot the landscape.

Nearby a platform with skulls carved around its base was certainly real enough; years later Rosan's slide of it became a staple in her Day of the Dead lectures, an emblem of the Mexican love of the skeletal and an intimate relationship with death from time practically immemorial.

Later we climbed up to the level of the rows of columns that dot the "palace" to the left of El Castillo where a German tourist—apparently assuming that I spoke no known language—gently but forcefully shooed me away from the Chac Mool figure I was standing in front of so that he could photograph it. That made for a good story, but we decided to push on to Old Chichen Itza across the roadway. Practically no one else went there, for it is less dramatic than the newer, Toltec-influenced city—no great pyramids, no cenote. It did have a feel of calmness that the El Castillo side of the road lacked, whether because it was deserted or because it had ripened more centuries in the tropical sun. Then we slipped down the road for a look at the luxury hotel that hides not far from the *zona archeologica*, offering cool verandas and comforts undreamed of by the sellers of straw hats and soft drinks just down the way, because we have a congenital tendency to seek out luxury, even if only as temporary interlopers. We sat on a veranda, possibly had a drink, enjoyed all the shade that good Yankee dollars could buy, and went back to get our public bus, waiting at a little soft drink stand.

A very pretty young woman, some sort of fair-skinned *gringa*, sat across from us, her face and shoulders looking genuinely ravaged by the sun in a way that made me want to wince with both aversion and sympathy for her sins of naïveté about the Mexican sun on her ruddy Northern European complexion. Rosan, more helpfully offered some sort of healing cream. Indeed, Janet Chapman was English, on a long-planned six-week holiday, and she suffered good-naturedly. The next night, she, Rosan, Dixie, and I had dinner at the Faisan y el Venado, which in those days was touted as Mérida's prime local restaurant. Rosan joked that I would be *muy macho*, squiring no less than three women. How the Mexicans actually saw me, of course, I don't know. But as the evening wore on, one local *boracho* (drunk) tottered over to our table, made salutatory noises, offered to buy me a tequila, and wound up paying a musician to dedicate a typical song to us. I think it was "La Peregrina," written by Felipe Carrillo Puerto, former governor of the Yucatan, who composed it for Alma Reed, his gringa lover; she was drawn to Mexico during the Mexican Revolution and he called her "the pilgrim." It is said—this bit of oral history hung around to haunt us with the past—that as he waited in prison the night before his political enemies shot him to death, they sang it to torment him.

Janet left us, and we boarded a bus that took us along the coast, a land of abandoned lighthouses, whole forests of palm trees swaybacked by the prevailing sea breeze, and the great, wide mouths of rivers disgorging brown torrents into a blue-green sea. At each river the bus disgorged us so that we could clamber onto a ferry that chugged us across to the other side; the bus made the same crossing without passengers. The intense sunlight even seemed to burn itself into my shaded, covered skin, and I looked upon my passage through this place with a mixture of fascination—this seemed to be the tropics indeed, the great rivers hinting of plantations, jaguars, and lost ruins in some remote interior from which these waters flowed, the lonely coastline weaving along the edge of a sea full of imaginary trade winds and ghostly bright islands—and profound discomfort. Discomfort won out, Dixie and I opting against Rosan's desire to stay on the palm-bedecked white sands of Isla del Carmen, or at least in Carmen itself, where we only half-heartedly sought accommodations and where, while we were at the bus station, a porter's loud public announcement that I was "puro Durango"— an apparent reference only to my height, though this became a story I later liked to tell, a story of cultural misunderstanding and the anxiety of being in foreign places and the situations that result—made me irrationally uneasy and snappish, as though I had been singled out in some untoward manner. After stumbling into Villahermosa, I was delighted to settle into a bleakly bland hotel room because it was hermetically sealed, and I enjoyed a throbbing air conditioner that sent out thrills of cold air.

Villahermosa was rather like the room—not hermetically sealed but bleak in a tackily modern way, at that moment a bit of an oil boomtown. Oil had, in fact, brought the city La Venta, formerly a great archaeological site down the coast, the mother lode of Olmec remains. A swampy place, it had proven to hold vast oil reserves further under its surface than the Olmec layers, so the drillers had torn into it to pump its subterranean pools. Officially reverential of their pre-Columbian past, however, Mexicans had gathered up Olmec artifacts and shipped them inland to a Villahermosa park—also called La Venta—and laid them out in a sort of reconstruction of the site. We wandered about it, on pathways that wound through a faux jungle that seemed far removed from the city that surrounded us, coming upon the enormous stone heads that the Olmecs wrought, which remind gringos of football players and which others theorize depict Africans, evidence of ancient contact with the other hemisphere's southerly parts. Startling enough in pictures, in reality they mesmerize like petrified gods, dwarfing our whole bodies with their heads alone. Intrigued, but feeling unable to contend with anything so powerful, we turned back to the more familiar Maya and grabbed a bus to Palenque. We arrived in the late afternoon, intending to see the ruins there on the following day.

Palenque, the town, was a dusty little village and the Hotel Palenque almost the only place to stay, and we checked into what seemed like a comfortable room—although a double, it even had a third bed conveniently set up for Dixie. In fact, this initial picture of comfort is an illusion and from that come stories, one of which flows from literary memories:

First, we arrive back at the room to discover that Dixie's bed has been removed! Rosan manages to negotiate its return. Then, infinitely ready for a comfortable read-in-bed before sleep, I turn on the lamp that goosenecks out over the bed. The lamp spits out the bulb like bitter fruit—shoots it across the room, where it smashes with a fragmented pop. Absolutely determined to read, I force Rosan to call the front desk to correct the problem. Eventually a maintenance man appears and spends long minutes examining and probing the light fixture. Finally he gets on the telephone and engages in a lengthy and spirited conversation. I imagine him to be earnestly seeking useful advice from some far-off electrician colleague. Then Rosan tells me he's obviously talking with his girlfriend about a date later. Then he leaves, unable to fix anything, though he does invite me to go out for a *cerveza* (with or without the girlfriend, I am uncertain). I decline—politely, I think. We decide to sleep, and we turn out the dim ceiling light and I put my head to the foot of the bed so as to better position myself under the blowy arc of the modern, white ceiling fan. I have learned Out East that if you get right under a fan, the mosquitoes can't get at you. My feet rest on what seems to be the wall at the head of the bed, but after a few minutes, I suddenly feel a great weight on them. The ceiling light goes back on, and we realize that the wall at the head of the bed—in fact, a sort of heavy board semi-attached to the wall—is collapsing forward. We jump out of bed and wrestle it into a leaning position from which we hope it will not fall, and then we do sleep.

In the morning, little is available in the dining room for breakfast, but Rosan spots a bunch of *plátanos* succulently hanging on the wall through the kitchen door and requests fried bananas with rice. The waiter says they have no bananas. Rosan points out the obvious existence of bananas. He says we can't have those. They are not ripe, though they look perfectly ripe to us. We repeat this request at several subsequent meals, but no bananas ever ripened sufficiently during our stay in Palenque. I imagine a Graham Greene-ish novel in which a young Englishman makes his way to some jungle hostelry where he orders bananas every day for two weeks and is told that none of those hanging nearby is ripe. Then the bananas, nearly rotten at that point, mysteriously disappear altogether and are replaced by a new but still off-limits bunch. An Old Jungle Hand explains that in the forty years *he's* been there, the hotel has *never* served bananas to anybody, and he's never learned why!

These minor events stayed with me in story, perhaps because I invented that imaginary literary connection and a bit of a fiction or perhaps because they spoke of the strange inconveniences that one comes upon in distant, so different places.

But the Palenque ruins were worth any starvation, any falling walls, any dangerously self-propelled light bulbs. Where Chichen Itza spread out across a hot plain, Palenque nestled into humid highlands so that one half-expected mountain mists to descend over the tops of structures with bottoms hidden by jungle. The pyramids seemed more human in scale but had little skeletal, cockscomb peaks, like vaguely Asiatic ornamentation. The site seemed a bit like the Lost World that some Victorian adventure story hero would stumble into in his quest for a hideously wrought idol or the elephant's burial ground.

German tourists swarmed here too. They have become so omnipresent in our sight that we speak of them and ultimately weave them into a story or two: We clambered over pyramids and temples and climbed one pyramid to find a gaggle of them at the top, clustered around a small Mexican guide lecturing in the shadow of a hulking tour leader. The Mexican would speak in Spanish for forty-five seconds and the tour leader would then translate into German for what seemed like five full minutes. I was so transfixed by this marvelous feat of linguistic skill, by how a Northern European language could overawe with its subtle complexity the evident childish simplicity of a Mediterranean one, that I at first did not notice the entrance down into the pyramid. Well, the German listeners *were* huddled in front of it, obscuring its existence. Sure enough, a stairway inside descended like a passage to some pagan nether region, and I felt my way down to the bottom. Here, illuminated by a spotlight helpfully provided by the Mexican archaeological service, was an extraordinary stone carving—a massive sarcophagus top of surprising delicacy and whiteness. I recognized it at once as the one Erich von Däniken—then at the apex of his fame as lunatic expounder of the theory that human civilization had been created by extraterrestrial visitors—argued bore the likeness of an ancient astronaut at the controls of a spaceship. Whoever or whatever the carved figure was—he was certainly scrunched up as if constrained in a constricted cockpit, and his expression suggested intense concentration or worry about a smooth take-off or the quality of the in-flight movie—I found him superbly beautiful. Then I turned about and hiked back up the stairs to the daylight. The Germans still gathered around the twin lecturers who continued their strange dance of language, the one still amplifying the other so that the audience surely got their money's worth of intellectual tourism.

The following day—another story—we sought to finally evade the German tourists and chartered a plane to fly us to Bonampak to see the murals at the temple there. It was a four-seater Beechcraft, or something of the sort, just fitting the three of us with the Mexican pilot, a reliable-looking stocky man in a tan guayabera (a shirt popular in the tropics, with a pleated front and worn outside the pants) who didn't say much. We took off and soared over hilly, jungly terrain thinking of the joys of aerial perspectives, of floating above a vast swath of earth imagining insignificant lifeways below and the only other way into Bonampak—by horseback or muleback, though today there is apparently a road that cross-country vehicles can use when it's not impassable. I myself also kept an eye on our fuel gauges and an ear cocked to the sound of our single engine. I was partly nervous and partly excited by my own nervousness, which gave our air excursion a further hint of adventure, the remote possibility of plunging to the jungle floor—lost for days, dead or alive! But we managed to wing into the little cleared strip at Bonampak, landing on the proverbial peso and bumping to a halt.

The wall paintings were a sensational find in 1946 because they were so well-preserved—the humid climate fixed a layer of lime over them like a cataract over an eye, protecting rather than harming them—and they have been of great value in documenting aspects of Mayan life. Their location, in the unprepossessing temple structure covered by a tin lean-to, made them difficult to see in the dark and cramped space—the well-lit reproductions in the National Museum of Anthropology in Mexico City are much more congenial to the eye—but the thrill of being in the presence of a still barely accessible Archaeological Find was sweet. Several other little planes landed while we were there, disgorging some of the selfsame tourists we'd been tripping over for a couple of days, but the glow of adventure seemed to stay fresh with us.

We rounded up our pilot and headed back for Palenque, and I eyed the fuel gauges and listened to the hum of the motor anew. We gradually lost some altitude around the time we should have been getting home, and then we realized that our man was stiffly craning his neck around. He was evidently trying to figure out where the hell we were. Then his body language relaxed, and he brought us down toward a dirt strip, and we hurtled for contact with terra firma. Until all at once a bus started lumbering right toward us from the other end of the strip, wheeling up dust and belching exhaust. And then we were precipitously making for the skies again in a quick upward arc, and the pilot was chuckling in a loud and unseemly manner, and before long he set us down on the real landing strip rather than the stray road he'd inadvertently tried to press into service. As we left him, his chagrin had a quality of high amusement to it, as though our near-mishap had been some Mayan in-joke to be savored in safe tranquility by all of us.

We did not see all the humor, but the incident provided a dramatic ending to our longer story of jungle adventures. As a story I told later, the tale spoke of foreign adventures, of a journey to a remote place reachable only by chartered aircraft, and of a last-minute kink in that journey—something that could only happen in a place like Mexico, with its ancient past and its present-day pilots. The Germans were there as a reminder of an outside world beyond this land of the smoking volcano and of forces that drove us deeper into the exotic.

We soon shook the dust of Palenque from our heels by boarding a train for Mexico City, on the move north again, drawn inexorably by the pull of our home country colossus. Our train arrived late, whether minutes or hours I can no longer recall, and I paced the little station where many *campesinos* waited more patiently than I, another antsy gringo. They paid little attention to us except for one who suddenly pointed at me—at my head in particular—and called me a hippie. Odd, I thought, because I'd had no beard for years and looked, I imagined, like any middle-class traveler. He was, of course—for reasons known only to himself—merely calling attention to the high quality of my hat, made of the straw called *jipe*, and then he wandered off. This time—unlike the Carmen bus station—I was only amused at being strangely singled out, though this became for me a twin story to Carmen. This time I was adapting or the heat had lessened or it was earlier in the day and the potential for misunderstanding was merely amusing.

The train did arrive, and it charmed me. A few years later we took the Aguila Azteca from Nuevo Laredo to Mexico City, and our train turned out to consist of old "Pennsy" Railroad cars from the 1950s, sleek reminders of childhood journeys or later grad school trips up from Baltimore in the 1960s. The train that clacked into Palenque was more like something that had wandered out of an old Pancho Villa movie—a coal-burning engine and all-open windows and *fin de siècle* shapes and, inside, cracked leather seats. It was devoid only of *soldaderos* and *soldaderas* hanging off the sides singing "La Adelita." I think that the line from that song about taking *un tren militar* may have slipped into my head as I watched the dull brownish cars shake to a stop in a puff of steam. Then we boarded, and the whole night-bound journey became an oral travel narrative for me:

We seemed to ride that train forever through an afternoon and then a night during which it must have wound around every hill and town in that part of Mexico. Later I found a map that showed what I think was our rail line and it did look as circuitous as the Plumed Serpent's tail. At first we were practically alone, then we started picking up hordes of people and letting them off and picking up more—definitely the local, not the express. We tried to sleep, to let ourselves be lulled by the distant *huff puff* of the engine, but I at least—Rosan has always been a more talented sleeper—cringed restlessly in my cracked leather seat. At one station a band of woodcutters got on with their axes and saws, one of which I remember as a ferocious-toothed, two-man implement they carried down the aisle like a stretcher, and sat with us until the conductor evicted them into second-class. Rosan said "Adios, amigos," which they seemed to appreciate as they shuffled off. At another station I was awakened from a minor doze by a woman selling hot coffee, and I reached out and bought some on the spot, a milky, sugary mix that reminded me of India, drinking it pleasurably until I realized with horror what I was doing: sipping from a plastic cup dubiously sanitized, with milk from who knew where. But it was lovely while it lasted, and I was still alive in the morning.

Alive but terribly anxious to get into Mexico City. And then we stopped somewhere on the outskirts in a vast and dusty rail yard on the edge of a barrio, and we sat and sat in exhausted and expectant silence. Finally I dozed off, slipping into the snooze that had been denied me all night, when out of nowhere—from the barrio? from another car? another universe?—a band materialized by my side like characters from bad science fiction, thumping guitars and scratching on gourds and singing like vaqueros on a tear, and I started awake bewildered by my own existence, fumbling for pesos to pay them off and make them go away. They went, but I never regained my slumber; eventually the train did lurch slowly ahead and deposit us at the main station.

And that was how we first came to the Hotel Monte Carlo, where D. H. Lawrence had written *The Plumed Serpent* and where, years later, we would drive through the lobby, endure the floating fiesta in the room next to ours, and enjoy the stern if solicitous ministrations of Panchito, the manager.

That first time I didn't learn to savor the Monte Carlo, and I mostly remember lying in a pleasantly bright room enjoying my narrow, probably lumpy but welcome bed with its yellow chenille spread, feeling like a refugee from the fearsome jungles we had just come through. Noisy Calle Uruguay seemed so safely urban to someone still at heart a New Yorker, distrustful of banana plantations and wild insect hordes and reassured by horns and the gentle waft of musky exhaust fumes.

We visited Sanborns, which was a visual treat, though I failed then to find the necessary accommodation to its rhythms, becoming annoyed by what I thought was the slow service of our waitress in her sweeping, fantasy skirt; failed to order the divine Enchiladas Suizas; failed to really comprehend this unique amalgam of restaurant and lunch counter and drugstore

Mexico

Photo by Rosan Augusta Jordan

Figure 9.2. The author, Mexico, 1990s.

and perfumery and newsstand and folk art gallery, often dismissed as "too American" by snippy gringos in search of some elusive ideal of authentic Mexicanidad, though *I*'ve never seen anything faintly like it in the States or anywhere else.

We also found our way out to Teotihuacan—the "Mexican Pyramids" of tourist fame, center of a still-little-understood civilization nearly contemporary with Imperial Rome—by local bus, somehow locating some bus station which Rosan assured me sat in the tough heart of the *vecindad* (neighborhood) where Oscar Lewis had found the Sánchez family.[3] It was near Easter by then, and we passed through one little village where I caught a tantalizing glimpse of a Good Friday procession—a Roman soldier in a leather helmet and shiny tin armor, Jesus bearing his cross along a dirt lane—until our bus shuddered past and this dream slipped away from us, as if we had rushed by a life-size Station of the Cross.

Teotihuacan was a dream of a different sort—religious, secular, vast, small, ancient, modern, off-putting, approachable. The obvious vastness hit me first, of course, the sweep of flat expanse punctuated by the great Pyramids of the Sun and of the Moon, unimaginably massive, great unitary blocks that ate up acres of horizontal and vertical space and sucked my attention out of everything else so that I hardly noticed at first the rows of little vassal pyramids or the neat geometry of the whole layout. Then the antiquity soaked in. Although I had only a vague idea about this pre-Aztec site, and no knowledge of how the *arriviste* Mexica gaped at what they found here while trying to conjure their own connection to its even-then ancient greatness, the antiquity overcame me and seeped into my imagination. I could envision great progressions of feathered priests and knots of near-naked runners, probably borrowed from old *National Geographic* renderings that accompanied articles by Sylvanus G. Morley. Thoughts of human sacrifice danced in my head once more. And when I slipped into the narrow space in front of the Temple of Quetzalcoatl and saw tiers of plumed serpent heads lined up and almost art deco, like an Esther Williams precision swim team, the sense of ancient mystery and spiritual power was nearly complete.

But in the presence of these gods the grounds also teemed with ordinary Mexicanos: spooning *novios*, picnicking families, soccer-kicking kids. It was an Easter-related holiday, Good Friday, and they used the place like a park, balloon sellers vying with the vendors of "genuine" pre-Columbian pottery. Constant lines of people mounted and dismounted the great pyramids, taking in the view. If the overwhelming size of the ancient structures made these folks look like armies of tiny ants on a trail of sugar water, the people in their way also dwarfed the pyramids—made them more human in scale—tugged them into the pleasantly mundane present, gave them a gently domestic mien and a modern, secular side. We ourselves poked into little architectural corners where the grandeur lessened, and Teotihuacan came to seem less huge, more modern, almost cozy despite being the great wonder of Mesoamerica. By the time we were having drinks at the onsite restaurant, the place seemed thoroughly homey.

Teotihuacan might have yielded a variety of stories, but only one emerged—the story of how we got back into town, which seemed to say something about our gringo luck and the kindness of strangers as well as our willingness to venture into the unknown and the unexpected:

The grounds of Teotihuacan were so enormous that by the time we finished our drinks and thought about getting back, we were uncertain just where we were. We headed off to try to find a different bus to return to Mexico City and finally found ourselves at a lonely, unpromising stop where we doubted *un autobus* would come anytime soon. Cars passed intermittently, and finally a taxi appeared, slowly cruising like it was on the lookout for lost gringos who'd stumbled off the approved archaeological zone into the wilderness. My New Yorker arm shot up on reflex. I was disappointed, however, to see the slight outlines of already-riding passengers in the backseat. The driver slowed down anyway, and soon he and Rosan were carrying on negotiations until the passengers—two *yanqui* guys—asserted their control: they had hired the whole cab for the day, but we were welcome to a free lift. It turned out they were businessmen flying back to the East Coast from California who'd figured out they could swing way south and do a free stopover in Mexico City and were seeing the sights. They liked it; next time they would bring their wives.

We all chatted away. Rosan chatted up the driver in Spanish; he seemed amazed and rather delighted to find a yanqui who could speak anything but English and was highly amused when she told him—he'd asked why I couldn't speak Spanish—that I "wasn't too smart." They dropped us off near the Basilica of Our Lady of Guadalupe, another place of mass pilgrimage—for tourist and devotee alike—where the Virgin Mary had appeared in colonial times to *indio* Juan Diego, conveniently fusing the spirituality of Spain with that of the local. We wandered around there, me a little dazed by the milling crowds and all the intense devotion of supplicants on their knees mumbling prayers and staring glassily into the divine. I don't even remember if I saw the miraculous cloak of Juan Diego that the Virgin had transformed before a skeptical bishop—this was in the days before the moving walkway glided the faithful in front of its famous folds—before we left.

Then—it must have been the next day—we got on a plane and were back in New Orleans, and I'd had my first Mexican experience and probably didn't know what the hell to think about it.

Perhaps I wouldn't have gone back, would have shrugged off the Third World—with its searing sun and confusing aromas—for good. But Rosan was very committed to Mexico, and that rubbed off on me. In 1974 we moved to Austin, Texas, when I taught for a year in the folklore program at the University of Texas. Our move was not an easy one, which is why a moving story came to some prominence in my repertoire, expressing in retrospect our frustrations: how North American Van Lines had delayed the delivery of our stuff, then finally hired our young neighbors as the "professionals" who off-loaded our worldly goods. We decided to take a break from it all—a trip down into Mexico, where we could chill out in colonial cities, and we spent time in Morelia, in the state of Michoacán, at a first-class hotel, in a fine corner room overlooking the cathedral where I could sit at a desk and write while Rosan siesta-ed or read Agatha Christie until it was time to venture out somewhere.

We made regular forays into Mexico after that, driving down a couple of times in early summer when gray clouds and scattered rain hung over the northern deserts with a certain damp coolness as we drove. We would stop to eat *natillas* (ladyfingers in a sweet cream sauce) at a certain restaurant in San Luis or buy *pulque* bread in a certain town famous for it. Once we went back to Morelia and stayed in a motel apartment on Santa Maria Hill, overlooking the city, strolling down the street to the posh Hotel Villa Montaña for the occasional meal, chatting up a Protestant missionary couple who wandered through trying to keep a low profile, listening to the incessant playing of an insipid Spanish translation of a Conway Twitty song that somebody obsessively played over and over through the central courtyard. A normal-looking street went past the front of the motel, but outside our back window was a semi-secret trail where muleteers ran pack trains transporting firewood and who knew what else. I wrote some fiction but we also made numerous little field trips to crafts villages of the area, Rosan taking careful notice of the various traditions, squirreling away information she would use for future courses, particularly those she taught in Mexico City a few years later.

That summer school summer was especially sweet, enabling us to stretch ourselves out in Mexican time, to lather ourselves with the atmosphere of Mexico City. The murals at the National Preparatory School, a sort of hidden early history of the whole mural movement that you stepped into via a single small door you feared might close and lock you in. Art galleries in the Zona Rosa. The artistic recesses of the Palacio de Bellas Artes. The bus that took Rosan and her colleagues Margaret and Juan to the LSU summer school site, with step-on vendors who became one of Rosan's stories because they so defied the stereotype of the lazy Mexican, walking the central bus aisle selling everything from needles to yoga instruction books to language manuals ("This contains all the English vowels and consonants, even the diphthongs!"). Dinner at Prendes, where Dwight Morrow had entertained Mexican artists and intellectuals and where murals of the period marked the spot as special, or at the Café de Tacuba, full of warm Talavera tile colors and the aromas of *tamales oaxaqueñas*. Drinks at the Hotel del Prado, in front of Diego Rivera's great mural of an afternoon in Alameda Park—with others by Miguel Covarrubias just around the corner by the front desk—or in the tucked-away corners of the Bar Opera. And a performance at the Teatro Juárez, seated high up in the precipitously sloping balcony, where as the intermission ends, the lights out, we hear the *thump thump thump thump* of someone obviously falling down the steep stairs, having missed their footing in the darkness, and an anguished woman calls out over and over again "mi hija, mi hija!," and doctors in the audience scurry toward the sound, performers who have come onstage standing transfixed until finally all calms down and the performance continues, though this gives me a dramatic story. Another night we go to hear *Lucia di Lammermoor* at Bellas Artes, again high up in a balcony, barely able to appreciate the wondrous glass curtain made by Tiffany, to Dr. Atl's design. Rosan goes off every day to teach while I remain at the Hotel Monte Carlo and write and usually go to a local Sanborns for lunch. One day, as I return to the hotel, all the traffic lights have failed; I experience chaos as I have never imagined it, every driver trying to assume control of uncontrolled intersections. Feeling great terror, I make my way across trembling streets and get home, to the Hotel Monte Carlo itself, where we originally had found a room because a friend knew an American painter whom the management seemed to revere who always stayed there; they fussed periodically at what seemed like the perpetual fiesta that went on in the room next to ours and where the narrow balcony outside our room and under the pendulously hanging "Hotel Monte Carlo" sign allowed a breath of fresh, if smoggy, air and an entrée into the heady mix of noise and light and fumes of Calle Uruguay and central Mexico City.

The students were farmed out in pairs to local families, the Monte Carlo was ours, and faculty and students met at some rented institute for classes while I sat in the hotel where Lawrence had sat. We all took the students to Taxco, where our room had a toilet without a proper seat—no frills for the LSU program—and where I discovered the Taxco Effect: so much precious silver looking so much alike that it becomes overwhelmingly uninteresting, unworthy of purchase; where the Bar Paco, overlooking the main church, beckoned with the sublime promise of cerveza and snacks, and to the government-run conference center at Huastepec, where a politically suspect old expat named Cuba Jones lectured the students while I, overcome by some equivalent of Moctezuma's Revenge, dozed in recuperative fashion on the bed in his house, feeling soothed by the warmth of the air and a healing drowsiness, hearing sleep-inducing voices some distance away, rather like Edna Pontellier snoozing at Chenière Caminada.

With our staid gray Ford Granada always at hand in the Monte Carlo garage, we could travel on weekends, and we wheeled it out a couple of times and made our way out of town, intrepid Rosan at the controls, zipping along traffic-diminished but still tricky Mexico City boulevards. Once we went to the superb sixteenth-century monastery at Tepotzotlán, north of the capital, a place not to be confused with Tepoztlán; a year or two before our colleague Miles Richardson (anthropologist, poet, and fiction writer)—the story must have gone back to him, though someone else told it to me and it became mine, told at least to those who knew him—had meant to go to the monastery but got on a bus to the other place, which was the site of famous anthropological studies so he had a good time anyway. We wandered through innumerable courtyards and chapels with masses of Mexicans on their own weekend outings, marveling at how little time the Spaniards wasted before setting about recreating Europe in the New World on the grandest of scales, or just enjoying the fine weather and the antiquity of the building stone.

One long weekend we dropped down toward the coast in Veracruz, feeling the steamier, more tropical air waft up to meet us as we perceptibly descended. We stopped for the night at a little coffee-growing town called Xicotepec de Juarez because of the commodious hotel there, a stopping place for everybody coming that way; at dinner, the dining room overflowed with noisy travelers. We walked the town's single long street and bought some of the local coffee liqueur, a concoction we savored for years. Then we hit Papantla, the vanilla capital, the smell of vanilla floating in the very air, and El Tajín, one of the greatest of pre-Columbian ruins, where *voladores* (flyers) performed for the tourists, climbing their soaring pole and spinning slowly down on ropes, like birds.

Back at the hotel, Rosan and I retired early while Juan and Margaret set off for a night on the town. As the night wore on, the air conditioner rattling away, we became increasingly worried when they didn't return. How much town could there be to have a night on? This was Papantla, a little provincial place. We worried some more. Finally they returned and told us that more was going on than met the eye. At another hotel they'd found not only a nightclub but a nightclub full of oil workers and vanilla buyers, and they all had danced the night away.

Juan and Margaret's experience, and our perhaps misplaced concern, appealed to me as a story: we were in an isolated, off-the-path place, yet life pulsed here if you looked; we ourselves hadn't looked but somehow became a part of it through our more venturesome friends and travel companions. I would go on to tell about it, as I would about our next stop.

We drove on to the coast south of the City of Veracruz and found a little beach resort called Tecolutla, where the beachfront hotel had no air conditioners—just ceiling fans—and a restaurant that served marvelous grilled shrimp while mosquitoes bit at us under the table in a sort of carnivorous circle of life.

On another trip I remember driving back over the mountains into Mexico City at night, in the rain, classical music playing on the radio, poor Rosan gripping the wheel, keeping us on track as the usual Mexican traffic shot all around us. We had driven to Puebla, where I got a story because our experience there seemed to be one of slightly bizarre cultural difference, of dealing with things very foreign to American norms (yet one that no doubt fitted a Mexican reality).

When we drove to Puebla this day we intended to be back over the mountains into Mexico City in daylight; we parked on the street and filled a parking meter with coins, then returned to the car ten or fifteen minutes after the meter expired. A meter maid had not only given us a ticket, but she swiped our license plate—the local practice, to ensure that people actually paid their parking fines to get back the plates. We found out where to reclaim the license plate and waited for several more hours for the maid to get back with a virtual stack of plates. Thus, we found ourselves going over the mountains in darkness, with grand symphonies playing on the radio adding a touch of majesty.

I remember climbing into and out of Mexico City a lot, once on a train to Pátzcuaro with the students, looking back from an outdoor observation deck, feeling like I had slipped into the frame of another time.

Another weekend we went to Chalma, the pilgrimage site, where we and our car were garlanded on the way into town, and we wended our way down a medieval-looking lane to the church and waited our turn to scramble up behind the altar to kiss some relic associated with the colonial black Christ who hung there on his cross. On another trip we drove to Ixtapan de la Sal via an improbable route, Rosan taking us up over a mountain on a shifty dirt road where we met only one vehicle coming the other way, a rickety bus signed "ACAPULCO" as though it were hauling tourists off to the seashore. In Ixtapan the resort hotels turned us away—they only booked package deals—and we wound up in a musty room up a dubious flight of back stairs.

On our next-to-final day in Mexico City, I raced over to the folk art dealer Victor Fosado V and bought a set of Aguilar pottery figurines depicting a funeral, which they packed in a cardboard box. Our car was so stuffed on the trip north that I carried that box on my lap the whole way, until we dropped Margaret and Juan off in Austin. No mishap except a flat tire on some Texas side road that we managed to change, though the trunk was still so jam-packed with luggage and artifacts that I first despaired of ever getting out the spare. But eventually Baton Rouge loomed in the night and we were home.

In later Mexico years we shifted our allegiance mostly to Oaxaca, initially to see the majestic ruins at Monte Albán and the more intimate ones at Mitla, then because our interest in All Saints Day in Louisiana made us want to see its Mexican counterpart—Día de los Muertos—and we trekked around to see elaborate altars that welcomed returning ancestral spirits with

Pepsi, mezcal, and cigarettes, Rosan taking rolls of slides in homes and markets and cemeteries for her class lectures.

Once we visited Oaxaca with a tour group organized by friend Gayle Younghein, and the drama of this journey produced a story—again one of cultural difference, of how Mexico responded to a crisis in a way very different from what we assumed would have been the American way—when, hurrying back to our hotel with armfuls of packages after a lecture at an art gallery, Rosan tumbled to the street, then stood up dazed, one hand a mass of blood. She thought it was broken. We dashed back to the gallery, a local woman wailing that she knew a *curandera* nearby, and Gayle bundled us into a taxi to the Clinica Carmen. The holiday was in full swing, but three doctors came in to tend to the wounded and broken one who had split the skin between fingers—hence, the profusion of blood. The radiologist used a portable X-ray machine while standing on a chair, unprotected by any lead cloak. We went back the next day for a final checkup and to pay the bill, a total of something like seventy-seven dollars. Rosan later wrote poems about both Teotitlán del Valle—the Oaxacan town—and the mishap, and I told the story.[4]

There were other journeys south of the Rio Bravo:

We traveled to a conference in Puebla, where we partied at the gracious home of a slightly mysterious American professor, then at the downtown apartment of some other strange gringo (who "adopted" young village men), where guitars were played and poetry was recited. Rosan accompanied a woman's group to a remote spot in Quintana Roo State, a little place on a lake where phone calls had to be patched through by radio and which she reached via Cancun, a place she dismissed as a "border town" full of gringo tourists baking in the sun and sitting in nightspots with onstage entertainers who asked where people hailed from. She drove one of the group's minivans, and upon returning to the airport, somebody forgot to lock the trunk and bags spilled out across the highway, a fact unnoticed until the end of the run. She told me about the luggage mishap as a story of her journey, and for me it became a tale of her own intrepid traveling and of the strange things that can happen south of the border.

And once, a trip with friends to tortured Chiapas, to San Cristóbal de las Casas, where the Mayan weavings for sale were marvelous things, but the people who sold them were so obviously full of tension and even hostility that it is easy to imagine that the rebellion that broke out a few years later was percolating to the surface even then; and on to Chamula, which we found so edgy and foreign and guarded that our visit there and to Zinacantán became one of my stories:

In Chamula the vendors whined about being given crinkled money, and the famous church where locals performed their very non-Catholic little rituals with egg and Coke bottle offerings was guarded like a fortress from our intrusions. Over in Zinacantán a festival turned out to be going on, splendidly dressed drunkards reeling about. View-Masters—those toy successors to the stereograph—were being offered for rent so the locals could catch little glimpses of the fabulously remote outside world captured by the strangely outdated View-Master technology. There was a wariness toward us outsiders that bordered on antipathy. Yet we possessed the bizarre knowledge that in this same little town there was a Harvard University tennis court, there for the benefit of those manning an anthropological field station.

The next day, the story went on, we emerged from our hotel to find that our Volkswagen had been stolen off the street—apparently stealing cars here and selling them in nearby Guatemala was not uncommon—and we spent the day dealing with the police, the rental car people, and our ambiguous rental papers ("Señor, esto es Mexico," we heard repeatedly). The matter was finally resolved the next day by the director of the airport at Tuxtla Gutiérrez after we spent a night in the restful and wonderfully named Hotel Flamboyant. But the whole experience made this far southern part of Mexico exhausting and unhappy for me.

As a story, this one seemed to take me back to my first, less than happy Mexican visit to the Yucatan years before, when I was unprepared for the humidity, the insects, even the people. Sometimes stories do seem to bracket life. Despite my years of Mexican trips, I seemed just a bit unprepared again, and the story expressed how easily the unknown exotic can still throw us off and how unknown and exotic Mexico can be.

That smoldering volcano by the surf-washed harbor never did appear. The closest we ever came to a volcano was during a drive in Michoacán, not too far from Paricutín—said to have erupted out of a corn field in 1943—on our way from Uruapan back to Morelia; guides tried to offer us horses or mules to the top. Then—and this is what became my story—somewhere along the road we were also stopped by the long-expected swarthy official in brown who was looking for drugs or guns and asked if we had any and peered into our trunk before letting us drive on. Because he reminded us so much of a Mexican version of folklorist Dick Bauman, we were unable to take him very seriously, for he seemed like an old friend and colleague—feelings that we hoped he did not detect. It was a good story to tell anyone who knew Dick, yet it also neatly juxtaposed the foreign and the familiar and imposed the known over the unknown land.

Mexico did become my Exotic Other, and though it became for me a familiar and comfortable place, it also was a place of otherness, of improbable events and unprecedented conditions, of experiences out of the American ordinary, in contrast to the lives we and others knew at home.

Certainly my Mexico stories emphasize that here is a place where planes attempt to land on roads, raucous musicians scraping on gourds appear on early-morning trains, license plates disappear from vehicles, women tumble down theater steps in the darkness, traffic lights suddenly fail and throw a whole city into chaos. We live in a motel apartment, but out our back windows is a whole other world: village Mexico with mule trains toting goods from some other century. We long for unattainable bananas in some imagined Graham Greene novel. A maintenance man makes a date on our telephone but fails to fix a light before a wall collapses on us. Hawkers mount buses to vend vowels and consonants. Ritual drunkards stumble and fall around us. We twist and careen on a dirt road over a mountain only to meet a bus supposedly going to Acapulco. A brown Dick Bauman searches our car on a lonely highway. Our friends disappear then resurface after merrymaking with traveling vanilla buyers. Gringo strangers appear in a taxi in the middle of nowhere to give us a lift to the Basilica of Our Lady of Guadalupe, as though guided by the *Virgen* herself. We do not experience Mexico as the German tourists do—intent on picture taking, dutifully listening to lengthy lectures—but in some more immediate and exciting way. There are the usual cultural misunderstandings: I mistake being called "tall" for an insult or a reference to the straw of my hat for being a hippie. Our friend gets on the wrong bus because of an easy linguistic misapprehension. But in some way we encounter something elementally unusual and wonderful—garlanded pilgrims, women who cry out for curanderas, doctors who climb on top of stools to take X-rays—which seem beyond ordinary cultural realities. We claim a vague kinship with earlier travelers who came this way—Alma Reed, La Peregrina; Edward Thompson buying Chichen Itza; D. H. Lawrence holed up at the Monte Carlo; the list increases as Rosan develops an appreciation of Edward Weston and Tina Modotti and Carleton Beals, and even the Vicks salesman escaping the Mexican Revolution for British Honduras—travelers who saw life of a different kind in a different time.

We told these stories to anyone who would listen, but I suppose that I always was telling them to myself, assuring myself that I had indeed visited a different place—a place of cultural landmarks far from my own—and had experienced these in a somehow intimate way.

We took many trips to Mexico. And we finally retired from LSU while Carolyn Ware and Solimar Otero took over folklore teaching in English—much to our relief—carrying forward and expanding on what we started. We moved from Baton Rouge to the Crescent City—New Orleans—in June 2004, settling into a 1950s house in the Garden District, down the street from what had been the famous Newcomb Pottery, amid great live oaks and Italianate mansions and ornate nineteenth-century cottages, a few blocks away from Commander's Palace and one block from bustling Magazine Street.

The timing was not entirely propitious.

NOTES

1. Probably we found it in that great guidebook of the time, John Wilcock's *Mexico on Five Dollars a Day* (New York: Arthur Frommer, 1960).

2. I like to tell the story of how years later we invited a friend, a geographer with Latin American interests, to dinner in Baton Rouge. Our house at the time had a nice swimming pool, and we told our guests to bring bathing suits, that we'd swim before dinner. When they arrived, however, a terrible thunder and lightning storm was in progress, ruining, we thought, the possibilities for swimming. On the contrary, our geographer changed into his suit and jumped into the pool, swimming vigorously back and forth, the lightning flashing intensively around him, the thunder rolling in loud accompaniment, the rain pouring down in typical Louisiana cloudburst fashion. He came out insisting that this was the most wonderful time to swim and went on with the story of an archaeologist friend whose joy it was to climb to the tops of pre-Columbian pyramids in the midst of storms; he loved to stand on the tops, exposed to the elements, taking it all in, participating in all the natural fury. Did the man still do this? I asked. Oh no, he had finally been hit by lightning and was dead!

3. Lewis's book, *The Children of Sánchez: Autobiography of a Mexican Family* (New York: Vintage Books, 1961), received considerable popular attention. Lewis followed up on his subjects in later publications as well.

4. Published in *The Folklore Muse: Poetry, Fiction, and Other Reflections by Folklorists*, ed. Frank de Caro (Logan, Utah State University Press, 2008). 207–9.

Ten

Long Ago and Far Away
Another Passage to India

A MERGING OF FORCES IN 1979 BROUGHT ROSAN AND ME—while we were still very much folklorists teaching at LSU—to the pub in Youghal on the west coast of Ireland and to the stories which a kind reader may remember from chapter 1.

We took on what we called the "sahib project" because we were intrigued theoretically by the sorts of folklore an elite group would have and by the idea of studying a folk group in past time. Rosan, from her interests in ethnicity and group identity, was fascinated by the possibilities of looking at a new sort of group. And so we set out to talk to retired colonial administrators and soldiers about a society in which they had spent large parts of their lives but that no longer existed except in memory and the stories that capture memory.

We chose India in part because I had lived in post-colonial India and, as an alien Westerner, I certainly had wondered about how earlier generations of alien Westerners had lived there and coped with the experience.

But I would not entirely discount the toy-soldier factor or the romantic cinematic and literary factors.

Beginning around 1950 I became enthralled with the little metal toy soldiers, made primarily by England's W. Britain, that flooded American toy stores, which sometimes lined them up in vast armies. Hollow-cast, light, and decorated in an array of uniforms, their exotic color and élan charmed me while their solid American-made equivalents, heavy and combat-ready, tended toward drabness. The British figures came in sets in wonderful, usually bright red boxes—like getting department store Christmas wrap every day. I managed to acquire a great variety of regiments from across a dwindling British Empire: mounted troopers with great yellow tunics from Skinner's Horse, some sort of Bengal Lancers, fez-wearing Anglo-Egyptian cavalry. A panoply of toy empire—ironically at a time when the real thing was in quick postwar decline.

And I was certainly aware of Kipling, perhaps more from films like *Kim* than from books, and boys adventure fiction set in imperial landscapes. Although films about British exploits in India were a rather minor genre compared to Westerns or gangster movies, I saw a small but steady stream of them: sahibs putting down inconvenient native revolts, stalking tigers on foot, wandering through bazaars full of snake charmers and holy men reclining on the usual beds of nails.

India stuck with me as a place where unflappable white men found strange destinies, or at least hung out at palatial clubs or in sophisticated hotel bars—in either case, under gently twirling ceiling fans—imbibing both cocktails and the steamy atmosphere (of course, maybe that was Hong Kong or Singapore; in popular culture, the empire conveniently blended together like a suave cocktail). I suppose that on some level, I wanted to see such people close up, though in reality they had Gone Home.

We got to London in 1979 in the dead of winter, reasoning that as we moved toward spring the cold British weather could only improve. We headquartered in Mecklenburgh Square at London House, since called Goodenough College, although it was not at all a college in the conventional sense: a superb location near the foot of Lamb's Conduit—one of those neighborhood streets with pubs, greengrocers, and an ironmonger—which still give parts of London the feel of a village. A footpath—our own secret passageway—led from Mecklenburgh Square behind Coram's Fields—a vast children's playground—over to Brunswick Square, or we could cut through St. George's Gardens, a former churchyard made into a park that still held old gravestones poking up here and there, advertising the deceased among the benches and flower beds. London House itself, along with its companion, William Goodenough House, had been set up to accommodate overseas grad students and medical interns, plus a few older scholars and researchers like us, and to provide to such poor, benighted people an approximation of English college life: a quad, chaplains and chapels, a dining hall with portraits and long, carved tables and chairs, a bar, a library, TV rooms, tennis courts in the square. It provided, in all, a splendid, self-contained life within walking distance of the British Museum, the National Theatre, and Sadler's Wells. From its portals, with an elaborate coat of arms over the gate, we could use the resources of the India Office Library—across the river, reached by bus, handy to the café in the Young Vic Theatre, where we always ate—the National Army Museum reading room, the Imperial War Museum, which had oral history interviews with Brits who had soldiered in

From The Graphic, *1881*

Figure 10.1. British family in India, after "Christmas in India" by E. K. Johnson.

India, or the BBC for transcripts from their "Plain Tales from the Raj" radio shows. And we set forth for a number of interviews with retired sahibs in London or the Home Counties or other places close enough to London to reach in a day.

We set out early on our fieldwork days, found our way to Waterloo or King's Cross or Victoria, took a train to the country, found our sahibs, and spent the day with them, tape recorders rolling. They almost always invited us for lunch and were charming and cordial. Often the men wore exquisitely tailored suits; the women, rather like the Queen herself, tended more toward frumpy. Often we'd still be there for tea or sherry—we usually took along a bottle as a gift—soon learning that Brits of this class liked the dry stuff and shunned the "cream." Then in the spring we "toured," traveling around England, Ireland, and Scotland, to parts not so reachable on a day trip. This was, we had learned, in the best traditions of sahibdom: district officers in particular spent a good part of their year—in the cool, winter months—"on tour," making the rounds of their territories, taking a *dekho* (look) at what was on the ground, settling disputes, hearing reports and complaints. They usually traveled on horseback—Indian Civil Service officers were required to take a riding exam even in the 1930s—and camped, an entourage of traveling servants and servitors moving ahead with their elaborate tents. We ourselves put up in bed and breakfasts and the occasional first-class hotel, and in Ireland and Yorkshire and the West Country kindly sahibs put us up for a few nights as well. In Yorkshire our hosts invited other old India hands to dinner, where the port-passing ritual was practiced, as it was in the West Country, where we enjoyed a particularly convivial evening over copious servings of whiskey and wine. It was a splendid way to do fieldwork: not only an exercise in what we came to think of as historical ethnography, but a great way to get a glimpse of British life— of a certain, perhaps atypical subset of Brits.[1]

Ultimately, the pleasure was not in the journey to the UK but in the journey to India and that other country: the past. And in particular, to the stories about the past that seemed to limn the experience of having been there, of having dwelt in a world of our own twentieth century that nonetheless seemed remote and Victorian. Of course, each person we interviewed told us his or her "story": what took them to India, how they got there, what they did over the years—which might be their whole adult lives or just some segment of it or, in a few cases, mostly their childhood years—how they lived, what they saw and did. Although each interview differed in some way, each constituted a loose narrative of one person's colonial experience.

The actual stories they told—mostly personal narratives and anecdotes but also legends and jokes, the little narratives within the grand narrative of life history—were, we thought, especially revealing in the way that stories tell us things both within and beyond themselves, sometimes with indirection, sometimes deliberately, often with more clarity and force than we intend or expect. Because we use stories—though not always consciously— to communicate essential ideas and observations about our society, our lives, our personal and communal pasts, and because stories "synthesize events in meaningful . . . whole" (as Anthony Paul Kerby puts it), stories offer a quite personal but intensely focused way of explaining ourselves and our social and historical contexts. "Narrative is the universal human language," writes novelist Laura Lippman. "We tell stories to make sense of our lives."[2]

Alessandro Portelli cogently notes how memory is not simply a collection/recollection of facts but an active creation of meaning; and indeed, memory is both fallible (foolable?) and part of a creative process.[3] The stories evoked by memory may or may not reflect historical truth, what "actually happened." But we thought that our sahibs' stories, however they refracted the memory they contained, did re-create a colonial context, with its actors, worldview, attitudes and ideologies, symbolic parameters, and conscious and less-conscious assumptions. By giving thought to the thematic threads running through these stories, we thought we could obtain considerable, if perhaps indirect, insight into a subculture that no longer existed but which once played a significant role in the world and certainly helped shape our own post-colonial one. We felt that oral historians, unless they were also folklorists like Edward Ives, had perhaps paid too little attention to the explanatory and expository powers of smaller, embedded narratives that emerged in the course of oral history interviews. Our late colleague T. Harry Williams, who won the Pulitzer Prize for his pioneering oral history–centered biography *Huey Long*, had specifically rejected the value of legends and anecdotes.[4] Years later Elizabeth Lapovsky Kennedy would note how relatively infrequently oral history looks to such stories, though she and Madeline Davis used them in their history of a lesbian community.[5]

We thought of our stories as indeed revelatory of certain things and that they offered personal perspectives on greater historical forces. We believed that the value of "embedded narratives"—that is, the "little" stories within larger life narratives—should not be ignored in oral historical contexts, especially in projects with a central ethnographic perspective. To us they provided an important supplemental means of determining attitudes about society and the past. And we found ourselves in another world of stories not our own.

Much as our interlocutors had found themselves in different world. It was more obvious from the stories than from anything else our narrators said that they saw going to India as an entry into quite another realm of life. That was clear from such stories as one Arthur (see chapter 1) told about mistaking papaya seeds for caviar on his first Indian journey, but even more so from a series of stories about acquiring sun helmets, notably the "wrong" sort of sun helmet.[6]

Sun helmets, or *sola topis* (*sola* is the name in Indian languages for "pith," the light material from which the hats were fashioned; *topi* simply refers to a hat), were developed in the nineteenth century as a European response to finding protection from the powerful and relentless Indian sun. So they have a long and detailed history. By the earlier twentieth century they had become a kind of headgear virtually universal for Europeans in India—a sort of "religion"; failure to wear one was thought to be madness, an invitation to sunstroke. Being identified with life in India caused sun helmets to become a symbol of that life, so it is hardly surprising that on ocean voyages to India, British passengers semi-ceremonially donned their helmets when their boats reached Suez in Egypt, the portal of the East; on return voyages they ceremonially removed and threw the hats into the Mediterranean as they steamed into its waters—a sign that they were approaching home.

But in acquiring a "wrong" topi, a newly minted sahib learned of his greenhorn status, and these stories indicate the entrance to the new and

Long Ago and Far Away

different world experienced by Europeans. In the stories the newcomer finds that he or she has purchased—not in India but in England or at Suez, the symbolic dividing line between East and West—a topi either outdated or not of the "correct" material. These stories may even be associated with missionaries, people who may have been admired but who were seen as out of step with the rest of Anglo-India. Hence, we recorded such stories and snippets of stories:

> You always used to stop at Port Said . . . and go to a shop called Simon Artz . . . And you bought your topi, your sola topi, which, having bought [it] when you got to India, you found quite useless because it was of the wrong design.

> I must have looked the most awful ass. I went out with an old-fashioned type of topi that no one wore at all. My mother [who had been in India long before] advised me; she gave me the wrong name. I got one of those cork topis. Everyone wore the "Bombay bowler."

In fact, a story from a bishop who in earlier Indian days became a missionary recognized the missionary stereotype from the outset of his having gone to India as a newcomer:

> In the early days, the topi was a fetish, it was a tribal symbol. If you didn't wear a topi, you were not merely silly, you were a cad, you were a traitor. I mean, I remember the first voyage, the first time I went out to India, my wife and I, we went on one of these old ships which took a month to get from Liverpool to Madras. And all the way up, till we got to Suez, life was perfectly normal. We were all living just like the ordinary civilized Englishmen live. The moment we entered the Suez Canal something totally different happened. The officers all changed into a different kind of uniform and all the Europeans started wearing topis. I remember Helen and I standing on the edge of the deck watching the sights as we went down the Suez Canal and an old India hand said, "You haven't been out East before, have you? You won't last long. You'd better get in and get a topi immediately." Literally. I mean, you were a cad if you didn't wear a topi. It wasn't just that you were silly, you had gone native. It was the white tribe's fetish. If you didn't wear a topi, then you were not part of the tribe.
>
> I remember on this same voyage—on a four weeks' voyage everybody got to know each other pretty well. We, with one other girl, were the only missionaries on this boat. The rest of them were all tea planters and people like that. The big people went out first class, of course, but the kind of crowd that were with us were tea planters and so forth, and it very clearly came to us that as missionaries we were regarded as oddballs. So when the

fancy dress dance took place, as always happened on these ships, my wife and I went as the missionary of fiction and his wife. And I put on an enormous, great white topi and dark glasses and I had a bag full of tracts, which I went round distributing. My wife put on an enormous, great hat with fruit all around, which the purser tied on for her, and an appalling purple dress with a pink slip which showed underneath. So this was a great success. We got the prize—a couple of dishes which we're still using.

The missionary stereotype and the experience of acquiring the "wrong" headgear, as well as accounts of this happening, were common enough that a joke, playing on the basic elements of the story, developed:

There is a story about two women who are buying [topis] . . . in London and an army officer insisted on pointing out to them that what they were buying was unsuitable, and finally they said, "Well, we like these, we like these." And he said, "I assure you, nobody wears these except missionaries." And they said, "Oh, but we *are* missionaries."

These stories about "wrong" topis are about the need for integrating into Anglo-India, which was certainly its own subculture with its own rules and mores, certainly British but also something else, a colonial enclave that required adaptation. The acquisition of a sun helmet, literally thought necessary for coping with a dangerous physical threat—the relentless sun—became symbolic of adapting to the subculture and recognizing its parameters and behavior patterns.[7]

Of course, why colonial and expatriate subcultures develop is a complex question, and Anglo-India took shape for many historical reasons over a long period of time. But in part it was a pragmatic response to the problem of culture shock—that is, to the intense anxiety felt by people who must operate within a cultural and social system not their own. In an imperial context this means not only operating within it but manipulating and controlling it. In such a context the threat of being overwhelmed—by a cultural reality obviously much larger than themselves, by the exotic and different, by dangerous physical forces, by The Other—can be very powerful, leading to the creation of counter systems that insulate the controllers, whether alternate social systems or imperial ideologies or both. Many stories told to us indicated a fear of being overwhelmed.

India certainly brought dangers and an awareness of death. Whatever the actual mortality rate for Europeans in India in the nineteenth and earlier twentieth centuries, their perception of it was that European survival was precarious.[8] At the very least, an array of threats to life and a healthy existence—threats unfamiliar in the home-country context—seemed to exist and await in India, in the transition from tame, cool, temperate island to wild, boiling subcontinent with disease, wild animals, a restive native population. Death was seen not only as omnipresent but often quite sudden. Although perhaps no one we spoke with actually said it precisely this way, we heard again and again this statement: she was playing tennis at the club in the morning and we had to bury her by tea time—the quick burial a result of how fast a body decayed in the tropical climate, as though sudden death itself were not the final indignity of living here or the final reminder of the dangers.

Thus, Margery Hall, from suburban London, and with no previous family connections to India, who had come to visit a friend and then wound up marrying an Indian Army officer, found herself early on encountering death in a particularly grim setting:

> The deaths. I remember little Tommy Rushton. He got up. He was playing in the garden in the morning, at eleven. He was buried at six that night. It was as quick as that. And one doctor said cerebral malaria, the other doctor said polio, and they went arguing and arguing, and the poor parents never knew. And he was buried in a downpour, where the grave was full of water. They just dropped the coffin into a lake. And mother insisted on going—a nice, delicate little woman. I knew why she went: because she wanted to see the end of it. And the chap who sprinkled the water on the coffin—[the container] was labeled "tomato sauce." Now, that sort of thing, it takes some forgetting. And when you saw and heard that, you thought, "Is mine going to be next?"

Or death could be even more exotic, not just unknown fevers but the deadly poisonous snakes that might crawl up the drain holes of primitive bathrooms or wrap themselves around light switches to be encountered in the dark. And great jungle beasts as well, though the threat of their depredations might not come to pass, at least not to the narrator. Of course, our narrators had survived. But we were told of close encounters:

> We decided to go up into Bihar and were staying in forest bungalows in a very jungly area. We very nearly ended our career because we arrived at a forest bungalow in the late evening, and we walked in. The bungalows always have a night watchman and a cook. We couldn't see any sign of the cook, so we decided he must have gone. We made our own food and everything, went for a walk in the gloaming through the forest, went back and spent the night with the windows all open. The next day we started off for the next bungalow, and I suddenly saw a man in a ditch by the side of the road with a rifle. I spoke to him and he was American. I said, "What are you up to?"

And he said, "I was after the man-eating tiger." I said, "Which man-eating tiger?" He said, "Oh, the one who took the cook from the forest bungalow."

* * *

I stayed in another bungalow once in Bihar that had no door. There were arches in a plinth about four-foot high. No doors, just arches. We were just about settled down for the night when a large chap with nothing very much on except a thing around his waist appeared and informed me that he was from the local superintendent of police. He spoke English. He said, "I am the police *darogha*. I have a message for you." I said, "Yes?" "Royal Bengal tiger is operating." I said, "What do you mean, it's operating?" He said, "It's a man-eating tiger, and it's killing people around here." Royal Bengal tiger is operating. A lovely way of putting it. So we became quite alarmed then because we had no doors to this thing. So we spent a rather troubled night, but we weren't operated on.

The humorous tone that may pervade such stories does not necessarily mask the anxiety expressed, for humor—especially after the fact of surviving dangers—can serve to conceptualize fear and other negative emotions. The close encounter with death, though perhaps laughed off, means that death came near and was perhaps barely escaped. Although such stories express a sense of relief and—perhaps like traditional legends about how the power of witches was counteracted in some way—provide reassurance in the face of a great threat, they also highlight the original threat. As did the oft-repeated anecdote told to us by Fergus Innes of the Indian Civil Service, but also found in print, about several nineteenth-century figures, including the renowned John Lawrence, who subdued the Sikh empire in the Punjab for British power:

Which reminds me of long ago, the story of John Lawrence, when he was despaired of. This was in about 1840. He was very ill with a fever, and the civil surgeon rode all the way out from the nearest cantonment, a long ride. He came out and he said, "I'm sorry to tell you, Mr. Lawrence, that you won't live till morning. I'm afraid I've got to go now. I'll be back in the morning. I can do nothing more for you." And off he rode. And John Lawrence, as he lay there, said, "Well, that bottle of burgundy I was saving up for a great occasion. There it is. I'm damned well going to drink that." He sent for his bottle of burgundy, and he drank the whole bottle of burgundy. Next morning, when the doctor came back, John Lawrence was sitting there at his desk in his shirtsleeves working. And, funny enough, I've heard the same sort of story from Calcutta, where bottled claret or burgundy drunk right off like that has cured a man who was despaired of with a fever. Anything can happen.

Long Ago and Far Away

There is humor and relief but also the doctor's grim death sentence and the prospect of a night tormented by fever only to end with one's demise.[9] Ghost stories, a staple of Anglo-Indian storytelling—a fact that may be reflected in some of Kipling's early tales like "The Phantom Rickshaw"— offer another facet of the fixation with death, though they certainly may reflect other things as well. Those stories that we recorded usually featured British, not Indian, ghosts and probably provided our informants with a further reminder of the many dead left behind in the dangerous colonial context after they personally had been fortunate enough to make it Home. But many of the ghosts stemmed specifically from the period of the so-called Indian Mutiny, the violent rebellion against British rule that took place in Northern and Central India in 1857–1858, a bloody series of events that transformed British perceptions of India and long lingered in the British imagination as symbolic of the potential for Indian political unrest. Indeed, the ghosts may return, as ghosts are wont to do, specifically to offer reminders:

> And everybody knew ghost stories of the Indian Mutiny, mainly Indian Mutiny ones. Cries and screams on May the tenth, which is the day the Mutiny broke out. People were herded into a church and set fire, and then right on through the years, a century later in the church they would hear screams and see flames reflected on May the tenth. And these stories are very common. A ghost, the guard commander. The field officer of the week goes around and turns out the guard, and he finds it rather slow, and he goes to fill in the book and he finds that it's already been turned out. And the sentry says, "Well, a sahib I didn't know came up on a horse." And this is the ghost who turned out the guard. There are a whole lot. They are practically all connected with the Mutiny. Or some of them pre-Mutiny.

* * *

> Saugor was a big Mutiny station and we had our little club there and we had one of the few Englishmen left on the railways. The railway administration was nearly all Anglo-Indian [Eurasian]. He was off somewhere down the railway line because there'd been an accident or something. And his wife was in the club in the evening. She was looking very ill and white and finally said, "I can't go back to that bungalow. I must sleep the night with somebody." And it transpired that Mutiny, in that very same bungalow, the wife of the Englishman was on her own and her Indian ayah had come in. "Memsahib, memsahib, get out, get out." But she didn't get out in time, and she was killed. And this had also happened to her the night before. An Indian ayah had come to her the night before. An Indian ayah had come to her and said, "Memsahib, memsahib. Go, go." It so scared her, she wouldn't go back to that bungalow.

Rather like the ghosts themselves, the ghost stories "come back" to remind, to keep tellers and listeners from forgetting that unrest and rebellion are other possible dangers in a colonial environment, that though the natives may seem contented, and though some may be loyal—like the warning ayah, that is, the real one of Indian Mutiny times who seemingly reappears in ghostly form—there can always be lingering unrest and betrayal and violent death. The stories betray an anxiety about deadly natural or social forces that can overwhelm.

Culture can seem equally overwhelming, a colonial environment inevitably meaning that one is dropped into the midst of a place not one's own psychologically or socially, a place in which one is vastly outnumbered by people whose mores contrast and clash with yours and threaten to call your own mind-sets and modes of acting into question. Things that happen may even be reminders of one's own insignificance, however much one may be the colonial master, as a missionary bishop recalled:

> Oh, I remember one delightful incident. We had for a short period an old doctor who was an old-style missionary. I mean, he was an old-style sahib with handlebar moustache and very much the colonel sort of attitude. He was accustomed to ordering everybody about and there was a beggar who was pestering him, coming back and back and back at him, pestering him. He was getting more and more angry and shouting at him and swearing, yelling at him and cursing at him and threatening him, with no effect whatever, and the beggar went on absolutely. And finally this clerk, this Brahmin, who was a very mild man, physically very weak—he had very bad elephantiasis; his legs were absolutely swollen up—finally he saw that the doctor was having too much difficulty, so he lumbered himself out of his chair and he walked to his door and he looked at the beggar and just said, "Get out." The beggar just absolutely disappeared. All the cursing and swearing of an English sahib meant nothing at all compared to one little word from a Brahmin.

Sahibs' numerous servants were a popular subject for stories, and one can see that as reflecting the superior social status enjoyed by Europeans in India, who could enjoy a standard of living they could not have in England. But such stories contain other elements as well.

> We had one quite funny thing in Kotagiri, where I had a sweeper—a woman. And I was going to have a little sort of party and I had some nuts, cashew nuts or peanuts or something, which had to be roasted. I gave all these orders and everything and went out of the kitchen. Then quite by chance, I happened to walk round back of the house later, and there I found the sweeper with her dustpan, which was used pretty well for most

things, I suppose—the floors, to say the least of it. There were my nuts all being rattled around in this thing previous to coming to the table. I nearly had a stroke.

* * *

The best story I ever heard concerned the Chatfield Commission. Just before the war, this was a thing that took place in 1938. They'd seen the war coming and were trying to get some modernization, buying more modern weapons for the Indian Army. Amongst the staff sent out to India was a Guardsman who'd been BGS of Eastern Command—Brigadier General Staff, Eastern India. He went back to England, where he was made a major general, and he was on this staff, the Chatfield Commission. The originator of it all was Auchinleck, who went to meet them. He flew out to the Middle East to meet them and then came on by ship to Bombay. All very hush-hush. No one knew anything about it. Standing on the dockside when the ship docked in Bombay was this old Guardsman's old bearer and he said, "Oh, sahib, I heard you were coming. Will you take me on again?"

The first of these stories is, on one level, one of those amusing stories about the outrageous things foreign servants do, stories popular with expatriates of various kinds. The second focuses attention on what our narrators clearly saw as one of the marvels of Indian servants: their seeming ability to know when their former employers were returning to India after home leave despite their not having been informed of this by the former employer, whereupon they would show up at some point of disembarkation and request to be employed again. Both stories may seem to be whimsical musings on relations with foreign servants but underlying each is something more potentially disquieting. The servants have their own fully developed worlds beyond that of the sahibs where they have the power to do things of which their masters are but dimly aware, whether something mundane like roasting food in a container also used for holding filth or something nearly mystical like somehow understanding employers' movements out of and into their world. The relationships with servants become almost emblematic of the relationship with the colonial governed who are, of course, a sort of servant/subservient class.[10] And the realization is inevitable that one is on the cusp of a much deeper world, that powerful forces operate beyond one's ken and control, that one may ultimately have little significance and power to control things, and that a local Brahmin may really have more influence than a transplanted sahib with all his supposed superiority. In the days prior to the Mutiny of 1857–1858, strange events never understood by historians seemed to be taking place—not only a rash of rumors regarding new British-made ammunition (that cartridges supposedly had been greased with polluting animal fats was a precipitating cause of the uprising) but also the mysterious passing of chapatis—the Indian flatbread—from place to place, some sort of symbolic signal of events to come and evidence of secret worlds that existed and threatened beyond the purview of colonial power, perhaps not unlike the secret worlds as close as that of one's own servants.

The fear of being overwhelmed had to be encountered and overcome as part of the very strategy of colonization. One response was to create a parallel Anglo-Indian world in the midst of but apart from the colonized society—a world with its own social structures and institutions that resisted those of the local culture. Another was to create ideologies that provided powerful ways of conceptualizing the rightness of the colonial endeavor and that ennobled the colonial presence and made braving the dangers worth the effort. Stories suggested this process coming into play in the memories of our narrators, such as one told by Maj. Gen. William Odling, who had been stationed in Northern India in the Royal Artillery:

> We [British] were very scattered about. These military stations, even in the populated parts, were few and far between. Hundred miles, couple of hundred miles. There was a great story of a village which was half Mohammedan, half Hindu, and some very holy man—I don't remember which side—came to visit his confreres and was carried in procession through the village through a very narrow street, the narrowest part. He was given such a welcome that he died—literally—being carried on the people's shoulders. So they said we must bury him here. He's obviously been sent by the gods. Of course it stopped all the trade of the high street. The village was completely, absolutely upset. Nothing could get through. The most ridiculous situation, and the other side didn't dare do anything about it because they knew there would be the most frightful communal riot. It never took much to spark off the two sides.
>
> They had one or two wise men on each side and they said, "Let us get an adjudicator." And they said, "Who shall we get?" They said, "Well, there is a white man who works the signal station at the great railway junction fifty miles away. He'll give a fair decision."
>
> Now this chap was a corporal—a two-striper—and he was there because he was an expert in telegraphy or something. It was sort of a signal junction, not a railway junction. They went there, and they asked him to come. And he said, "Is there any shooting [i.e., good hunting in the area]?" They said yes, and he brought his shotgun and down he went, and they said, "Now this is the problem, and we will accept your opinion." He walked down the street, and he saw this ridiculous thing covered with marigolds in this narrow street, and he just said, "Take the old bugger

Long Ago and Far Away

away!" Like that, and it was done. This was the sort of respect you had, because we did try to be just.

The general's story was really part of a little narrative complex that commented upon the very basis of empire. It begins by calling attention to how scattered the British were in India, and our narrators often pointed out that they were "thin on the ground." It stresses that the British need not even be numerous to carry out their imperial task, indirectly suggesting a sort of effortless superiority, for they are so highly respected by the "natives." The empire is held together not by force of power but by respect, such that a corporal here and there is sufficient to maintain it. And the respect stems from a basic imperial quality—justice—the story ending with the assertion that "we did try to be just." The imperial ethic is essentially a beneficent one. And, of particular import, is an emphasis that the British are badly needed here as arbiters. The natives are hopelessly divided into Hindus and Muslims, and fanatical at that. Left to their own devices, their lives will grind to a stalemate; the commerce in the high street will cease; they will cancel each other out but for the just and trusted British who, unlike the natives, know how things are properly run and what really matters—not dead holy men.

Yet I say that the story partakes in a little narrative complex because Major General Odling went on to tell another story, a personal narrative about needing to consult the dentist who only infrequently passed through the area where he was stationed. The story went like so: He was driving with a fellow officer who was Indian when they ran into a huge anti-government demonstration blocking the road—perhaps reminiscent of the high street of his earlier tale. The Indian officer became terribly agitated, but our narrator merely strode up to the crowd and explained that he had to get to his appointment.

> They came down, they pushed my car the whole way through the village, I collected two flags they gave me, and two Gandhi hats, amidst cheers. This was a subversive, anti-government [meeting]. They were such nice chaps.

As with the signals corporal, the authority of the Englishman again prevails, even over anti-government, pro-independence Indians, whose essential goodwill comes through.[11] The general also told the story of how, as head of the "tent club," which locally organized the sport of hog hunting (spearing wild pigs from horseback), he would drive out to villages to scope out the hunting territory but bring along a medical kit to "doctor" the villagers. His group of stories clearly suggests a vision of what the entire imperial enterprise rested upon: an essential beneficence—whether medical assistance or justice—an unflappability on the part of the colonizers, and acquiescence and goodwill on the part of the colonized who, being "nice chaps," on some level recognize British goodness even as they seek to separate from it. These stories, we thought, commented on the very ethic of empire—though perhaps not in obvious ways—and one must look beyond the surface textures to see that it expresses an ideology of empire that justifies and ennobles the British presence, suggests Indian acquiescence and recognition of the British as useful arbiters, and posits an inner British power that cannot easily be overwhelmed.[12]

Another such story was told us by Col. William Alexander Salmon, who had served in India with the Highland Light Infantry, whose family had Indian connections going back to East India Company days. The story speaks of his early time in India as a subaltern officer:

> That was another funny thing. There's a terrific amount of entertaining, naturally, in the cantonments, and as bachelor officers—subalterns—you were asked out, and then there came a time when you felt you had to return the hospitality. And there came the time when four of us sharing a bungalow in Peshawar said, "Look, we've had a lot of hospitality. Let us throw a dinner party." So we called our bearers in, and of course, they loved it. We said, "Look, we want dinner, and we're inviting twelve people. We had one big sitting room that we shared and we said, "Tonight, bearers, make this the dining room." And then we turned out the largest of our bedrooms to get furniture. Again, you said "*bandobast karo*" [loosely, "get the business done"] to get what you wanted. He'd *salaam* and off he'd go and do it.
>
> Well, of course, living on your own and feeding in the mess, you didn't have any silver or forks or spoons. But when the time came, the table was beautifully laid. Well, we had the CO and his wife, and we had various other people. And as the dear ladies sat down, one turned across the table and said, "I think I recognize the salt cellars." And another said, "Yes, the candlesticks are rather familiar to me." Well, of course, the bearers had gone all around the cantonment and borrowed everybody else's bits and pieces. But they all went back the next day.
>
> But the real joy of it was, we were lingering on rather a long time at the table. It was the peak of the party, going very well. And we saw the bearers hanging around. So I was the senior, so I said, "Hamid Khan, what's the matter?" He came and salaamed and he said, "Please, will master and master's guests go into the sitting room?" I said, "Oh, well, we're enjoying ourselves." We were drinking our port or whatever. He said, "I know, sahib, but we want the sheets to make the beds." It was marvelous the way they could improvise.

Long Ago and Far Away

The sheets doubling as tablecloths merely tops off the rather makeshift manner of the whole bandobast and the story, which on one level is "just" an amusing account of making-do, presents something of a metaphor for empire as a bit of a patchwork affair, of arrangements cobbled together. It also both confirms and challenges a stereotype of British colonial life as being very grand. The dinner party has an elegance, yes, but the elegance is rather tenuous, based on borrowing and temporary arrangements. Indeed, those we interviewed often noted that people "at home" thought that life in India was more glamorous than it usually was. The story also expresses much about other attitudes. There is the idea of sacrifice made for the cause of imperial service—an important theme throughout our interviews—though here it may be a small sacrifice: those who serve in the far outposts may not even have enough possessions to mount a proper dinner party. But there is also a fine sense of a community whose members are supportive of each other and of the common good, held together by Indians who are subservient but ingenious and supportive of the whole enterprise—indeed, essential to it. Again, Indian acquiescence plays an important role. Can India be overwhelming when the Indians themselves are so supportive?

And the British role becomes one not of rule and manipulation but sacrifice in the face of grave dangers—though the dangers in these stories may not in themselves be so great—and service. Our narrators saw themselves as undertaking service and certainly not profiting monetarily, as they got transferred about to difficult stations, had to rent their meager household furnishings, had to separate from their children who were sent home to England for education and proper acculturation. The very names of the organizations that structured British administration—Indian Civil Service, Indian Forestry Service, Indian Political Service—suggest such an ethic. Certainly European life in India had its pleasures—the signals corporal looked forward to having some hunting—but even these could be cast into the mold of service. One of the joys of Indian service *was* the availability of sport, particularly hunting (riding to hounds in selected places but more so ready access to shooting, whether "for the pot" or "big game"), though even this, like the hog hunting expeditions organized by Major General Odling, could be rendered a form of service to the native population. John Stubbs, who we interviewed in his Irish manor house, spoke of his days as an ICS district officer:

> I had two man-eating leopards in the last district I was in, Garwahl, in the Himalayas. The trouble with these leopards is they're scavengers, and if they pick up a dead body they sometimes get a taste for human flesh.

When I got to Garwahl I found there was one leopard that had been operating for nine years without anybody doing much about it, and I spent an awful lot of time after that one. I didn't actually shoot it. I shot several leopards when I was trying to get it. I spent an awful lot of time sleeping in villages and sitting up in trees at night.

In periods of three or four days, out and back again, I suppose I was after it for three or four months. When I finally got it, I'd shot two or three without it being the right one. I finally got this one, but I didn't shoot it. I poisoned it because I was using every kind of method I could to get it. You've no idea what terror they inspire. Nobody would leave the door open at night anywhere in the village. There's no sanitation at all, so that anybody taken short in the night didn't dare go out and you could smell the smell of human excrement in that village . . .

Then I went on and shot another one, which I had quite a bit of excitement with because I had to follow it up for a couple of miles across the hillside. Then I got nearer again to the man-eater near a house where it had killed a boy earlier on, so I went and sat up over these beasts outside the house and my torch let me down. I knew the animal was there. I could hear something. I got down off the tree and I poisoned the kill, and I went up to bed, and we found him dead later on.

There was a very sporting effort by one of the officers of the local regiment. He and his brother sat up. One of them went to bed on the veranda, the other one sat up over him. It was a very sporting effort.

Well, you see, these were all the troubles a DO [district officer] had on the job. I didn't want to sit down and have people in my district eaten!

However, I got a very nice lot of skins, made a coat, which a niece now has, and I tell her if anyone complains of her wearing leopard skins to tell them that they weren't shot except in a good cause. That's the last thing I did before I left India. I was determined to get rid of this animal.

The stories told by Colonel Salmon, Major General Odling, and others might be in one sense "small" stories of their personal encounters, stories such as we all tell about amusing things that happened to us—or, in the case of Odling's narrative of the corporal or Fergus Innes's anecdote about John Lawrence, a story heard from others—they nonetheless may express grand themes. Those grand themes might be hidden a bit below the surface of a more everyday reality, but often stories work for us on more than one level; and it seemed to us that these stories were in fact powerful statements about a mind-set that influenced many developments in the twentieth century. That they were personal statements rendered not by the theorists of empire but by men who played simple and ordinary roles in the imperial endeavor makes them all the more interesting. However, the stories that we heard tracked many aspects of the imperial experience, at least insofar as

India—the "jewel" in the imperial British "crown"—is concerned, not only the thematic threads of empire itself; and I have only touched on the stories here, looking at some central elements: recognizing how to go to India, however "British," was to enter another world where powerful, potentially overwhelming forces offered dangers of several kinds; then trying to understand the worth of being there and reassuring oneself of one's own strength, power, and goodwill.

Indeed, the stories take us from India and back Home, for several narrators recounted events that transpired not in India at all but in England, and which reflect the perhaps inevitably fading influence of one-time imperial connections on Britain itself. Major General R. C. A. Edge, who headed the Survey of India that mapped the subcontinent, told us of one post-imperial encounter, though not his own:

> Did _____ tell you the story about his father's dress uniform? When his father retired from being governor of Burma, he came back to this country, and being a Scotsman he thought he would realize as many of his assets in cash as he could. And he thought, "Well, I shan't need this full dress uniform anymore, and I'll flog it." So he took it up to Moss Bros. and offered it to them. And they looked at it and said, "Well, it is in beautiful condition, but of course you must realize that it's not very often that we get any requests for the full dress uniform of the governor of Burma. I'm afraid we can't offer you very much for it, but we'll give you ten pounds." So he thought, "Well, ten pounds is better than nothing." So he took the ten pounds, handed over his best dress, went home, and a month or two later, one of these enormous envelopes—with the royal household seal on it—appeared in his letter box, saying that Her Majesty commands you to attend a levee at Buckingham Palace/St. James Palace on the occasion of your handing over your duties as governor of Burma. So he thought hard, and he said, "Well, I'll have to go and hire a uniform." So he went back to Moss Bros. and he said, "Well, I've got to attend a levee as governor of Burma, and I wonder if I could hire the uniform." And they said, "Well, you must realize that it's not very often—you know, we keep these things in stock, but it's very expensive to keep them in stock because there's not much demand for them, and I'm afraid they *are* rather expensive to hire. The fee will be ten pounds." And he was so impressed by the perfect justice of it that he paid up and hired his own full dress back.

India—Burma was at times administered as part of the Indian Empire—continues to loom back at home, asserting its presence through a ceremonial occasion. Yet, in the passage of time, India also becomes less significant, the uniform as something for which there is less and less demand until—we can imagine, in the present day—the demand has entirely ceased. Inevitably the stories will change and British stories of India will pass out of active repertoires of narrative. Colonel C. A. K. Innes-Wilson, the last British director of the Survey of Pakistan, remembered hearing Indian stories during his own childhood from his grandfather, who had served in India:

> My grandfather used to tell us a story every night—he used to tell me a story in bed—he used to come up—what we used to call our "jungle stories," and they were all very exciting, about hunting and going off after elephants. I used to think this was exactly what had happened to him, but—looking back on them—he must have thought them up. They were fascinating. When he died I can remember that I thought, well, no more will I hear the jungle stories that he used to tell about India. They were mainly about going out on hunting expeditions and watching animals. One sort of got the flavor of India somehow.

These were stories told early in the twentieth century, when a life in India was still a British reality, and Colonel Innes-Wilson went on to live his own Indian stories. What we heard in the 1970s, however, were the last vestiges of a narrative tradition; very few who remember and tell such stories remain in the twenty-first century. Stories are ephemeral. That is an inevitable but regrettable thing because stories communicate ideas and experiences and perspectives and now-lost worlds in ways that touch our imaginations; they have the potential to give us important knowledge and understanding. We certainly came back from England in 1980 with a new appreciation for the power of narrative to communicate many complexities.

NOTES

1. Fortunately other friends took us in—notably, Helen Taylor, a former LSU grad student, then teaching at Bristol Polytechnic, and Fran and Robert Whittle in Lewes in East Sussex, close friends of close LSU friend Margaret Parker. And we were grateful not only for their hospitality but also for visions of British life different from those of our informants.

2. Anthony Paul Kerby, *Narrative and the Self* (Bloomington: Indiana University Press, 1991), 3; Laura Lippman, "Shut Up, Memory," in *Life Sentences* (New York: William Morrow, 2009), n.p.

3. Alessandro Portelli, *The Death of Luigi Trastulli and Other Stories: Form and Meaning in Oral History* (Albany: State University of New York Press, 1991), vii–ix, 1–26.

4. T. Harry Williams, *Huey Long* (New York: Knopf, 1970).

5. Elizabeth Lapovsky Kennedy and Madeline D. Davis, *Boots of Leather, Slippers of Gold: The History of a Lesbian Community* (New York: Routledge, 1993).

6. Rosan Jordan and I discuss the "wrong" topi stories at greater length in "The Wrong *Topi*: Personal Narratives, Ritual, and the Sun Helmet as a Symbol," *Western Folklore* 43 (October 1984): 233–48. In this essay we also note several fictional sources that emphasize the uniqueness of life in British India (which was thought to be insular and very hierarchical), including Berkely Mather's 1977 novel *The Memsahib*, which contains a whole chapter in which one character explains the makeup of Anglo-India to a newcomer to the extent of unintended comedy. A more recent novel makes a similar attempt, perhaps because modern readers in particular are removed from such strange mores. See Carolyn Slaughter, *A Black Englishman* (New York: Farrar, Straus and Giroux, 2004), especially 40ff.

7. That they had entered a rather different world is also echoed more obliquely by such a story as this one, told to us by Patricia Edge, whose husband was a member of the Royal Engineers and eventually, the Survey of India:

> You had to learn the language even as a woman, or you missed so much otherwise. It was essential. I had a *munshi* [teacher] to teach me, but he always taught me along military lines, because that was what he was used to. He would say, "Go to the adjutant and tell him that number three company has mutinied." And all I wanted to know was how to say, "The meat is tough."

That is, language takes on the specialized usage of the colonial subculture that must be adapted to. Of course, this story may also reflect the fear of being overwhelmed: even in the 1930s there is both a memory of the "Great Mutiny" of 1857 and the ongoing concern with Indian unrest; everyday matters like the tenor of the food become subordinated to the fear of mutiny.

8. On European mortality in India, see Theon Wilkinson, *Two Monsoons* (London: Duckworth, 1976).

9. In another version we recorded the fever victim, after drinking his bottle of wine, awakens the next morning feeling well but disturbed by the sound of hammering. He goes outside to find that a local carpenter has been constructing something. He asks what it is and is told, "It's a coffin." "For whom?" he asks. "It is for your honor."

10. In addition to their own servants, the British were particularly intrigued by Indian royalty and aristocracy—that is, by both ends of the Indian social spectrum (indeed, they did not relate particularly to the middle class or the intelligentsia). The rajas and feudal nobility enjoyed positions that gave them common political and economic interests with British rulers, but additionally they seemed similar to the European landed classes with whom the British in India often identified. However, in story, even the rajas proved problematic and in need of British rule and guidance. Of the following two stories, G. N. Jackson, who served in the Indian Police, told the first; Kate Smith Pearse, whose husband headed a college for young Indian princes, told the second:

> There was another extraordinarily good maharaja who had a very fine administration, wonderful roads and schools and communication, hospitals. He had the unfortunate thing that his oldest son—he was the heir apparent—fancied himself an amateur doctor. He was liable to go into the hospitals where they had some appendix cases and would operate himself—to his father's infinite chagrin.
>
> * * *
>
> A friend and I were asked to stay in one state before the visit of the governor. We went along to see that everything was all right. The bathroom was about the size of this, lovely, all tessellated, the floor, and the bath and the basin. But no outlet. You lifted up the plug of the bath, and the water just swished over the whole place. Your clothes would be floating about. We did say to the raja—this was the

royal guest suite that we occupied before the governor came—"You know, you really ought to have a pipe attached." But he never did.

Even the best of the native princes may be hobbled by dangerous eccentricities. Not even a raja can necessarily manage to master the intricacies of modern plumbing, not even in the face of a governor's visit. Even the exalted princes remain somewhat childlike and, of course, in need of British guidance and control. And even they, who have power and prestige and who might be expected to share cultural norms with the superior British, clearly partake in cultural realities which are difficult to understand and thus threaten to overwhelm with otherness. An Indian Civil Service man, John Shattock, spoke of his time as prime minister in one small, hill state:

> I was posted to Chamba as *dewan*, or chief minister. The Raja of Chamba had died; he left a small son and you had a minority. Always with a minority someone had to rule the state while he grew up and was trained. In Chamba there was a series of dewans . . . for a number of years, and I was the last. The way I arrived was a very strange and unusual thing.
>
> The road did not go into Chamba, the capital. The last bit I had to do on horseback. It was a hill state up in the Punjab. Just before you reached the town, you had to go right downhill to the river, and then you had to go back up the other side to where there was a flat *maidan*—an open playing field—and lined up were all the state officials. There was the raja to greet me and his private secretary (whom the viceroy had made him appoint to look after his monetary affairs). The raja introduced me to all these people and at the end of the line—this is something that has always fascinated me since—there were four young men. I shook hands with the first two, and the raja suddenly pushed me back. "Mr. Shattock, you can't shake hands with those last two." I was mystified. I bowed and they bowed. Late that evening I said to the private secretary, "Would you please tell me why I was allowed to shake hands with the first two of the young men and why not the last two?" And his answer was, "Well, you see, the first two were the sons of the recognized concubines of the late raja. The last two were the sons of the unrecognized concubines." I said, "Such a subtlety is beyond my understanding."

Another story comes from Lady Daphne Dalton, who was with her husband, at the time serving with the British Army:

> We were invited to go and spend the weekend to shoot crocodiles by the Pir of Makhad. The crocodiles lie out on the banks sunning themselves. We floated along in this boat and the idea was to shoot the crocodiles before they got into the water, but they're fairly difficult to shoot. We stayed the weekend at his place, and we had this tremendous dinner given for us by this man, the Pir of Makhad, who was a sort of local squire sort of chap. And he thought he was going to do us jolly well. So we all went in to this supper after having spent the day on the boat, and we sat down on the floor, and we were given a delicious Indian meal—rice and all sorts of stuff—so we did ourselves quite well. Then there was a pause, and suddenly a whole English meal appeared, including roast beef, Yorkshire pudding, and, topping it all, Christmas pudding!

The British in the story are almost literally overwhelmed—by food, by cultural misunderstanding, by misplaced norms of hospitality. The host means well—an aristocratic ideal of generosity—yet clearly also represents a cultural reality beyond that of the British narrator of the story.

11. That the Indian officer accompanying Odling got into "a terrible state" over the subversive rally suggests several things, among them that only the British possess the truly unflappable spirit of sangfroid that allows them to prevail.

12. I have written at greater length about this complex of stories in "Differential Uses of Narrative," *Fabula* 29 (1988): 143–49; however, because I had recorded a very similar story from an Indian physician in India in 1966, the article is concerned with comparisons.

Eleven

Katrina
We Leave, We Return, Stories Abound

We leave New Orleans, running away from Hurricane Katrina, on Saturday, August 27, 2005, before the big rush of people, well before the deadly rush of water. We are not tied down to jobs, a business, cats, aquaria. The road out is an easy drive, not yet clogged by later refugees; dear friends in Baton Rouge, Margaret and Juan, take us in, even giving us their own grand king-size bed. Although Baton Rouge takes a hit, Juan and Margaret's street never loses power; we have A/C throughout and some TV, though the cable service has been knocked out. The day following the blow, we help our hosts clean up some storm debris and watch what television we can. All looks OK in New Orleans and we wonder how many days before we can get back. Two? As many as four or five?

Then the images of inundated neighborhoods and desperate, stranded people appear on the screen, and we hear snatches of cell phone calls to the media from people even more desperate, trapped in attics. Helicopters buzz in the air above the flood, a few boats seem to be reaching folks, though much is just chaos. It becomes clear that we, too, are stranded people, cut off from home for who knows how long. Thus begins an odyssey of displacement, until we finally get back to Camp Street in early November.

At first we are in Baton Rouge, moving at one point to the upstairs semi-apartment in the nice old house on Ferndale of friends Anna and Neal, making our way around a city (now clogged by refugee traffic, threatened for a few days by gas shortages) that we know even better than we know New Orleans, grateful for the opportunity to hang out at our beloved Highland Coffees. Then we take the opportunity to get on the road and head west, staying for over a week outside Oklahoma City in the house of Rosan's cousin Paul Pettigrew while he and his wife are in Europe. We leave soon after their return; we are grateful to be there but feel particularly displaced. Their small

Photo by Rosan Augusta Jordan

Figure 11.1. 2848 Camp Street, New Orleans, November 2005.

town feels simultaneously remote and suburban; Oklahoma City somehow seems like some western place of thirty years ago—not much happening—though we go to the theater and like the Cowboy Hall of Fame, where we stock up on Christmas gifts. And no Whole Foods, just a funky old health food store. After that we spend a week with cousins in Austin. On the way we pass through Fort Worth, Rosan's hometown, and stop for a night at the grand Fort Worth Club downtown.

In the meantime Hurricane Rita has come too, missing New Orleans but hitting the Gulf Coast further west, so we're reluctant to head back to Baton Rouge by that coastal route and opt instead to go cross-country through East Texas. For the first time—this is practically our only story of exile—we feel not just a bit displaced but like real refugees. We begin to notice felled trees. Rita's winds passed through here. Then as our gas gets low, we pull into the town of Lufkin. Gas is suddenly unavailable here, evidently a temporary, Rita-caused shortage. We spot people lining up at one gas station. It seems that a shipment of fuel is on its way and we are directed to a spot not too far from the front of the line. Others pull in behind us until we're a mob of supplicants all waiting in the heat for gas. A tanker truck arrives, hooks up, and slowly, slowly pumps its liquid cargo into the ground, after which we all start pumping our own tanks full, a few at a time. And then we're finally on our way into Louisiana. First the no-man's-land that used to be the dicey frontier between Spain and France that still today has a strange, empty heft to it; we're feeling like we've escaped, like the huddled masses in some old newsreel lined up—if they're lucky—to board some ancient, overcrowded ship that may take them to safety or to further disasters.

Back in Baton Rouge, we manage to get into New Orleans on October 5—that one day designated for quick visits—and find the house in one piece. Amazingly, the electricity pops back on virtually as we enter, so at least we have A/C as we perform the dreaded task of cleaning out our rotting fridge. Then we have time to do a few other things like took around our street before we have to be out of town by a six p.m. curfew—another little reminder of our tenuous status. This becomes a story of several meanings: our strange good fortune in getting much-needed electricity at the very moment of our temporary return, our joining in the task shared by so many other returnees of cleaning out an abandoned fridge, our sense of sharing exile in this temporary, limited return.

We then drive up to DC, where our friend Leslie Prosterman has very kindly offered us her late mother's apartment; it's up for sale and being cleared out but is available for a brief stay. It turns out to be six most comfortable rooms, with valets who park our car and lovely artwork on the walls, so that our ongoing exile seems a painless one; and this experience of being taken care of becomes a story that counterbalances my tale of uncomfortably waiting for gas in Texas, as if I need one story that says our exile was mostly a painless one and another to highlight the difficult uncertainties of the experience.

We return to New Orleans on November 10, after more than two months stretched in those various places between Baton Rouge and Oklahoma City and Washington, DC, and naturally, the stories begin to flow—because stories provide order, sequencing the flood of chaos into smaller, more contained meanings.

When we return, our house in the Garden District appears to be largely undamaged, though the goldfish have mysteriously disappeared completely from our pond and the yard is full of layers of debris. A lot of it consists of magnolia leaves, as though the Old South veneer of the neighborhood has been carefully and deliberately dripped all over us, landing symbolically at our feet in a mass of postmodernity. I do not suspect that I am about to

Photo by Rosan Augusta Jordan

Figure 11.2. Building damaged by Hurricane Katrina, New Orleans, 2005.

stumble into a key story—with someone else's story inside my story of meeting him—of our return and of the whole Katrina disaster:

At one point we begin to smell gas in the front yard and finally realize that the smell is coming from our lantern on a post that always gave off an odd light, sort of like a super-magnified bug zapper. We thought it was a strange sort of electric light, installed by the previous owner of the house for unknown reasons. We realize now that it's a gas light fitted with some sort of device that emitted not a flame but this odd, bug-zapper glow. We have no idea how to relight it and, in fact, realize that, hapless householders that we are, we have no idea even how to turn off the gas. Obviously we need expert advice (not always easy to come by; in the post-Katrina days experts are often in short supply), and that takes us to the Yellow Pages and ultimately to a shop in the French Quarter, which has been making decorative gas lamps (most far more decorative than ours, a somewhat pedestrian black metal affair that looks like it was ordered out of a catalog) since 1945. And that is how we happen to have come to the place where we hear our first Katrina-spawned urban legend.

The proprietor of the shop is a young man in his thirties, son of the late founder of the business. The shop itself is a spacious but simple affair, with bare brick walls and an air of having survived from an earlier time into our current Vieux Carré era of T-shirt shops and galleries of souvenir art. There are a few display cases and sample lanterns hung on walls. The proprietor tells us that our lamp is fitted with something called a mantle, which creates the sort of glow we had, increasing the amount of light emitted. However, he can sell us, if we prefer, the more standard fitting that can turn it back into a gas light, as conventionally conceived, so that our lamp will emit the flickering flame that is more romantic and more decorative. This appeals to us (we do, after all, live in one of the neighborhoods where Olde New Orleans is most avidly evoked for tourists and locals alike). We buy the fitting, eventually install it ourselves, and even learn how to turn off the gas; but that's another story, far less interesting than the one the proprietor tells us.

In the post-Katrina moment there is an impulse to talk, to exchange war stories, to say where one has been, when one came back to the city, what one found. The proprietor tells us, among other things, that his wife is still in Houston with their child and is very reluctant to come back to New Orleans. She has taken a regular job there without his "permission" (which we take to mean without discussing it with him or against his wishes). He is concerned about getting his business back up and running, something which would presumably smooth the way for his family's return. And he asks who we are and what we do, and we say we're folklorists. That's an answer that often stirs uneasy interest, and we talk a little about folklore. He has a Katrina story, he says. He is aware that it falls into the realm of folklore, and he may mean to be commenting on the gullibility of those who believe such stories.

It seems that in the Superdome, in the aftermath of the storm and flood, gang violence broke out as gang members reunited within the Dome. But to stem this tide President [George W.] Bush sent into the place the Secret Service, who "executed" all the gangsters. Then, to cover it all up, they were listed in death as just more "drowning victims."

We aren't doing fieldwork, we're just trying to get our front yard lamp up and running. We don't probe too much about further details or what he thinks about the story he has told us—and which I make into my own narrative, including our coming to him because of our light and his telling of it. Yet it's not hard to immediately see possible meanings emerge within the narrative. New Orleanians have been burdened with belief in a drastically high crime rate for a number of years. Indeed, local newspaper obituary columns do seem to have been remarkably full of death notices for young people shot down, and news stories remind a local audience of the same grim reality. Gangs have been on our minds, so it's hardly surprising that they should emerge into our narratives, another worry in the midst of our worries about the disaster that has just happened.

A few days later we have lunch with a visiting Baton Rouge friend at the Savvy Gourmet on Magazine Street, just uptown from Napoleon. That lunch is being served here at all is a Katrina consequence. This emporium for cookware/cooking school/catering business was in the process of opening just as Katrina approached. When the owners returned following Katrina, they began offering lunch; they decided that the city needed more places to eat. Its look is high tech, gleaming with polished woods and metals, a sort of tube of modernity inserted into what was an old warehouse or garage; a large plasma TV on one side of the restaurant displays the Cooking Channel.

This day we run into friends having lunch, a married couple that lived in Lakeview, an area of the city hit especially hard by the flooding from the Seventeenth Street and London Avenue Canals. Their lovely house (she is a decorator by profession) has been virtually destroyed by floodwaters and a falling tree. Then what was left of their house was looted. The houses of their grown children, also in Lakeview, have been destroyed. They don't know whether their businesses can survive in the current economic climate, and they may have to leave New Orleans, where their families have lived for generations. They are remarkably cheerful and we join them to chat over food. They also have a story, about something that happened to friends of a friend.

These friends of a friend returned to their house in Lakeview to find it looted. Their silverware and the wife's jewelry were gone. But after they pumped the mucky water out of their swimming pool, they recovered their lost treasures. They were in a sack at the bottom of the pool, with the looter who took them still clutching the bag in his dead hand. Evidently he had been making his way through the world of water that covered everything, was unaware of the existence of the pool, and plunged into its depths when he reached the edge. Unable to swim, he drowned and stayed under water, held down by the bag of silver and gems he couldn't let go of.

Not long after our lunch we hear another version of the same story from another friend, an educator quite aware of urban legends who has been flooded out of his own house and is staying in the suburbs in a borrowed residence. In this version (told to him by a friend) the story is essentially the same, but the location is Uptown, the dead looter has taken a pillowcase from the house for the loot, and the looter is specifically noted to be a black man. (*The New York Times* quotes TV star-turned-vocal-French-Quarter-saloon-keeper

Harry Anderson as saying "with disgust" that many of the white people who have come to makeshift town hall meetings held initially at his bar probably hope that blacks will not return to the city in appreciable numbers; they say, "There's a lot less crime now that the Black people are gone"; indeed, some whites viewed New Orleans crime as a black problem, but with this exception, the race of the looters and gang members did not appear in any of the stories.)[1]

We have the story happening to a friend of a friend; we have a plot where faint possibility vies with improbability—elements that would mark it as urban legend even if the story didn't echo the themes of other such narratives: the dangers that invade our personal places, the ironic justice that catches up with those who do wrong.

Then we are on our way to dinner in the Quarter with other friends whose Uptown apartment has flooded but who have a house in Baton Rouge; they are living and working there and come into the Crescent City periodically. Did we hear about the looters who broke into an old lady's apartment while she was home? Noticing that she had nothing worth stealing—in fact, virtually nothing at all—they went out, stole a plasma TV, and brought it back and gave it to her!

Finally, much later, our educator friend puts me in touch by telephone with the friend who told him the story of the looter in the pool. This man is in town working for a big cleanup and restoration company, an outfit that arrived in town early and has people working all over who hear lots of things. As for the looter in the pool, he just adds that the man dashed out the back door carrying "something heavy" and plunged into the water. But he has a lot to add to the story of the executed gangs. He says that 350 armed gang members were shot in New Orleans, that when newspeople were busy looking into stories in one part of town, Special Forces would slip into other areas and kill gangsters. At the Superdome people congregated by neighborhoods but were purposefully split up and placed on many different buses during their evacuation, so they wouldn't notice who was missing. He says that a friend of his who works in a retail establishment talked to someone from the coroner's office who came into the store and said that "a hell of a lot of people drowned by being shot" and that no investigations were made into any deaths during Katrina.

That all of these stories relate to crime is probably not surprising. Nationally, a number of urban legends deal with crime and criminals, and it might well be argued that the general function of many urban legends is to warn us of the dangers that can befall us in the modern or postmodern world (much as American ballads once warned of the nearness of sudden death—in the mine, on the railroad, on the logging drive). Crime is one such danger, and fear of it is expressed in other genres as well. In fact, when we shop for a new hall rug, the proprietor of *that* store tells us his personal narrative of his business being looted: they left his huge inventory of valuable carpets untouched but stole a picture of Jesus among other small items. But crime has weighed especially heavily on the New Orleans consciousness in recent years. The whole nation has been aware of the city's high murder rates, and drug violence in particular has been blamed for waves of maim. After Katrina news stories of widespread looting and great violence and disorder inside the Superdome (an iconic building and an official evacuation center) and the Ernest N. Morial Convention Center (a more makeshift haven for those caught in the city by the disaster) rocked the news media and their audience. News stories, in part fueled by rumors, claimed that New Orleans gangs had shifted to Atlanta and that the skyrocketing crime rate in Houston resulted from New Orleans criminals settling in there.[2]

As New Orleanians returned home many complained that their houses had been devastated by both natural forces and looting, although the police expressed ambivalence regarding verification. The police devised a special code for reports of such looting—21K. The "K" stood for Katrina and the "21" meant "lost or stolen." It indicated that the police felt they could not be certain whether objects had been looted or simply lost in the destruction. "The chaotic landscape made it difficult to separate legitimate looting complaints from storm losses and, to a lesser extent, false insurance claims," according to one report.[3] How much looting actually took place was difficult to determine and early reports of dreadful violence in the Superdome and convention center were later claimed to have been wildly exaggerated.

But belief in the early lawlessness and in the widespread prevalence of looters (bits of graffiti warning "Looters will be shot" or just "Looters shot" were still in evidence months later) does not depend on verification, and it has been noted that belief in high crime rates and fear of crime may exist beyond all reality of crime; although in New Orleans crime was certainly a serious, real problem. Clearly the urban legends express that belief, and that fear carried over into the context of Hurricane Katrina, to a time when people felt overwhelmed to begin with. The gangs that marked life pre-Katrina thus show up in the context of the Superdome chaos. The looting reported by the media—and no doubt experienced by some people, whatever the police codes may suggest and though to folklorists what "really happened" may be largely irrelevant—becomes central to the narrative. The legends can be seen as a statement about the criminals that threaten us. On top of the crushing disaster of storm and flood, crime is still a powerful, tormenting force in our urban lives, as gangs form anew and looters pillage our cherished possessions. One French Quarter shirt proclaims: "I went to New Orleans and all I got was this lousy tee-shirt, a new Cadillac and a plasma TV," echoing both an older shirt inscription and prominent reports of items particularly popular with looters, supposedly including expensive cars "borrowed" by police officers.

Yet these stories contain another element as well, and perhaps they offer more needed hope than dispiriting despair in the face of great collective tragedy. The looter perishes in his looting; he slips into the pool because the flood has literally muddied terrain he does not know in the first place. The natural disaster itself brings destruction and looting but also punishes his evil deed. The lost possessions are not even really lost. The Superdome gang members conveniently gather themselves in a neatly confined space so the Secret Service can pick them off. Or the Special Forces fan out to do the same when the media is conveniently not looking. Because gangsters are listed as drowning victims, the natural disaster—in a sense—also punishes them for their evils, or at least makes it easier for the forces of justice to do the deed and cover their own tracks. Katrina has actually made it possible for gang violence to be eliminated. But of course, the final story even tells us that not all looters are completely evil. Some have a Robin Hood streak. When some of them perceive that a potential victim has nothing, they steal from the rich and render their loot unto the poor.

All of this suggests that, however much these stories recognize the problem of crime, they emphasize hope and a kind of redemption—not for the criminals but for the law-abiding rest of us. The looter is thwarted by his grim plunge into the pool and is eliminated forever. The gang members are likewise done away with and so, presumably, is their reign of terror. If their elimination is grim and even a bit sinister, the means by which it was accomplished—by the Secret Service dispatched by the president himself or by Special Forces from the US military—suggests a further note of hope.[4] Although our national government failed the victims of Katrina in many ways—failures exposed rather spectacularly in the national media—nonetheless it has done something positive here: crushed the local gangbangers. The president has not been as indifferent to New Orleans as some have charged; the city is not as alone as some have feared; the message is, overall, reassuring. And even though most of the looters may have escaped the terrible retribution of the lurking swimming pool, some weren't so bad after all. Some were Robin Hood-like and gave plasma TVs to the poor, an act that certainly takes the edge off—with a note of bemusement, perhaps—the terrors of a crime spree.

This is to say that the legends display a kind of balance. There is a recognition of the local crime problem and our fear of it even in the midst of the greater problem of terrible, widespread physical destruction. But there is also a note of hope that the worst crime is behind us: some looters must have perished, the Secret Service has—indeed *secretly*—disposed of the gangs. Those criminals who may be left may at least be Robin Hoods at heart. Katrina has not been all bad. Planners and visionaries suggested that Katrina might have been that blessing in disguise—an event precipitating new, more positive directions for the city. In almost evangelical language, one candidate for the city council declares, "As devastating as the Hurricane was, it has washed us clean of our former political sins and given us a unique opportunity."[5] The narratives re-enforce possibilities of redemption and new beginnings, though they do so as an extension of an earlier discourse on the threat of local crime. While such a vision may be little more than wishful thinking about escaping the past, narratives do often function to frame pictures of what we wish to be and may even influence what comes to be.

Of course, that does not address what may be the most significant urban legend of all, one that we encountered only through media reports of it—namely, that the levees that had protected the Lower Ninth Ward were in fact deliberately dynamited to drive out the African American residents of that area; the perpetrators probably being the white economic elite of the city. Reports circulated that people actually heard the explosions—attributed by those who debunked the story to the explosive sound of the levees breaking and of a huge barge plunging through the breach. The story echoes actual events during the Great Mississippi Flood of 1927, when levees below New Orleans were deliberately blown up to relieve the pressure building upriver that was threatening the city—at least in the view of the New Orleans economic elite. It also reflects African American feelings that minority white New Orleans would as soon be rid of them and that wealthy white developers covet their land. Indeed, the predominantly black St. Thomas housing project, near the Garden District, had already been torn down well before the storm, its site redeveloped, and developers were thought to be eyeing the Iberville Projects, so close to the valuable real estate of that other historic, tourist-oriented district, the French Quarter.

All of the other stories noted here we heard from white informants while the dynamiting story seems to come out of the African American community. The rumors and legends told by whites and blacks in modern America are often quite divergent, as Patricia Turner and Gary Alan Fine have argued more than once.[6] Given the very limited sampling of stories noted here, it would be rash to declare that the crime legends are "white" and the dynamiting story is "black." But if the crime legends offer a vision of hope, that vision may be of a white population that has more resources to rebound from the Katrina tragedy. The story of the dynamiting of the levees—an act that would be even more horrendously criminal than looting but something not conceived of as *crime* in the most conventional meanings of the term—suggests a much darker vision: a terrible distrust and a terrible division of the New Orleans community, which will make recovering from Katrina even more difficult.

That recovery proceeds but may yet prove problematic. The population of New Orleans just before the storm was close to 500,000. Today it may be closer to 343,000, or possibly 368,000 according to some recent estimates. Although the population had been declining for years, the Katrina disaster may have caused a sudden loss of as many as 140,000 people, not only the over 1,500 who died—some of whom yet remain unaccounted for—but the many more who were forced to evacuate and have never returned. Vast numbers of former New Orleanians continue to live in the places that took them in, like Houston and Atlanta; many would prefer to return to the Crescent City but cannot do so because of lost homes and a lack of resources. In the city itself, the balance between white and black populations has radically shifted while the Latino population has grown and become more of a presence.

Our gas lamp flickers romantically. Our new hall rug (hand-knotted in China) is quite handsome. The Savvy Gourmet went through several transformations and finally closed. But none of us here can keep from wondering about and worrying about the future of New Orleans. Those of us who are folklorists can't stop thinking about what the narratives may be telling us about that future—or at least our local visions of it. For me personally, those stories seem part and parcel with the many others that shape and add meaning to memory, as do all our stories.

NOTES

1. John Schwartz, "Next Trick: Bring Back the Magic," *New York Times*, February 18, 2006.

2. See Trymaine Lee, "Haven and Hell," *Times-Picayune*, February 12, 2006.

3. Michael Perlstein, "Police Reports Conceal Looting," *Times-Picayune*, February 7, 2006.

4. As did the arrival of Lt. Gen. Russel L. Honoré, who assumed control of a joint military task force in the city and imposed order on a chaotic situation, gaining a certain degree of positive media exposure. Probably his being a Louisiana native, as well as a Creole, added to the favorable light in which New Orleans cast him. We later heard stories from a friend

who had never left and who lived not far from the convention center, scene of an impromptu refugee encampment, who encountered Honoré. She told us that they chatted about their common Creole heritage (though she is a "White Creole" and he self-identifies as "African American Creole"), and he offered to send her ready-to-eat meals because she was feeding her neighborhood.

5. Shane Landry, campaign flyer for City Council District B, 2006, in author's possession.

6. Gary Alan Fine and Patricia Turner, *Whispers on the Color Line: Rumor and Race in America* (Berkeley: University of California Press, 2001) and Patricia Turner, *I Heard It Through the Grapevine: Rumor in African-American Culture* (Berkeley: University of California Press, 1993).

Contexts and Meanings
A Brief Afterword

WRITING RECENTLY IN *THE NEW YORKER* ABOUT BUSINESS theorist Clayton Christensen, Larissa MacFarquhar notes that her subject's success lies partly in that he is "a master storyteller." The CEOs he has influenced "learned through stories, they remembered stories, and they repeated stories to the people who worked for them."[1] Christensen presented his stories in written form, in his published work; the CEOs presumably picked up the stories from there and carried them into the oral realm. But the point is that stories, which convey understandings, are likely to be remembered and repeated and are particularly effective as a means of communication. They provide something that people like—namely, narrative while they present ideas and express to teller and listener life themes and perhaps self-observations.[2] This is hardly news to anyone, let alone folklorists, but it does call attention to the fact that we have just begun to consider how stories work, what meanings particular stories can convey, why we remember some happenings as stories and forget some stories we hear or even have told.

Folklorist Amy Shuman writes, "Storytelling promises to make meaning out of raw experiences; to transcend suffering; to offer warnings, advice, and other guidance; to provide a means for traveling beyond the personal; and to provide inspiration, entertainment, and new frames of reference to both tellers and listeners."[3]

She is careful to point out that these are *not* presented as the functions of storytelling, but rather as promises that have been made for storytelling in more than a few works on narrative. We assume that stories may do these things, though in fact we have seldom demonstrated the actual doing, have seldom analyzed, for example, how stories do in fact convey meaning in being told. Part of the reason for that—at least as far as orally told narratives are concerned—is that often enough we have simply ignored the contexts in which stories exist. In this book I have hardly explained stories or storytelling as cultural phenomena, but I have attempted to provide one context— my own life or parts of it—as a "venue" in which stories have played a role, giving me some of my memories, providing some of my interactions with other people, serving to help me personally in making meaning out of what I've known. Probably everybody has such stories that play a role in memory generally, and in our larger life narratives, and this book has mostly consisted of my larger life narrative.

That larger life narrative is obviously something I have told in writing—it too is a narrative and thus, I hope, something that people may like and perhaps prefer to abstractions—not through the spoken word. Clearly it has its oral components, and like most of us I have on occasion spoken bits and pieces—notably stories—and listened to other people's bits and pieces, sometimes incorporating those into my own. The smaller narrative components inform the larger narrative, and in this book I have tried to call attention to those smaller components—the stories one actually tells—and to make some sense of how they explain my conception of the bigger whole, how they render meaning, if you will. Of course, they also may say something about how I, in narrative, present myself to the world. That is, I am indirectly writing here about how stories, both my own and those of others, came to me. The memoir form not only allows me to look at my life as context but also to order my stories.

In a sense my family stories come first, giving me my past—the past before I myself existed. Many of us have such stories, stories that situate us in time and place, whether tales of our literal ancestors that have come down to us or legends of other sorts, perhaps of the places that gave us early life or even of the local heroes who came before. Mine, of course, set the stages of the past: the Kansas frontier, nineteenth-century New York, New York and Connecticut in the 1920s, the Europe of visitations and origins. They provide some literal "facts," accounts of key players and what they did. Obviously they provide me with the background we all seek and explain forebears and events that eventually had an impact on me.

But I also prefer to see them as commenting on assimilation and inclusion, on how my ancestors became part of the grand American experience. The stories speak of these ancestors as immigrants and pioneers. These people get off the boat and have to sleep on park benches or see their first black people. They ride west in covered wagons and help sod-house dwellers or get kidnapped by Indians. That is, elemental, mythic American forces—what we may think of as basic historical memes—engulf them. They climb the ladder of success, changing the pronunciation of names, promising brides (and their parents) comfortable lives. That growing success morphs into country life in the 1920s, against a backdrop of the "roaring" times, as the next generation paddles to dances or tears about in speedboats, which they sometimes boldly or cavalierly run aground. The families again blend into a larger American pageant, if perhaps a somewhat mythic one, until they, like the nation, grind to a halt with the depressing 1930s—though the stories tend to focus on the transgressions of one ancestor—my maternal grandfather—as if his very actions caused the sudden end. Stories do simplify.

My seeing these family stories as thematically stressing some sort of absorption into the American mainstream and thus of tying us and myself into our culture may itself be a great simplification. So too may be my attitudes toward the stories that recall my own early years, whether of my thinking of how I marveled at my native place—New York—and its inherent possibilities or of my surprise at realizing that more than one of my stories from this time seem to reflect an awareness of the time's obsession with communism, something I would have thought I myself had largely ignored. Yet I can only offer my own perspectives on my stories and, in doing so, perhaps provide some insight into a teller's (and a listener's) outlook upon what his narratives mean.

When it comes to the oral narratives of others, such as those of my British sahibs, I offer something different. These are "my" stories only in the sense that I collected them, recorded them on tape, evoked them with my questions. When I offer interpretations of them, I am acting as any commentator/critic might. Yet I have internalized a lot of the relevant background context for these stories, and I cannot help but feel that those I have recounted here reflect a concern with culture shock, with dealing with the experience of being an alien in a strange land—a land that one was expected to control. Stories of death and the threat of death, whether from dreaded disease or wild animals or restive locals, reflect a fear of being in the strange place. A lack of the implements for entertaining can suggest how far out one was on the edges of existence. The puzzles of local plumbing or social order or even food indicate the inherent possibilities for confusion. Indeed, I see the same concerns in Kipling's India stories, which the young writer published for a British-Indian readership.

Perhaps I am thus imposing a limited view of "my" stories, but of course, others can propose alternative interpretations. I have included them here because they have been an important part of my consciousness of people's stories, and I could not include them without trying to somehow "make sense" of them, to suggest something more about how our stories lay down patterns of understandings. Likewise, the urban legends that I heard following my return to New Orleans after the exile wrought by Hurricane Katrina are stories that have an existence largely beyond my own telling of them—they are not my personal narratives. I included them because they seemed to come into my life, as stories do—I did not "collect" them for study—and relate to important aspects of my own larger life narrative. They explained something about what had happened to my city in a time of grave crisis. These stories were not literally true, or so it would seem, but they did say much about what people thought might have happened. They were musings on alternate possibilities, and those possibilities said much about some psychic realities that I had to live with.

To return to my own stories, some of them, too, deal with the realities that I had to live with. I would say that my stories of living in New York's East Village in the 1960s are useful in part as reflecting that time period—also written about by others—but that they are stories of coping with the realities of those times. Cataclysmic blackouts must be endured, a problematic landlord dealt with, a suicide noted. Then in India, the realities changed, as swarthy customs officials palmed patent medicines, cobras threatened bowel movements, or camels proved elusive acquisitions. Personal stories surely do not speak only of life's difficulties, though many obviously do, difficulty certainly being one of the dramatic pegs upon which we hang stories.

In other phases of my life I have found stories that tell me other things. My stories of life at Indiana University do, I think, speak of my journey into the American heartland, where the local provincials might eye my beard skeptically but where the tensions of the time could be played out in destructive fires. Or in the small world of folklore study I might encounter the eccentricities of a major player like Richard Dorson, with his fake beer glass, or of my fellow grad student who maintained a jungle cat. As I think back to the prosaic world of Baton Rouge, my stories remind me of my stranger moments there: a colleague who would buy expensive champagne at the drop of a hat; another who took pride in hanging Stalin's picture upside-down; a governor who shimmered in rhinestones, threw gigantic parties for voters, or chased young women about. My Mexican stories provide a contrast to Baton Rouge, assuring me that I encountered another cultural world, where gringos once bought archaeological zones, planes try to land on roads, and broken traffic lights visit chaos upon existence.

Stories are multivalent in their functions and meanings, and I do not claim that the meanings I have coaxed out of mine are the only ones that reside there. I mean only to indicate that I see these particular meanings as central, as informing me about what my narratives are trying to tell me and how I think I am being projected to the world by my stories, and indeed, how some stories that I've heard from others or share with others tell me things as well.

Obviously much of what I have written here is not about stories as such but about my life, in which we might say the stories are embedded. This is clearly a work of memory, as a *memoir* is bound to be, that has been motivated by what usually motivates such writing, including perhaps a certain vanity about one's interest to others as well as a desire to commit one's existence to the human record, to become slightly less ephemeral by converting gauzy memory to surviving testimony. I do seek to make the point that our grander memories are wound up in our smaller stories. And because I do believe that *everyone's* memory matters, I hope that what I have set down here ultimately will be useful to someone—not as some sort of wise musings but as a tiny part of what might be recollected about the past and about things that happened and places that were.

NOTES

1. Larissa MacFarquhar, "When Giants Fail," *New Yorker*, May 14, 2012, 88.
2. As humorist Dave Maleckar notes, "We want a narrative, not just one thing happening after another for no good reason." "100 Word Rant: Tails Have Something to Prove," *Funny Times*, August 2011, 4.
3. Shuman, *Other People's Stories*, 1.

About the Author

FRANK DE CARO is Professor Emeritus of English at Louisiana State University and editor of *The Folklore Muse* and *An Anthology of American Folktales and Legends*.